POWERPRO SERIES

Supercharging, Turbocharging, & Nitrous Oxide
PERFORMANCE HANDBOOK

EARL DAVIS AND DIANE PERKINS-DAVIS

MOTORBOOKS
INTERNATIONAL

First published in 2001 by Motorbooks International, an imprint of MBI Publishing Company, 380 Jackson Street, Suite 200, St. Paul, MN 55101-3885 USA

Motorbooks International titles are also available at discounts in bulk quantity for industrial or sales-promotional use. For details write to Special Sales Manager at Motorbooks International Wholesalers & Distributors, 380 Jackson Street, Suite 200, St. Paul, MN 55101-3885 USA

On the front cover: A 1987 Ford Mustang LX with an ATI supercharger installed by author Earl Davis blows smoke at Speed World Dragway in Orlando, Florida.

On the back cover, main: Author Earl Davis assembled this three-stage supercharged Mustang 5.0-liter engine to illustrate the versatility of forced induction. The ATI centrifugal blows into the Paxton supercharger, which blows into the Kenne Bell positive displacement blower. **Top left:** This 400-horsepower, 2.3-liter, 4-cylinder engine sits in a 1987 Mercury Merkur XR4ti and is complete with a Garrett T04 hybrid turbocharger. **Bottom left:** A nitrous bottle for an NOS Stage II kit. **Bottom right:** This Ford Mustang Cobra 4.6-liter four-cam has been modified with an OpconAutorotor supercharger that generates an additional 100 horsepower. This application is an excellent example of a reliable and powerful blower kit for the street-performance enthusiast.

About the Authors: Earl Davis and Diane Perkins-Davis are automotive enthusiasts who have owned, modified, and enjoyed more than 55 cars to date. Earl is a member of the Society of Automotive Engineers (SAE) and studied Advanced High Performance Engine Engineering at the University of Denver. A former senior technical editor for Mustang Monthly and Super Ford Magazines, he coauthored the popular 1964 1/2-1973 Mustang Restoration Guide.

Diane manages, programs, writes, and records script for an Audiotex system in the New Media Department of The Press-Enterprise newspaper in Southern California. They live in Moreno Valley, California.

Library of Congress Cataloging-in-Publication Data Available

ISBN 0-7603-0837-3

Edited by Chad Caruthers
Designed by Dan Perry

Printed in the United States of America

Contents

Introduction

Forced Induction for the Masses

A number of very informative books have been written about supercharger, turbocharger, and nitrous oxide injection systems. Most offer a *Reader's Digest* version of high-performance engine engineering by addressing everything from metallurgy to chemistry. Some of these books post more complex mathematical equations than a third-year engineering textbook. A well-funded racer bent on designing a one-off supercharger, turbocharger, or nitrous oxide injection system from scratch could no doubt put these teachings to good use. To overstate the obvious, engineering an efficient forced induction system is as difficult as it is costly.

Few of us, however, have the time or the means to envelop airflow engineering as a second vocation just to support a hobby. Instead, we want instant gratification without all the hard work and study. And we want it

all at minimal cost. We are truly the drive-through fast-food generation.

Most enthusiasts are street-driving fun seekers who own one or two street-legal cars. They are not, nor do they aspire to be, professional automotive engineers. This same group of power-hungry drivers is not willing to sacrifice comfort or durability in exchange for large amounts of power. Some insist the air conditioner be as powerful and efficient as the engine. Driving a stripped down racing car or off-road truck is fun now and again. But having to endure the noise, heat, and the rough ride every day is somewhat masochistic. Further, few of us want to spend every Saturday working on an exotic car just so we can drive it on Sunday. Recognizing the need, automobile manufacturers now produce a record number of powerful sports cars, high-performance touring cars, and ultra-luxurious trucks we call sport utility vehicles.

If you count yourself among the throng of carefree, performance-minded drivers, this book is for you. There are many ways to get from here to there without spending a quarter of your life immersed in complex algebra. Many creative professionals have greatly simplified the arduous task of engineering and building an efficient forced induction system by taking their creations from the drawing board to store shelves in the form of "bolt-on" kits. As a result, well-engineered blower and nitrous kits are becoming more popular, fueled in part by the needs and wants of non-technical auto enthusiasts.

A large number of companies around the world engineer and market laboratory-tested and race-proven supercharger, turbocharger, or nitrous oxide injection kits. The availability of a particular application seems to be the only limitation. That is, not every make, model, or year of car is a qualified candidate. To make the mass-production process pay off, kit makers must select popular vehicles purchased in large numbers. Fortunately, the ever-increasing volume of popular vehicles provides the aftermarket forced induction performance manufacturers plenty of room to expand.

Nitrous oxide injection kits are the exception to the "application specific" rule, because each includes the same basic components. For these reasons, nitrous oxide kits could be considered nonapplication specific. Basic off-the-shelf nitrous kits can be installed on almost any internal combustion engine, regardless of the make, model, or year of the car. The same 50-horsepower nitrous kit will add 50 horsepower to a Dodge, a Buick, or a Lexus.

There are plenty of reasons to install a forced induction kit. The cost is affordable, the installation procedures acceptable, and an engineering degree or mechanical certification is not required. Purchasing a well-designed forced induction kit is like hiring a team of engineers to modify your personal car at a fraction of the cost. Once calibrated to deliver optimum performance, the benefits are exhilarating.

About This Book

Some material contained in this book may contradict information offered in some automotive periodicals or magazine advertising. The most obvious reason is simply opinion. Like noses, everybody has one and not all are alike. The least obvious is somewhat political. The information contained in this book is not influenced by advertising dollars.

Most magazines are advertising driven, which means their profitability largely depends on advertising sales. Advertising budgets can range from thousands to tens of thousands to hundreds of thousands of dollars, depending on the size of the company and the publisher. Subscription and newsstand sales typically will not support a magazine publishing company, which means publishers are somewhat beholden to advertisers. As a result, using advertising dollars as leverage, advertisers can influence editorial content about their respective products or their performance potential. Likewise, advertisers can say pretty much whatever they want in the space they purchase from the publisher.

The material contained in this book is the product of experience and research. Every effort has been made to report factual information based in sound engineering theory. If there is an error in this book, it is just that—an error. No product, no money, no favors were solicited from any supplier or source represented in this book.

Chapter One
Fundamentals

Some people think all engines suck. Not that they dislike engines, but rather they think engines suck air in the top and force it out the bottom. The concept can be debated, but it really isn't worth the time or the paper.

Engines take in air with help from an energy source we call gravity. No, gravity doesn't pull the air *down* into the carburetor per say, but rather gravity creates atmospheric air pressure, which is roughly 14.7 pounds per square inch at zero elevation. To put it another way, we live in a pressure canister.

Atmosphere has mass, which means it also has weight. The closer you get to the earth's center, the greater the atmospheric pressure. Conversely, atmospheric pressure becomes less and less the further you go away from the earth's center. Atmospheric air pressure forces air into the engine.

An engine is basically a vacuum pump on the inlet side and a pressure pump on the exhaust side. Vacuum is created in each cylinder as the piston travels down the bore during the intake stroke. Air, driven by atmospheric air pressure, rushes in to fill

In 1901, Sir Dugald Clerk first used the theory of supercharging to create an artificially dense atmosphere to feed a two-stroke engine in an attempt to lower its combustion temperature. He discovered the blower produced a 6 percent power increase compared to the naturally aspirated version.

the void. The process defines "natural aspiration," under which air at any given pressure will travel toward an area of less pressure. Vacuum creates the need, and atmospheric air pressure satisfies that need. For those who might think gravity pulls air down into a carburetor, explain how updraft or side-draft carburetors work. The fact is, atmospheric air pressure will move air in any direction until the pressure equalizes. Movement will stop once the pressures become equal.

The effect forced induction has on a naturally aspirated engine is very profound. What drives the piston drives the engine, and that is the combustion of fuel. The amount of fuel an engine can burn depends on the amount of air it can take in to mix with it (which must be balanced—neither too rich nor too lean—for optimal performance). Forcing an engine to ingest more air/fuel mixture will net more powerful combustion and a predictable horsepower gain.

All high-performance modifications, like all internal combustion engines, incorporate some level of compromise. This rule applies to superchargers, turbochargers, and nitrous oxide injection systems. In addition, each has its advantages and disadvantages.

The Basics of Superchargers, Turbochargers, and Nitrous Oxide Injection

Supercharging, turbocharging, or nitrous oxide injection will enhance your engine's power output, no question. Although any of the three will force-feed an engine a large amount of air/fuel mixture, each system is unique by design, and each operates and installs quite differently.

Fortunately, with little exception, any spark-ignited (SI) engine can be supercharged, turbocharged, or injected with nitrous oxide. Even a single-cylinder Briggs & Stratton engine can be supercharged. Properly sizing a supercharger, turbocharger, or

nitrous oxide injection system for any engine can be complex, time consuming, and expensive, but it can be done. Calibrating the air/fuel or the nitrous oxide/fuel mixture is the most difficult part of an installation.

Superchargers and turbochargers are essentially air compressors that force more air into the engine than it can process at one time. Picture the intake manifold or plenum as a holding tank. The compressor (the supercharger or turbocharger) forces air into the inlet of the tank, and the intake

valves control the outlet. The intake valves allow a small amount of compressed air to enter the engine during each cycle. To generate pressure in the intake, the compressor must be of larger capacity than the naturally aspirated engine's requirements. An undersized compressor, one that is too small for the application, will not pressurize the intake manifold or plenum because the engine will ingest the air faster than the compressor can compress it. Conversely, an oversized compressor, one that is too large for the

Forced induction systems can be further defined as "draw through" or "blow through." Fuel introduced ahead of the blower by any means is a draw-through system. Carburetors calibrated for naturally aspirated applications *must* be reworked and recalibrated for blower applications. *Blower Drive Service*

application, will create an abundance of pressure in the intake manifold or plenum because the engine cannot ingest air fast enough. A properly sized compressor will generate the desired amount of pressure in the intake manifold or plenum. This residual pressure in the intake manifold or plenum is called boost.

Superchargers and turbochargers require more installation time than nitrous oxide systems and are comparatively difficult to calibrate, but perform well under all loads and at any throttle position. Unlike nitrous oxide systems, superchargers and turbochargers react to load. In addition, their recharge rate is equal to the size of the fuel tank in the car. When properly sized, boost should arrive gradually, then increase at a calculable rate as the engine speed increases.

The more gradual the boost inclination, the smoother the drive. If boost comes on too early, the transition to power will be too harsh and abrupt, making the car hard to handle. If it comes on too late, it will be ineffective, and performance will suffer accordingly. For that reason, a supercharger or turbocharger will perform well during part-throttle opening and at comparatively slow vehicle speeds.

As the name implies, nitrous oxide injection literally injects an extremely potent mixture of nitrous oxide gas and gasoline into the engine. The molecular makeup of nitrous oxide is further defined by its scientific acronym, N_2O. The scientific formula indicates each nitrous oxide molecule contains two nitrogen atoms and one oxygen atom. Combining N_2O with the just the right amount of fuel produces a condensed, highly volatile air/fuel mixture. The nitrous oxide gas provides the oxygen needed to burn the extra fuel.

Superchargers

Compared to a typical turbocharger system, a supercharger is easier to install on most applications.

The mechanism used to drive the compressor is a controlling factor, in that it must be efficient, accessible, and reliable. Because most superchargers are crank driven, the compressor (or a portion of its drive system) must be in line with the crankshaft. Locating the drive assembly parallel to the crankshaft (like all other accessory drive components) imposes a level of restriction. Besides the drive mechanism, superchargers require a fuel-enhancement system and enough plumbing to complete the airflow circuit.

Superchargers can be classified as one of three types: centrifugal, positive-displacement (rotary), or sliding vane. Centrifugal superchargers and turbochargers are similar by design in that both spin a contoured compressor wheel inside a conical housing. The conical housing is positioned in the air intake system somewhere between the air filter and the throttle control. Turbo and centrifugal supercharger assemblies are usually remote mounted and integrated into the airflow path via a series of tubes and hoses.

The power needed to drive the compressor wheel further defines centrifugal superchargers and turbochargers. Turbochargers use the exhaust gas flow to drive a turbine wheel, which in turn is connected to the compressor wheel via a shaft. The compressor wheel in a centrifugal supercharger is typically driven by mechanical means.

Positive-displacement superchargers consist of a pair of overlapping paddles or screws (picture a wood screw) that rotate inside the confines of a specially designed housing. A given amount of air is trapped between recesses of the rotor lobes or screws and the housing. The fixed volume of air is moved toward the discharge or delivery port. Positive-displacement blowers pack a fixed volume of air into a given space in rapid succession. Like centrifugal chargers, positive-displacement blowers are commonly belt-driven, although not all are remote mounted. The power needed to drive the compressor is minimal compared to the power they generate. Blower Drive Service (BDS), Eaton Corporation, and Whipple Industries manufacture positive-displacement superchargers.

Since sliding vane-type superchargers are not widely used for automotive applications, covering them in great detail is somewhat pointless. But for identification, relatively thin, rigid vanes are radially mounted along an

Fuel is introduced behind the compressor in a blow-through system. In this application, the carburetor is enclosed in a pressurized box. Blow-through systems work reasonably well under low-boost conditions. From a practical standpoint, they are better suited for boats than cars.

axis (rotor). The rotor and vanes spin inside an elliptical housing. Centrifugal force holds the vanes against the wall of the housing. Because the housing is elliptical, the space between the vanes grows larger and smaller as they rotate around the axis. Air trapped between the vanes is then compressed into a progressively smaller area.

Turbochargers

Turbochargers are more efficient compared to superchargers, in part because they use energy that is otherwise expelled through the exhaust system.

In addition, turbochargers are not limited to any specific location, because they do not require a mechanical drive mechanism. Therefore, the turbocharger itself (or turbochargers in the case of a multiple system) can be positioned in any convenient area near the engine. However, the additional piping needed to funnel the exhaust through the turbine housing offsets the benefit.

Routing the piping is by far the most difficult and time-consuming part of a turbo installation. If the exhaust manifold is not designed to mate directly with the turbine housing, the two must be joined with pipe. From there, the exhaust must be plumbed to an acceptable location, preferably to the rear of the car. Fresh air should be filtered and collected from a source outside the engine compartment, then piped to the turbo inlet port. Another tube is usually needed to connect the outlet of the turbo to the intake manifold or throttle opening. Add an intercooler, and the piping can become overwhelming, particularly in a tight engine compartment. Smaller but equally important tubing must channel engine oil (for lubrication) and water (for cooling) in and out of the turbo bearing housing. Turbochargers, because they are not mechanically driven by the engine, can also exhibit "turbo lag."

Because their power output is related to load, superchargers and tur-

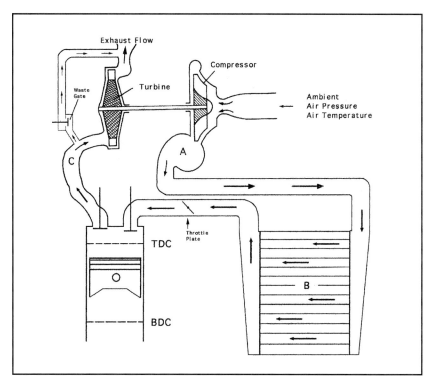

Turbocharger systems are somewhat more complicated because additional plumbing is needed to drive the exhaust turbine. Ambient air is compressed and heated by the compressor wheel (A). Air is cooled as it passes through the intercooler (B). Energy contained in the superheated exhaust gases (C) drives the turbine wheel.

bochargers do little to degrade drivability, provided the system is sized and calibrated properly for the application. For this reason alone, superchargers and turbochargers are the power enhancer of choice for a large number of street-performance enthusiasts.

Nitrous Oxide Injection

Nitrous oxide injection is more of a straight-line, full-power wide-open throttle power source. Applying a number of staged events provides some level of rpm versatility, but for the most part, a nitrous oxide system is similar to a toggle switch: It's either full-on or it's off. In fact, it can be dangerous to activate nitrous oxide injection at any time other than wide-open throttle operation, and only after the engine has attained a safe speed. For that reason, most nitrous kits activate the "on" switch with the throttle linkage. When adjusted properly, the nitrous oxide/fuel mixture will flow only when the throttle is wide open.

Nitrous oxide injection is the least expensive of the three and can be installed quicker and easier than a car stereo and four speakers. Liquid nitrous oxide and gasoline is delivered through high-pressure hoses and tubes to a properly sized jet or jets. Storage bottles are heated with electric blankets to ensure an adequate supply of nitrous is delivered at sufficient pressure. Storing nitrous oxide in a liquid state under pressure solves two important problems: It compresses a large amount of product into a very small space and provides the propulsion needed to inject the chemical into the engine. Nitrous oxide can also be considered power on demand because it is onboard at all times and activated with a simple flip of a switch.

Nitrous has an added benefit that further enhances its effectiveness. When stored under pressure, it is condensed into a liquid. As the liquid nitrous is released into the intake system, it absorbs heat as it vaporizes. The

This NOS Stage II kit for 1986 to 1994 Ford SEFI 5.0-liter engines converts the dry-flow intake manifold into a wet-flow system by injecting the nitrous oxide and fuel ahead of the throttle body. *NOS*

refrigeration effect cools the combustible charge, which further improves the overall efficiency of the process.

But, unlike superchargers and turbochargers, nitrous oxide injection systems have a very limited range of operation, dictated mostly by the size of the storage container. Frequent users will need one or two spare storage bottles. When you are out of nitrous oxide, you're out of power. Also, nitrous oxide injection systems don't work well at part-throttle operation, which somewhat limits nitrous oxide's serviceability to straight-line performance applications such as drag racing. Further, nitrous oxide is expensive. It doesn't take long to burn up $20 worth of nitrous gas. A user addicted to street racing will need a large bank account and several spare bottles to feed the need.

In spite of its shotgun approach to performance, nitrous oxide injection

kits remain very popular, if for no other reason than their comparatively low cost. Pound for pound, dollar for dollar, horsepower for horsepower, nitrous oxide injection will deliver equal performance at a fraction of the cost of a supercharger or turbocharger, at least initially. In addition, nitrous oxide kits are easy to adapt to any spark-ignited engine, regardless of size, application, or manufacturer, and a kit need only be calibrated to deliver the proper amount of nitrous oxide gas and fuel for optimum results.

Assessing Power Needs

Is it possible to generate too much power? Most automotive enthusiasts would probably say no. However, there are mechanical limits, cost restrictions, and safety issues to consider. Theoretically, the more air/fuel mixture stuffed into the engine, the more power it will generate. Obviously

this is not an open-end scale. At some point, durability becomes a limiting factor, as does the cost of maintenance and repairs. No one wants to drive an overpowered hand grenade or pay someone to put it back together again after it explodes. Moreover, it's important to strike an acceptable compromise between brute power and overall performance. High performance should always include an acceptable level of drivability and durability. Otherwise, the car can become unfriendly to drive when you're not on the racetrack.

To oversimplify a number of physical and chemical variables to make a point, for now we'll say a pound of boost is a pound of boost. If the fuel calibration is correct and the system is operating at near-peak efficiency, the engine will respond accordingly. Six to 10 pounds of boost from a supercharger or turbocharger will blow an extra 100 horsepower out of 300 cubic inches with relative ease. The same results can be achieved with a modest shot of nitrous oxide and fuel. How you get from here to there is a matter of choice, safety, cost, and many other considerations.

Functionality

Which system you install should depend on what you plan to do with the car. There are many applications for increased power—weekend cruising, street racing, drag racing, off-road, monster truck stadium racing, Formula One, freeway commuter, show car, daily driver, weekend quarter-mile warrior, garage queen, and so on. If you plan to enter any form of sanctioned racing, the rules will define the legal modifications in great detail. A few classes of amateur and professional racing accommodate forced induction, but most do not. Some offer open classes that allow no-holds-barred modifications as long as minimum safety standards are met. Everyone engaged in unsanctioned events must rely on common sense

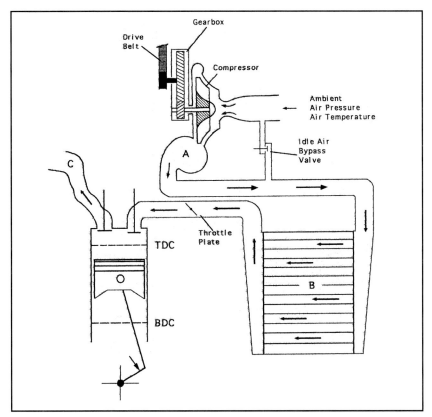

Centrifugal superchargers compress air in much the same manner as a turbocharger, though the compressor wheel is driven mechanically. The belt drives a gearbox, which in turn overdrives the compressor wheel. The airflow through the system is basically the same, except the exhaust gases are not contained.

Nothing should circumvent safety. Consider how the car will be driven and the effect the power enhancements will impose on the other systems. Give the brakes and steering at least as much attention as you give the engine and transmission. Install a drive shaft loop, four-point seat belts, and at least a four-point roll bar, especially if the car is a convertible.

Factory safety equipment works reasonably well under average conditions, but it is no match for a car operating on an overabundance of steroids. Traction or the lack thereof can turn a turn a powerful car into an unguided missile. Further, DOT-approved street tires will always be a limiting factor on a car that is capable of delivering 500 horsepower to the rear wheels. There is an old saying, "Power is nothing without control," which could be interpreted as "Power without control is foolhardy." Spend the money needed to improve the whole car proportionately, or limit the power modification to a reasonable level.

Cost

A supercharger or turbocharger kit can cost between $2,000 and $30,000, depending on the level of performance, the application, and the electronic controls needed to manage the power through a normal range of operation. Conversely, nitrous oxide kits can be owned for hundreds of dollars. For those who keep as keen an eye on their checking account balance as their tachometer, nitrous oxide is the bargain boost, at least in the short run. Compared to a supercharger or turbocharger system, a nitrous system is like making payments on a power allotment. The initial outlay is small and you pay for refueling as you go. Conversely, the cost of a supercharger or turbocharger system demands a rather large up-front expenditure, but the cost from then on is minimal.

Most automotive enthusiasts are savvy shoppers. All of us have spent more on a project than its total net

and an evaluation of his needs to get from here to there as quickly and safely as possible.

Engine Limitations and Safety

As you plan your performance upgrade, keep in mind your engine's present limitations. Attempting to push 30 pounds of boost or five gallons per minute of nitrous oxide into nearly any factory production engine is an exercise in durability, not feasibility. Stock engines will tolerate a certain amount of abuse, but there are mechanical limits. Remember that the transmission, drive shaft, rear axle, and tires must also survive the rush of power. Components of factory-engineered thresholds will not support a 300-horsepower hit for long.

Be sensible in your approach to power modifications. Some factory-assembled engines are designed to take a higher level of abuse; others are not. Durability testing is both frustrating and expensive. Further, any car, high-performance or not, is only as reliable as its weakest part. If that part happens to be a 10-cent roll pin holding the distributor gear to the shaft, then overkill elsewhere is for naught.

If you plan to build the engine, don't skimp: Use high-quality parts. Cast pistons are not as durable as hypoeutectic pistons, which are not as durable as forged pistons. Applying overkill to the long block will not only make it more stress resistant in the short run, but will also provide thousands of trouble-free miles under average driving conditions.

Also, do not allow your need for speed to compromise safety. Overpowering a factory production car is unwise, but unfortunately it is so common it could be considered an epidemic.

worth at one time or another. Leaning from one's mistakes usually creates profound memories. There is nothing more humbling than discovering you paid too much for something. Conversely, most of us have a "best buy for the buck" story to counter any past feelings of vulnerability. Make sure the return you seek is worth the investment.

If cost is the primary consideration, you should work the plan backward. The amount of disposable income available will greatly influence the answers to the other questions.

Legal Issues

It's still a free country, but there are also legal issues to consider. If you plan to modify a licensed street car, know the laws in your state regarding emissions compliance. Most engine modifications are illegal according to federal standards. The California Air Resources Board (CARB) set strict standards in California. Other states and cities have emissions laws with varying degrees of latitude. The strictest environmental restrictions state that it is unlawful to modify a motor vehicle in any way if the changes cause exhaust emissions to increase; it is unlawful to disable, tamper with, or remove any emissions control device; and it is unlawful to remove or bypass a catalytic converter.

Many aftermarket high-performance assemblies, kits, and individual components are emissions legal. Make emissions compliance part of your build-up and have the car tested regularly to ensure it meets emissions standards set forth at the time of manufacture. Emissions laws and compliance are covered in greater detail in chapter 8.

Be Real

The builder's insights and mechanical prowess will play an equally important part in the project. Do you plan to build an engine from the ground up or modify a factory production engine? Space, tools, time, and experience will also affect progress. Do you plan to install the kit yourself? If not, is the hired mechanic experienced and qualified? Who will service and maintain the car in the future?

One final thought on assessing power goals: No one ever won a race using advertised horsepower. Advertised horsepower is only good for competing in a bragging race. It's relatively easy to build a 1,000-horsepower engine by adding advertising horsepower claims to the factory performance numbers, i.e., a 50-horsepower cam plus 75 horsepower from a pair of free-flowing cylinder heads, added to the 60-horsepower intake manifold means a 200-horsepower engine so equipped will now generate 385 horsepower. If it were that easy, most mildly modified V-8 engines could produce 500 horsepower, as some claim.

Realistically, increasing the power output of any engine by 25 percent is notable. Fifty additional horsepower coaxed from a factory production 200-horsepower engine is a respectable achievement. Expect a 25 to 45 percent power gain from a typical street-legal forced induction kit. Don't assume all advertised horsepower numbers are obtainable. Some, but not all, are real.

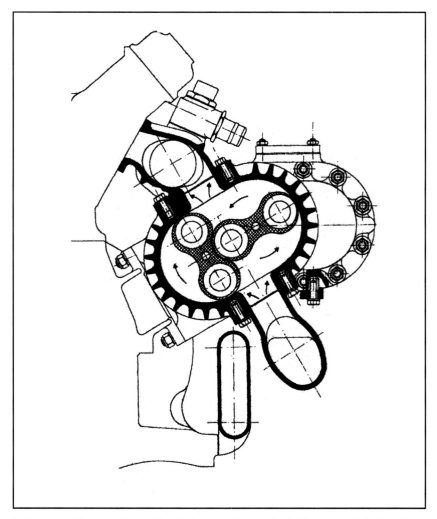

Leakage around the rotors in a positive-displacement blower is inevitable, because their edges do not contact each other or the housing. Pumping losses grow less significant as speed increases. Boost increases to a predictable level with engine speed, then levels off until it is substantially constant in the top-most portion of the working speed range.

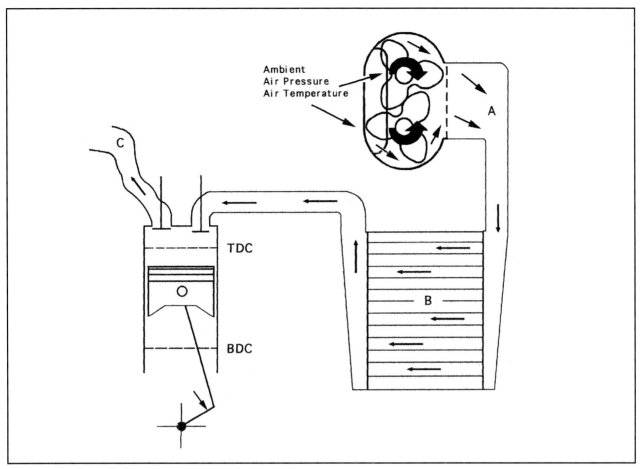

Atmospheric air pressure forces ambient air into the supercharger, where it is compressed (A). The heated, compressed air is directed through an air-to-air heat exchanger (B). The cooled, compressed air enters the cylinders. The spent gases are then expelled through the exhaust port (C).

Service After the Sale

Addressing the fundamentals is somewhat like going to class. It's something you must do if you're to succeed in your chosen endeavor. Most automotive enthusiasts simply want to enhance performance, the sooner the better. For that reason, a lot of would-be street/strip racers will cut class to save time. Why learn the science behind the system if you can achieve optimum results without knowing how it works? Because of our busy lives, we apply this approach with so many things, such as any TV, VCR, or stereo. To succeed one need only to learn the owner's manual, not the circuitry.

But what happens when you don't obtain optimum results? Is the problem the operator, the equipment, or a combination of the two? And what is the best solution? The more you know about how your system works, the better you'll be able to decide how it should be fixed, and by whom—or whether it should be upgraded or replaced because it no longer suits your needs. The more you know, the faster you can go, and the less it is likely to cost because you'll avoid making changes and buying parts that don't solve the problem. In the end, you may decide to pay someone else to service the system, but you'll know what's involved and you can make sound decisions.

Upkeep, in the form of maintenance, diagnosis, and repair, is an important part of owning a supercharged, turbocharged, or nitrous oxide-injected car. Keep "service after the sale" in mind when you build or purchase a highly modified car. Who will you turn to when your one-of-a-kind, highly modified car needs repair? The original manufacturer covers each individual part, subassembly, or kit, but the person best suited to know the complexities of the finished product is likely to be the one who built it.

The point is that a sophisticated high-performance car requires an equally sophisticated owner. The more sophisticated the car, the higher the minimum requirements for ownership. The busiest phone at any high-performance aftermarket manufacturer's business is always the tech line. Knowledge is power. Believe it. Don't skip the fundamentals. Learn everything you can about a modification before you buy or build.

Chapter Two
Technical Basics–
How It All Works

Embracing the benefits of forced induction leads to a learning process that explains how a system works. But before we can discuss the hardware, we must first understand the terminology used to describe and define the process of efficiently converting chemical energy into mechanical energy. Fortunately, the physical laws that influence, and in fact dictate, the operation of a naturally aspirated internal combustion engine also apply to an engine equipped with forced induction. In other words, understanding how and why a naturally aspirated engine converts liquid fuel into mechanical energy will lead to a better understanding of forced induction and how it is used to increase power output.

Horsepower, Torque, and Weight

Skilled advertising has taught us to crave big horsepower numbers. The term horsepower was coined at the start of the industrial revolution to describe the amount of work a machine could do compared to the standard power source—a real, live horse. Scottish inventor James Watt estimated that an average horse could lift about 550 pounds in one second. Multiplying this out, he figured that in one minute, it could lift 33,000 pounds. One horsepower is a unit of power equal to 745.7 watts or 33,000 lbs-ft (of torque) per minute.

Torque is defined as "the moment of a force; the measure of a force's tendency to produce torsion and rotation about an axis, equal to the vector product of the radius vector from the axis of rotation to the point of application of the force." In simpler terms, torque is a measure of an engine's ability to do work, and horsepower is the rate at which work is done. Drag racers say torque pushes the car off the starting line and horsepower drags it through the lights. The point is, torque is equally as important as horsepower. Torque makes a car fun to drive because it typically occurs early in the rpm range. Without torque, every car would be a slug off the line. Torque and horsepower are computed using the following formulas:

$$\text{Horsepower} = \frac{\text{RPM X torque}}{5,252}$$

$$\text{Torque} = \frac{5,252 \text{ X horsepower}}{\text{RPM}}$$

High-performance, naturally aspirated street engines can be built to generate one horsepower per cubic inch (16.387 cc) of displacement. Divide the factory-rated horsepower by the displacement to determine your engine's horsepower-per-cubic-inch ratio.

$$\text{Horsepower per cubic inch} = \frac{\text{flywheel horsepower}}{\text{displacement}}$$

For example, a 1994 5.0-liter Mustang (it's actually 301.59 cubic inches, or 4.94 liters) generates 215 horsepower at the flywheel, according to Ford Motor Company. Dividing 215 horsepower by 301.59 cubic inches equals .713 (rounded to the nearest thousandth) horsepower per cubic inch. A 5.0-liter Mustang has long been considered a reasonably good factory production performance car, but not because its 5.0-liter V-8 generates .713 horsepower per cubic inch. The 5.0-liter's big advantage is that it generates .945 lbs-ft of torque per cubic inch (285 divided by 301.59) at a relatively low 3,400 rpm.

$$\text{Torque per cubic inch} = \frac{\text{torque measured at flywheel}}{\text{displacement}}$$

Pushing a 3,258-pound car around with 285 lbs-ft of torque is worth the cost of admission.

Toyota's new 4.7-liter dual overhead cam (DOHC) V-8, installed in its half-ton Tundra pickup, generates .854 horsepower per cubic inch (245 flywheel horsepower) and a neck-snapping 1.098 lbs-ft of torque per cubic inch (315 lbs-ft). Comparing the numbers, Toyota's 4.7 is hotter than Ford's 5.0. Why then isn't a Toyota Tundra pickup considered a muscle truck? It is in the truck world.

The major difference is the weight

of the two vehicles, which points to another measurement of performance—weight-to-horsepower ratio. If you divide the weight of the vehicle by the amount of horsepower (or torque) the engine generates, you compute the amount of weight each horsepower must move. The aforementioned Mustang has a 15.153 weight-to-horsepower ratio (11.43 pounds per lbs-ft of torque). In a way it's like saying every horse must pull 15.153 pounds. At 4,276 pounds, the Toyota pickup is closer to 18 pounds per horsepower. If you are picking nits, lightening a vehicle by approximately 6 pounds is equal to adding one horsepower.

Squeezing one horsepower out of each cubic inch is relatively easy and equally painless. One-and-a-half horsepower per cubic inch is doable, while pushing two horsepower per cubic inch will tax the limits of most factory production engines. Two horsepower per cubic inch requires performance head gaskets, aftermarket head bolts or studs, O-ringed combustion chambers, and so on. More on those subjects later.

Vacuum, Atmospheric Pressure, and Boost

Vacuum, atmospheric pressure, and boost describe pressure differentials. Atmospheric pressure measured at sea level (approximately 14.7 psi at 32 degrees Fahrenheit) is regarded as a baseline. We say approximately because normal weather conditions and altitude will cause atmospheric pressure to fluctuate. Atmospheric pressure diminishes at a predictable rate as you travel away from the center of the earth. Psi and PSIG mean basically the same thing. PSIG is pounds per square inch gauge. Any value above normal atmospheric is positive pressure or boost. Any value below normal atmospheric is negative pressure or vacuum.

On a standard gauge, zero is equal to the atmospheric pressure (one atmosphere), which means zero on a

The higher the incremental calibration, the less accurate the gauge. Separate, large-dial boost and vacuum gauges calibrated in very small increments are more accurate, and they are easier to read. Electronic instruments calibrated in tenths, hundredths, or thousandths offer the highest degree of precision.

pressure gauge is equal to the current atmospheric air pressure. Assuming the current atmospheric air pressure is 14.7 psi, 1 pound of positive pressure would be equal to 15.7 psi, or one pound of pressure above atmospheric. Normal atmospheric air pressure will fluctuate up and down as weather conditions change. Some gauges take this normal atmospheric fluctuation into account by allowing zero to cover a small range on the scale. Instead of positioning zero at a single mark, zero will represent the widest range on the gauge. When the needle rests against a post, zero represents an average atmospheric pressure value. Any positive pressure is then added to the atmospheric pressure.

One pound of positive pressure is actually 1-psi over the atmospheric pressure. One pound of positive pressure is one pound of boost. In the United States, negative pressure, or vacuum, is commonly measured in inches of mercury. Some gauges will indicate both positive and negative pressure. Vacuum can also be presented as a decimal equivalent, as in .8 (8/10 of an atmosphere), or as kilograms per square centimeter, kilopascals (kPa), or millibars. If you are

interested in accurate monitoring, install a high-quality pressure gauge graduated in 1 psi increments and a separate vacuum gauge. A quality pressure gauge divided into 1/4-pound increments will be more accurate, and a digital gauge graduated in 1/1,000 pound increments will provide even greater accuracy. Pressure gauges designed to measure in 2-, 4-, or 5-psi increments deliver a comparatively wide range of approximation. Larger increments can be compared to a boost light: the light glows when manifold pressure changes from negative to positive. Otherwise, it remains off.

Overall, once a forced induction device is set up properly, measuring residual pressure in the intake manifold is of minor importance. Yet a lot of automotive enthusiasts crave big numbers. If some is good, more is better, and too much must be just right. In reality it's better to think that the right amount is just right and any more is too much. Residual pressure is just that–residual pressure. While the "more boost makes more horsepower" theory holds true to a point, the efficiency of the engine is more important—that is, how efficiently the engine converts chemical energy into mechanical energy.

The maximum output (boost) of a forced induction system is somewhat fixed once it has been calibrated. For example, a stock 1990 5.0-liter Ford engine equipped with a base supercharger might produce a maximum of six pounds of boost when bolted to a totally stock 5.0-liter engine. Improving the efficiency of the engine will cause the residual pressure to decrease. After installing a higher-lift camshaft, a pair of high-flow aluminum cylinder heads, an Edelbrock intake manifold, and a pair of long tube headers, maximum boost might be from four to five psi. These results are predictable, although some statisticians may suspect a problem. Remember, the output of the blower is somewhat fixed. The blower still pumps the same volume of air, even though the amount of residual pressure (boost) went down. The discrepancy is the result of the engine modifications, which greatly improved its ability to process a larger volume of air. On the flip side, the enhancements will likely add from 75 to 100 extra horsepower. It's worth remembering: boost is residual pressure, not an indication of results. In this example, six pounds of boost forced into a stock engine might generate, say, 100 additional horsepower. But it's possible to gain an additional 50, 75, or 100 horsepower with four pounds of boost from the same blower by increasing the overall efficiency of the engine. The approach that is best for you would depend on your needs, desires, and budget.

Air/Fuel Ratio

Achieving and maintaining an accurate air/fuel ratio calibration for a naturally aspirated engine is difficult enough on a good day. Add a supercharger or turbocharger and the problem is compounded to the point of madness. Carbureted engines are more difficult because modifying the calibration requires a working knowledge of a carburetor's integrated systems. Simply installing larger main jets will not provide an accurate recalibration in all situations. In addition, because carburetors are somewhat linear, maintaining an ideal air/fuel ratio through a broad rpm range is difficult. This problem is inherent to carburetors in general. Carburetors are fixed-orifice drip meters. Their ability to adjust to a wide range of variables—atmospheric conditions, air density, load, airflow, and so on, is limited. Adding a compressor to a naturally aspirated carbureted engine compounds the problem. Electronically controlled fuel injection systems are somewhat easier, because they are self-adjusting, at least to a point.

Air/fuel ratio, the octane rating of the fuel, and the compression ratio of the engine, work hand in hand.

Higher compression ratios require higher-octane fuels. Most of our discussion will focus on pump gas with a 91 octane rating or above.

Air/fuel ratio is a numeric value indicating the concentration of fuel in a given amount of air. It's the amount of a specified substance in a unit amount of another substance. Thus, a 14:1 air/fuel ratio indicates there are 14 parts of air combined with a single part of fuel. The ratio is commonly written with the air component first. Reducing the amount of air has the same effect as increasing the amount of fuel. An 8:1 mixture is considered rich, while a 20:1 mixture would be very lean. The correct mixture for complete combustion, known as the stoichiometric air/fuel ratio, is approximately 14.75:1. The stoichiometric mixture is approximated because different engine designs and adverse operating conditions require slight adjustments to achieve efficient combustion. Equal in importance is the fact that different fuels burn at different rates and release different amounts of energy per unit mass. The chemical properties of pump gas are of little concern because they are strictly controlled by the processing plant. However, the quality of pump gas does vary from supplier to supplier; therefore it is wise to purchase the highest-quality, name-brand fuel available.

Even though 14.75:1 is considered an ideal air/fuel ratio to achieve the best compromise between power and economy, more power can be extracted from a slightly richer mixture. A 12:1 ratio will generate approximately four percent more power because the flame travels through it, releasing the fuel's energy, approximately 17 percent faster. Extreme mixtures, such as a very rich 8:1 or a very lean 20:1, slow the flame travel so much that the engine will run poorly.

Enriching the amount of fuel to achieve more power sounds reasonable

enough if it were not for one important adverse side effect: a rich mixture raises the amount of pollutants the engine expels. An ideal calibration will promote complete and total combustion, meaning all of the fuel entering the engine is burned completely. Complete combustion is not only efficient; it's the smartest way to minimize harmful emissions. Complete and total combustion can be attained only if all the chemical and mechanical variables have been optimized.

Compute air/fuel ratio by applying the formula:

A/F = <u>Air Mass Flow Rate</u>
<u>Fuel Mass Flow Rate</u>

As you will see in the chapter on electronic controls, the true problem is not obtaining a stoichiometric mixture, but rather maintaining an optimum mixture throughout the entire operating range of the engine. A running engine behaves according to many physical and chemical laws. In addition, conditions inside the engine change with engine speed, load, and varying atmospheric conditions. A stationary engine running within a very small rpm range greatly minimizes the challenge. A drag race engine is similar in concept because its useful rpm range is relatively narrow, compared to a street engine. In these two examples, all of the variables can be optimized so an engine, while running within its optimum rpm range, will run at peak efficiency 99 percent of the time.

Conversely, engines that power road vehicles must endure a host of variables.

An automotive engine must operate acceptably and reasonably efficiently from idle to 5,000 rpm, in any and all weather conditions, at almost any altitude, and under varying load conditions. For these reasons, and others, calibrating a street engine for optimum efficiency and drivability is considerably more difficult. Modifying the engine further complicates the issue. Because of these variables, many automotive professionals identify the implementation of computer engine controls as the greatest automotive achievement since the invention of the Otto cycle. If it were not for computers, engines would be mechanical or electro-mechanical nightmares. Emission controlled production cars with carburetors built between 1974 and 1984 exemplify the point.

Applying this knowledge to the subject at hand, force-feeding an engine with a supercharger or turbocharger effectively raises the stakes. Naturally aspirated fuel calibration is designed to operate with negative intake manifold pressure. Engine dynamics dramatically change when intake pressure switches from negative to positive. Fuel calibration must also adapt in equal proportions and with extreme precision.

Nitrous oxide injection is considerably easier to calibrate for optimum results, in part because the formula for combining the two agents (N_2O and fuel) is somewhat fixed, as is the chemical composition of each. When calibrated properly, a nitrous oxide system will deliver a near-ideal mixture of fuel and oxygen. Nitrous oxide injection is calibrated by controlling the pressure of the liquid nitrous oxide and fuel and by fine-tuning the size of a metering orifice. A main power switch is used to activate the system when the driver is ready to make a nitrous power run. A purge switch can be installed to ensure the nitrous and fuel lines are full and ready. A wide-open throttle (WOT) switch opens the solenoid valves, which allows the nitrous gas and fuel to flow into the engine when the throttle is pressed to the floor. A basic system can be activated anytime the throttle is held wide open, regardless of engine speed, although dumping a healthy shot of nitrous into a stock engine running at a very low rpm can place a tremendous strain on the head gasket(s) and the rotating assembly.

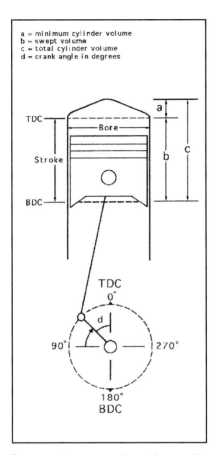

a = minimum cylinder volume
b = swept volume
c = total cylinder volume
d = crank angle in degrees

To compute compression ratio, use the measured values A, B, and C. A is the combustion chamber volume plus the thickness of the head gasket (minimum cylinder volume). B is the length of the stroke. C is the combined, or total, cylinder volume. Compression ratio equals A + B ÷ C.

Static Compression

To a point, the more a given amount of air/fuel mixture is compressed, the greater the energy released when it is ignited. Compression ratio is a numeric comparison of the maximum volume in the cylinder with the piston at bottom dead center (BDC) to the minimum volume when the piston is at top dead center (TDC) on the compression stroke. Because more compression means more power, it seems natural to raise the compression ratio to the mechanical limits of the engine.

Unfortunately, the relationship between compression ratio and thermal efficiency is not governed by any straightforward law of physics. For example, serious high-performance engines can utilize compression ratios in the low- to midteens by raising the octane rating of the fuel they burn. An average compression ratio for an average street engine will range from approximately 8.0 to 9.5. Compression ratios over 10:1 can be considered high by today's standards. A modern engine will run with a compression ratio less than 8.0, but performance will suffer dramatically.

Compression ratio may be calculated using the following formula:

CR = maximum cylinder volume / minimum cylinder volume

To put it another way:

CR = (Cylinder Volume + Chamber Volume) / Chamber Volume

To calculate the cylinder volume, or swept volume, use the formula:

CV = (pi)/4 x Bore^2 x Stroke

Note:(pi)= 3.1415927
(pi)/4 = 0.7853982

On the downside, high compression ratios adversely affect long-term durability. Forcing 14 parts of air/fuel mixture into an area the size of one part places severe stress on engine components. Extreme compression ratios can literally hammer the piston and pin, the rod and bearings, or the crankshaft, to the point of failure in a relatively short period of time. It's also harder to keep the cylinder heads sealed to the block because high compression is ever-present any time the engine is running.

High compression also requires ultra-high-octane racing fuel. Fuel must burn evenly in a controlled environment through ignition by the spark plug. Low-octane fuel will detonate too early from high pressure and temperature, causing the explosion to resist the piston before it reaches

TDC. This condition, known as pre-detonation, can destroy an engine from within. Fuel, rather than mechanics, limits compression ratio. More specifically, the compression ratio is limited by the fuel's tendency to detonate under pressure. The higher the octane rating of the fuel, the more resistant it is to detonation.

Think of forced induction as force-feeding the engine with compression. Stuffing more air/fuel mixture into each cylinder is somewhat like increasing the static compression ratio when the engine is under boost. But unlike a high static compression ratio, forced induction is compression on demand. A 12.5:1 static compression ratio is full-on at all times when the engine is running. An engine enhanced with a supercharger, turbocharger, or nitrous oxide injection system can cruise comfortably with a relatively low compression ratio during low- or no-boost conditions when the need for speed is not as great. A forced induction system is a power-on-demand option: It doesn't operate at full capacity until needed, but it's there when you want it.

Save Money—Don't Speed!

Excessively high engine speeds have an equally negative effect on durability. High-speed stresses can cause a reciprocating assembly to fly apart.

A piston and rod assembly is similar to a slide hammer. The piston races toward the end of the bore at lightning speed, slows to a dead stop, then reverses direction. It attains its highest speed roughly halfway through its stroke at peak rpm. Piston speeds between 2,500 and 3,000 feet per minute at peak rpm are common. Breaking it down further, a piston will accelerate from a dead stop to approximately 42 feet per second within a distance between 1.5 and 3 inches, depending on the length of the stroke. Needless to say, the inertial forces on the piston, pin, and crankshaft are tremendous. Is it any wonder a solid

Piston Speed and Crank Angle

This graph illustrates piston speed in relationship to crank angle. A piston accelerates from a dead stop at top dead center (TDC) to its highest velocity near midstroke, then decelerates to a dead stop at bottom dead center (BDC). Inertial forces are greatest at TDC between the exhaust and intake strokes and BDC between the power and intake strokes. Calculate piston speed in feet per minute (fpm) by multiplying 2 times the stroke (in inches) times peak rpm, then divide by 12.

Piston speed is an indicator of g-load force. The velocity of the pistons in a 350-cid Chevy engine running at 9,000 rpm is 5,220 fpm. Assuming a reciprocating weight of 1,029 grams, estimated critical tension occurs at 8,211 rpm. Limit piston speed to 4,500 fpm when running stock cast crank and rods and 5,000 fpm with forged crank and heavy-duty rods and main bearing caps. An engine built with high- quality aftermarket rods, steel crankshaft, and forged pistons will withstand higher piston speed for a limited amount of time. Forced induction promotes peak power earlier in the rpm band, which reduces the need for excessively high engine speeds.

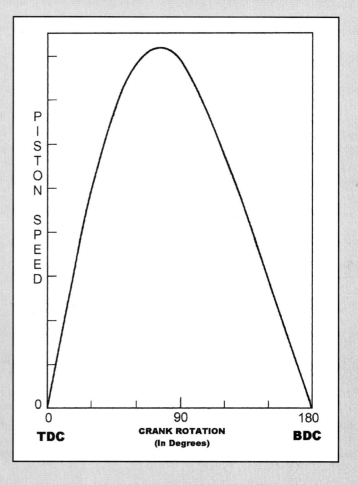

connecting rod will stretch to the point of failure when engine speeds exceed engineering limits?

Use the following formulas to calculate piston speed:

Velocity (in feet per minute) =

$$\frac{stroke \times rpm}{6}$$

A piston in a 350-cubic-inch Chevy engine is traveling 3,480 feet per minute when the engine is running at 6,000 rpm.

$$\frac{3.48 \times 6,000}{6} =$$

3,480 feet per minute

The highest inertial forces in a naturally aspirated engine occur when the piston is at TDC at the end of the exhaust stroke. An 8-ounce piston exerts an inertial force on the wrist pin approaching one ton when the engine is running at 6,000 rpm.

In human terms, it's like drawing a five-pound barbell up to your shoulder, then thrusting it out away from your body as fast as you can. When your arm reaches its full length, the weight stops. Your upper arm and shoulder represent the crankshaft and your forearm the connecting rod. The bar between the weights is the wrist pin and the weight is the piston. If the weight could be accelerated to a speed of 42 feet per second, it's doubtful you could maintain a grip on the bar when your arm reaches its full length. If you could hold on to the bar, chances are your shoulder or elbow would separate or one of the bones in your arm would break. The same thing happens inside an engine when the inertial forces become too great. Excessive inertial force can cause the weakest component in the rotating assembly to pull apart, resulting in engine failure.

Inertia is one of many evil forces that can destroy an engine. Lowering the maximum rpm of the engine, or reducing the weight of the moving parts, lessens the inertial force. High-revving engines are built from the strongest, lightest materials available. Available also means affordable. There are probably stronger, lighter space-age materials out there, but few racers can afford to mold them into engine parts.

Harmonics, or vibration, is another destructive force caused by high speed. The movements and forces produced by vibration work against the proper movement of the engine's parts, undermining the engine's efficiency. Harmonics create excess wear and stresses that can destroy an engine. To minimize harmonics, the reciprocating assembly must be balanced to a high degree of accuracy.

Obviously, slower engine speeds promote longevity. Slower engine speeds also promote economy. Broken parts and the damage they cause are expensive to repair or replace. An average, well-engineered modern-day engine will easily and safely spin to 6,500 rpm. Therefore, using 6,500 rpm as a high speed limit, peak horsepower should level off somewhere between 5,000 and 6,000 rpm.

Forced induction negates the need for high-speed operation in most street applications. A forced induction engine can generate high, relatively flat torque and horsepower curves very early in the rpm range. It's possible to generate 700 horsepower, or more, without spinning an engine over 6,500 rpm.

Volumetric Efficiency

Volumetric efficiency (VE) indicates the total amount of air/fuel mixture each cylinder takes in during the intake stroke. VE is actually a percentage of cylinder filling. One-hundred percent VE means the total area inside the cylinder is filled with a fresh air/fuel mixture during each intake stroke. Obviously, 100 percent VE is considered optimum for a naturally aspirated engine. A typical 5.0-liter V-8 engine achieving 100 percent VE would consume 5 liters of air every 720 degrees of crankshaft rotation.

Attaining 100 percent VE during each and every intake stroke would be ideal, but it isn't that easy. A number of related events combine to reduce the overall VE, including valve timing, inertia, and inefficient exhaust scavenging.

Maximum VE for an average passenger car engine will typically measure between 80 and 90 percent, well below its 100 percent potential. VE also varies with engine speed and, as you might imagine, is directly related to power output. VE is an extremely important measurement when discussing performance. Attaining 100 percent VE 100 percent of the time would be virtually impossible when considering all of the variables. It is possible, however, to improve VE at critical points in the power band.

High-performance engine builders improve VE by optimizing exhaust scavenging and by taking advantage of inertia. Velocity—the speed of the air traveling through the intake runners—is compromised by the diameter of the runner (cross-sectional area), its length, and its shape (straight versus curved, and so on). The intake port, the valve, and the surrounding area also influence the effects of velocity, as does the displacement of the cylinder(s). Typically, a long, small-diameter runner promotes velocity while a short, large diameter runner impedes velocity. In short, small-diameter runners deliver speed at a limited volume, and large-diameter runners deliver volume with limited speed. High velocity through the intake runner fills the cylinder at an incredibly fast rate. The weight and speed of the oncoming column of air forces extra air/fuel mixture into the cylinder. The intake valve is slammed closed before the column of air stops moving, thereby trapping a larger amount of air/fuel mixture in the cylinder. A well-engineered naturally aspirated race engine can attain peak VE values over 100 percent by taking advantage of high velocity.

Improving VE is as difficult as it is expensive, and naturally aspirated race engines are traditionally ill-tempered beasts. Driving through any rpm range outside the power band is usually an exercise in frustration. It's difficult to extract large amounts of power from a naturally aspirated engine without sacrificing drivability.

Forced induction improves VE numbers with little or no adverse side effects. A force-fed engine performs normally at idle, during normal acceleration, and at legal cruising speeds. It's possible (although not advisable) to double the VE of a stock engine with a supercharger, turbocharger, or nitrous oxide injection system. Conversely, when either system is not called on, the engine runs in a docile, naturally aspirated mode. A blown street engine can realistically achieve 125 to 175 percent VE numbers.

Overall VE can be calculated by applying the formula:

VE = 2 x mass airflow rate
air density x swept volume x rpm

Volumetric efficiency is affected by variations in:

-Fuel type, fuel/air ratio, the amount of vaporized fuel in the intake manifold and fuel heat of vaporization;
  -Mixture temperature, as
    influenced by heat transfer;
  -Exhaust to intake manifold
    pressure ratio;
  -Compression ratio;
  -Engine speed;
  - Intake and exhaust manifold
    port design;
  - Intake and exhaust valve timing,
    geometry, size and lift.

Decreasing compression ratio is best accomplished by adding a dish to the piston crown. The volume of the dish is added to the minimum cylinder volume, effectively lowering the static compression ratio. Installing a thicker head gasket will have the same effect, although to a lesser degree. Although machining a dish into a stock flattop piston is doable, it is not recommended.

Air Density

The power output of any engine, no matter how big or how small, is limited by the amount of fuel that can be burned efficiently during each cycle. The air-charge density, (i.e. the amount of air and fuel contained in a given space), is a huge variable factor. Compressing air increases its density by forcing a larger number of molecules into a smaller space. Increasing air-charge density is the essence of forced induction. In theory, the higher the air-charge density, the greater the power potential, provided that all of the fuel can be burned efficiently. In scientific terms, air and fuel are both fluids, (i.e., either can be made to flow at a calculable rate). Don't confuse air-charge density with airflow. Forced induction increases air-charge density, not airflow. Getting the air-charge into and out of the engine (airflow) as efficiently as possible is another subject altogether.

Allen Lockheed, noted high-performance engineer and an expert on computer modeling, emphasizes, "The airflow through an engine remains the same whether or not it is supercharged or turbocharged. The power comes from the increase in air-charge density."

Computing air-charge density is somewhat complicated, in part because there are so many variables such as temperature, atmospheric air pressure, and humidity. Engineers begin with a standardized value appropriately called dry air. Used as a scientific baseline, dry air consists of 20.95 percent oxygen, 78.09 percent nitrogen, 0.93 percent argon, and trace amounts of carbon dioxide, neon, helium, methane, and other gases. Each mole has weight, which is further defined in the *Concise Encyclopedia of The Sciences* as:

mole or mol (mÅl) n., 1. The amount of a substance that contains as many atoms, molecules, ions, or other elementary units as the number of atoms in 0.012 kilogram of carbon 12. The number is 6.02257 x 1023, or Avogadro's number. Also called gram molecule. 2. The mass in grams of this amount of a substance, numerically equal to the molecular weight of the substance. Also called gram-molecular weight.

In engine engineering, it is acceptable to regard the composition of dry air as 21 percent oxygen and 79 percent inert gases. Put another way, there are 3.773 moles of atmospheric, or apparent, nitrogen for each mole of oxygen in dry air. The molecular weight of atmospheric nitrogen differs from pure molecular nitrogen because the trace amounts of the other gases are included in the final measurement. Given these accepted variables, dry air has a molecular weight of 28.962 (typically rounded up to 29), and atmospheric nitrogen has a molecular weight of 28.16. Using these measurements, the density of dry air can be computed by working the formula:

Pressure in pounds per cubic foot =

$$2.699 \times \frac{\text{pressure in pounds per square inch}}{\text{Temperature}}$$

Therefore, dry air weighs 0.0739 pounds per cubic foot at one atmosphere (14.696 psi) at 77 degrees Fahrenheit.

Ambient air usually contains water vapor. The amount of water vapor in a given volume of air depends on the temperature and the degree of saturation. The normal proportional mass is from 1 to 4 percent. Relative humidity is the ratio of the partial pressure of water vapor actually present compared to the saturation pressure at the same temperature.

Acceptable values for all inputs must be established when computing the output of a new engine design. To obtain standardized results, all variables must be assigned a fixed value. The values for computing air density listed above exemplify the point.

Mean Effective Pressure

While torque depends on engine size, mean effective pressure (MEP) is a more useful measurement, in that overall torque—the engine's ability to do work—is broken down into work per cycle. Mean effective pressure is a relative engine performance measurement derived by dividing the work per cycle by the cylinder volume displaced per cycle—units of force per unit area. It is a perfect example of converting one form of energy (chemical energy) into another form of energy (mechanical energy), and it illustrates the force exerted on the piston by the expanding gas.

For a four-stroke spark-ignition engine, work per cycle equals power times the number of crank revolutions for each power stroke per cylinder, divided by crankshaft rpm. Therefore, the mean-effective pressure equals power X 2 ÷ V (swept volume) X rpm. To calculate mean effective pressure as it relates to horsepower, use the following formula:

Mean effective pressure =

$$\frac{\text{power} \times 2 \times 396,000}{V(\text{in}_3) \times \text{rpm}} = \text{in-lb2}$$

To calculate mean effective pressure as it relates to torque:

Mean effective pressure =

$$\frac{75.4 \times 2 \times \text{torque in lbs-ft}}{V(\text{in}^3) \times \text{RPM}} = \text{in/lb}^2$$

Mean-effective pressure values for a typical naturally aspirated spark-ignition, four-stroke engine will range from 125 to 150 lb/in² at the rpm where peak torque occurs.

Forced induction increases the air-charge density, which effectively increases volumetric efficiency and in turn increases the mean effective pressure. Forced induction produces an artificially high compression ratio, i.e., the actual compression of the intake charge is greater than the geometrical compression ratio as determined by cylinder volume.

To show that power, torque, and mean effective pressure are proportional to inlet air density:

Power = $\frac{\text{(fce)(ma)(rpm)(hv)(A/F)}}{2}$

Conversely, adding a dome to the top of the piston effectively reduces the minimum cylinder volume, which increases the compression ratio. The volume of the dome is subtracted from the volume of the combustion chamber. Installing a thinner head gasket will also increase the compression ratio.

Where (fce) represents the fuel conversion efficiency; (ma) represents the mass of the air inducted into each cylinder per cycle; (rpm) represents revolutions per minute; (hv) represents the heating value of fuel, which further defines its energy content; (air/fuel) is the air/fuel ratio; and 2 is the number of crank revolutions for each power stroke per cylinder.

Brake Specific Fuel Consumption

Fuel consumption over time can be used to measure efficiency as well. Fuel consumption is represented as a flow rate in pounds per hour, (i.e., mass flow per unit time). Brake Specific Fuel Consumption (BSFC)—fuel flow rate per unit power output—is the industry standard and measures how efficiently an engine uses the fuel to generate work. BSFC is another measure of how well an engine converts chemical energy into mechanical energy. It is computed as follows:

BSFC = $\frac{\text{fuel flow in pounds per hour}}{\text{brake horsepower}}$

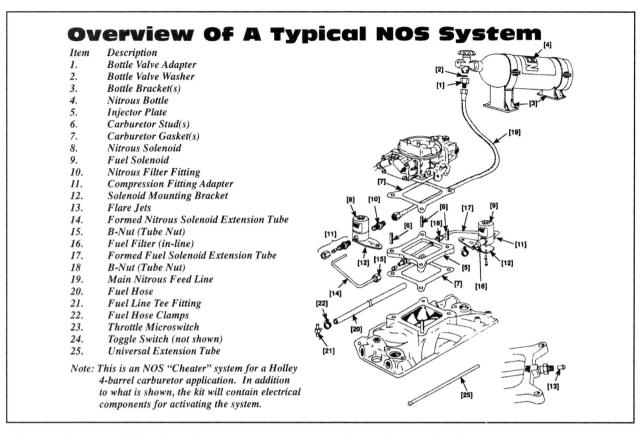

Overview Of A Typical NOS System

Item	Description
1.	Bottle Valve Adapter
2.	Bottle Valve Washer
3.	Bottle Bracket(s)
4.	Nitrous Bottle
5.	Injector Plate
6.	Carburetor Stud(s)
7.	Carburetor Gasket(s)
8.	Nitrous Solenoid
9.	Fuel Solenoid
10.	Nitrous Filter Fitting
11.	Compression Fitting Adapter
12.	Solenoid Mounting Bracket
13.	Flare Jets
14.	Formed Nitrous Solenoid Extension Tube
15.	B-Nut (Tube Nut)
16.	Fuel Filter (in-line)
17.	Formed Fuel Solenoid Extension Tube
18	B-Nut (Tube Nut)
19.	Main Nitrous Feed Line
20.	Fuel Hose
21.	Fuel Line Tee Fitting
22.	Fuel Hose Clamps
23.	Throttle Microswitch
24.	Toggle Switch (not shown)
25.	Universal Extension Tube

Note: This is an NOS "Cheater" system for a Holley 4-barrel carburetor application. In addition to what is shown, the kit will contain electrical components for activating the system.

This nitrous oxide system (NOS) kit is designed for a single four-barrel carburetor application. The make and model of the engine are of little concern. Nitrous oxide and liquid gasoline are delivered under pressure to a jet tube that runs through a spacer sandwiched between the carburetor and the intake manifold.

The BSFC will vary with rpm. A BSFC of .50 or lower at peak torque is acceptable and considered normal. The lower the number, the more efficient the engine. A number of variables, such as frictional losses, parasitic drag, and pumping losses, will reduce overall efficiency.

Soft Power

Supercharging and turbocharging promote another less obvious benefit called "soft power." Nitrous oxide injection systems are exempt here because they do not pressurize the intake manifold.

The destructive forces caused by high engine speed or high compression ratio have already been detailed. Fortunately, forced induction all but eliminates the need for either. This accomplishment is a major advantage and reason enough to use a blower to make horsepower.

Earlier we determined that the highest inertial force of the piston occurs at TDC at the end of the exhaust stroke. At this moment, an event occurs that is known as overlap, during which the intake valve is opening at the same time the exhaust valve is closing. Overlap is represented in degrees of crankshaft rotation defining the length of time both valves are open simultaneously.

The inertial forces are greatest at overlap because the piston meets very little resistance as it travels toward the cylinder head at high speed during the exhaust stroke. The resistance offered by the exhaust gases as they are forced out is measurable, but it is very small. This resistance can be calculated into what is called "pumping losses," which do little to reduce the inertial force the piston must endure.

Forced induction reduces this inertial force. When the intake runner is pressurized, the air/fuel mixture is forced into the combustion chamber under pressure as soon as the intake valve leaves its seat. The intake valve opens before the piston reaches TDC, allowing this pressure to push down on the top of the piston. Although small by comparison, the compressed air/fuel mixture acts like an air bag or shock absorber and creates a soft landing for the piston as it decelerates to a dead stop at TDC.

Applying pressure to the top of the piston during the intake stroke offers yet another advantage: the pressurized intake charge actually pushes down on the piston. Multiplying that small force times the number of cylinders equates to a minute but measurable amount of power transferred to the crankshaft.

In addition, a typical naturally aspirated high-performance camshaft will extend the length of time the valves are off their seats (duration) by opening the valves earlier and closing them later. This extended valve timing causes a negative side effect known as intake and exhaust reversion. Reversion is reverse airflow either through the intake or exhaust ports. Intake reversion occurs at the beginning of the intake stroke, which happens to be near the end of the exhaust stroke.

To promote cylinder filling, engineers open the intake valve as early as possible and hold it open as long as possible. Exhaust gases are forced into the intake runner by the piston as it nears the end of the exhaust stroke because the intake valve is opened early in the cycle. Exhaust reversion occurs at the end of the exhaust stroke, which is also the beginning of the intake stroke (overlap). The exhaust valve remains open past top dead center to help scavenge residual exhaust gases lingering in the combustion chamber. The incoming intake charge actually helps the process by purging residual exhaust gases from the chamber. At slow engine speeds, a small amount of exhaust gas can reenter the cylinder as the piston changes direction. Reversion occurs mostly during low-rpm operation, when air velocity in the intake and exhaust runners is relatively low.

Long duration, high-lift cams also produce a very long overlap period. During overlap, the fresh air/fuel mixture entering the cylinder can escape into the exhaust passage because both valves are open at the same time. This negative side effect is called "blow through." Besides wasting fuel, blow through increases harmful emissions by allowing raw fuel to enter the exhaust passage.

Extended cam timing lengthens valve overlap, which promotes reversion and impedes complete cylinder filling at slow engine speeds. The side effects of overlap make the engine sound rough and hesitant at idle—even though it's ferocious on throttle.

Contrary to what you may have been told or sold, air filters do not make horsepower. A paper air filter will not restrict airflow into the engine if it is properly sized. An undersized air filter can restrict airflow and power. The material that the filtering medium is made out of is of little concern as long as it filters dirt particles out of the air-charge.

Opening the intake valve later can minimize or eliminate intake reversion, but at the expense of high-rpm performance. Closing the intake valve earlier also reduces volumetric efficiency (VE) by shortening the critical time needed to fill the cylinder. Reversion decreases at higher engine speeds because higher velocity in the intake and exhaust runners somewhat overpowers the reversionary force.

Forced induction all but eliminates the need for an excessively long duration, high-lift cam profiles because the compressor can force more air/fuel into the cylinder in a shorter length of time. Shorter valve duration also limits overlap, which in turn reduces harmful exhaust emissions caused by blow through. A typical OEM or emission-legal aftermarket camshaft will eliminate overlap completely, in other words, zero degrees overlap.

From Mild to Wild

It's easy to see why the advantages of forced induction far outweigh the disadvantages.

A comparatively docile naturally aspirated engine will make an ideal blower motor, provided it is strong enough to withstand the pressure, so to speak. And because it is docile, it will deliver good overall performance and fuel mileage during typical low-power driving conditions. Our engine should have a static compression ratio lower than 9.5:1, a camshaft with zero overlap, and it should make peak power under 6,000 rpm. With a cursory understanding of the fundamentals, we can now turn our attention to building a mild street engine that will complement a 200-horsepower forced induction system.

Chapter Three
Engine Preparation

Building a super-strong long-block is a matter of sweating the details. The rules of thumb are to keep it light, to use strong parts, and to make them fit right. The primary consideration is durability, with secondary emphasis on reducing reciprocating weight and parasitic drag.

The stresses imposed on a four-stroke reciprocating assembly change with rpm and load. Balancing and blueprinting procedures address these stresses directly. Still, inertial forces and the transference of energy impose tremendous stress on hard parts, no matter how well the engine is built. Consider, for example, that during the power stroke, a piston must endure approximately five times as much transferred energy as during the compression stroke. Connecting rods, pistons, and crankshafts routinely fail when exposed to excessive or prolonged stress, even on the strongest rotating assemblies. Force also causes wear. Wear compromises integrity, which makes the engine more susceptible to stress. As a result, all internal combustion engines eventually hammer themselves to pieces unless they are renewed periodically.

Adding bulk in high-stress areas such as wrist pins, piston pin bosses, and connecting rod beams makes them stronger, but it also adds weight. The heavier the rotating mass, the slower it accelerates. Therefore, engineering for durability is a compromise between weight, strength, and efficiency.

Sometimes focusing on the "cause" side of the cause-and-effect equation can lead to efficient methods of reducing stress. Eliminating or redistributing an opposing force is more efficient than engineering a strong defense against it. For example, responding to a weight reduction campaign, Ford trimmed a sizable amount of weight from the 5.0-liter HO crankshaft and cylinder block castings. The change was implemented for the 1982 model year. To balance the lighter crankshaft, offset weight was increased from 28 to 50 ounces. More important, the firing order changed from the standard 298/302 1-5-4-2-6-3-7-8 to the 351 Windsor 1-3-7-2-6-5-4-8. Converting the firing order reportedly redistributed undesirable stress from the rear of the crankshaft to the front. This is an unconfirmed report, but after comparing the late-model crank to an early model, the theory makes sense.

Improving durability, like increasing horsepower, is also a matter of cost. Original-equipment engines are engineered to be mass produced, which means manufacturing costs are every bit as important as the quality of the materials used. As a result, today's engines are considerably lighter and much more efficient compared to their buffed-up ancestors.

Eliminating weight, however, can have serious repercussions. Trimming bulk can lower the durability threshold. Most new engines cannot withstand the added stress imposed by

Inside measurements are checked with a dial indicator or universal telescoping gauge. Cylinders must be set to the correct center-to-center spacing, be straight (no taper) from top to bottom, and perpendicular to the crankshaft centerline. In addition to wear, stress and heat cycling over time causes the block and all its measurements to become distorted.

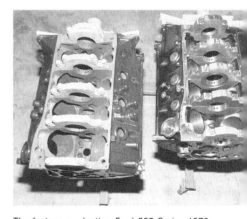

The factory production Ford 385-Series 1970 and 1971 SCJ and 1971 CJ block on the left have cast-iron main caps and pressed-in core plugs. The Motorsport 460 block on the right has forged steel main caps, screw-in core plugs, and thicker cylinder walls and decks. Unless you already have an SCJ/CJ block lying around, the Motorsport block is a better choice.

Blueprinting

Literally every machined surface in an engine should be adjusted to a blueprinted measurement. Holding those measurements to the smallest possible tolerance is the essence of "blueprinting." Some measurements correlate. Referring to the line drawing, A (throw) plus G (rod length) plus H (compression height) equals N (deck height). Subtracting D from E gives the rod bearing clearance. Likewise, J minus C indicates main bearing clearance and M minus 2 times P computes the connecting rod side clearance. These clearances are checked, not just computed.

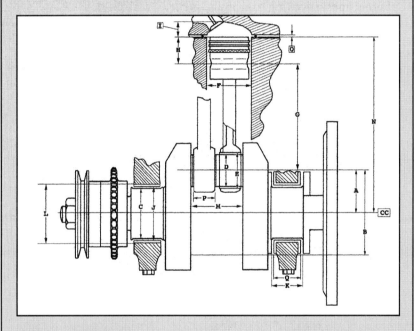

A — Throw
B — Stroke
C — Main journal diameter
D — Crank pin journal diameter
E — Rod bearing bore diameter
F — Cylinder bore diameter
G — Connecting rod length (center to center)
H — Compression height
I — Clearance volume (combustion chamber plus head gasket)
J — ID main bearing diameter (crushed)
K — Thrustbearing land
L — Main bearing bore diameter
M — Crank pin width
N — Deck height
O — Head gasket thickness
P — Connecting rod width
Q — Thrust bearing width
CC — Crankshaft centerline

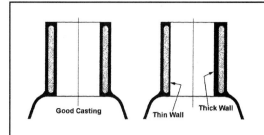

Core shift occurs when the molten iron is not properly supported or positioned during the casting process. Core shift can cause thin spots in cylinder walls, decks, and/or water jackets. Overboring can further weaken cylinder walls, making them porous when areas become excessively thin. Sonic testing can detect thin spots.

Cross-bolted Ford FE 427 blocks offer serious performance potential, but they are very heavy unless you opt for aluminum heads and intake manifold. This particular stroked FE sports a forged-steel crankshaft.

long-term forced induction as well as their heavier counterparts. That's not to say *all* late-model engines are fragile. Some engines can endure large amounts of power and abuse. With that thought in mind, remember that not all engines can be built for endurance because the main component, namely the block, is simply too meager to handle the stress, even if the reciprocating assembly will. Any engine is only as strong as its weakest component, and if that component happens to be the block, its strength will limit the durability threshold, as will any other component.

Research is your best defense against building up an unsuitable block. Some engine blocks can be reinforced while others cannot. More accurately, some blocks cannot be reinforced economically—almost anything

Blocks should be bored with a steel deck plate bolted to the gasket surface. Solid plates simulate the stresses imposed on the block when the heads are installed with the bolts tightened to the recommended specifications. Main bearing caps are installed and torqued as well. All cylinder measurements are indexed to the crankshaft centerline.

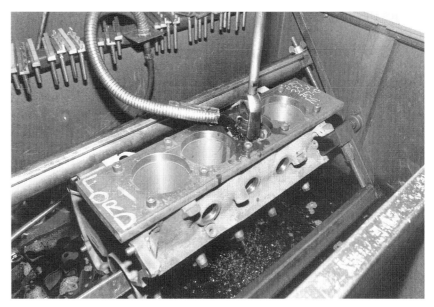

The same conditions apply through the rough honing process. Bores are undersized to allow for finish honing. Some portable cylinder hones rest on the deck and index on the centerline of each cylinder. These machines cannot adjust bore spacing, and they will not bore a perpendicular hole if the deck is not parallel with the crankshaft centerline.

Each piston is prefit to its respective cylinder. Each cylinder is then finish-honed to obtain a blueprinted piston-to-wall clearance. Depending on the composition of the piston material, tolerances must be adjusted to compensate for heat expansion. It is common to fit traditional forged pistons loose in anticipation of normal expansion.

can be accomplished within given engineering parameters if someone delegates enough time and money to the project.

As stated earlier, you don't want to build up your engine for maximum conceivable horsepower—no matter how appealing that may at first sound. Overpowering a factory production engine pushes its dependability threshold and shortens its useful life. If you plan to add forced induction to a factory production engine, research the engine's limitations before ordering the first part. Most factory production engines will withstand a small increase in power, and some will tolerate larger amounts, but many are engineered strictly for economy. Don't invest thousands giving a mediocre engine more power than it can handle; instead, get a different engine, or a different car!

Research requires a little time, but it is inexpensive. Mistakes can be very costly and time consuming.

Few people know more about a particular engine than someone who builds them to race. Locate a high-performance machine shop or engine

builder who specializes in a particular engine model. If the person or one of his customers runs a competitive car, chances are they know the engine's limitations. I have yet to meet a determined racer who doesn't push the threshold of endurance.

As a general rule, people like to share information and the Internet is a great place to begin your research. Search the Web for race teams that run your particular engine. Query newsgroups for information. Check car clubs, application-specific parts houses, tuners, and personal sites. Go to the manufacturer's Web site. Most accept e-mail and/or offer links to recommended high-performance parts stores, race teams, and service shops. If you probe deep enough, sometimes you can get inside an original-equipment manufacturer engineering group. Start with the Society of Automotive Engineers (SAE) at www.sae.org, and while you are there, shop its bookstore for printed material.

Because weight has a direct effect on fuel mileage, manufacturers are always looking for places to trim excess pounds. As a result, factory production engines have gotten lighter over the last 15 years. The widely accepted use of aluminum, plastic, and other lightweight materials have contributed to the great weight-loss effort. But unfortunately, some manufacturers choose to lower the durability threshold by removing material from blocks, crankshafts, connecting rods or pistons.

To avoid this austerity program, if you plan to build a small-block Ford or Chevrolet V-8 engine, research the benefits of the older engines. For example, a Ford 302 installed in Mustang before 1980 is more durable than one built after 1982. (Ford didn't offer a 302 Windsor in 1980 and 1981 Mustangs). Mustang 302 blocks built in 1979 (engineering number D8VE-6010-AA) weigh 135 pounds while those built in 1982 (E0AE-6010-DD) weigh just 120 pounds. Mustang 302 blocks built between 1982 and 1985 (E0AE-6010-DD – 1982; E2AE-6010-KA – 1983/4; E5AE-6010-HA – 1985) should be avoided because they are lightweights. But 1986 and newer 302 blocks (beginning with E6SE-1610-DC) are okay because the cylinder walls and decks are thicker and the cylinders are joined together in the water jackets (siamesed bores). If you plan to force-feed a Ford 4.6-liter engine (4-valve or 2-valve), limit boost to six psi. Ford's 4.6 is a difficult and expensive engine to repair.

GM took a similar view back when the term "musclecar" was new. For example, all 350ci small-block Chevrolet engines installed in 1967 Camaros were equipped with a very desirable forged-steel crankshaft. Many large truck engines were also equipped with steel cranks, four-bolt main bearing caps, and stronger blocks.

Toyota has a special "factory engineered" program called Toyota Racing Division (TRD). Special TRD dealers offer application-specific supercharger kits for popular Toyota models, which can be dealer installed.

What's better, these kits are covered by a factory warranty.

Learn anything and everything you can about your engine before you spring for a forced-induction kit, and be prepared to revise your plans at any time. If a 50-horsepower nitrous kit will meet the need, why spend $4,000 on a supercharger kit?

Durability Versus Time

Internal stress increases as power output, engine speed, and load increase. Assuming the effects of stress are cumulative—(i.e., each burst of maximum power output shortens the life of an engine by a given amount)—then durability can be factored in as an element of time.

Consider a 5.0-liter engine bolted to an engine dynamometer. For this example, assume that the cooling and oiling systems are capable of maintaining constant and safe operating temperatures. With the engine loaded to produce maximum horsepower at wide-open throttle and held there for an unlimited amount of time, how long would it survive? Five minutes, five hours, or perhaps five days? One thing for sure, eventually it will break. It might not completely destroy itself, but it's safe to say some part in the engine will fail in a relatively short period of time.

How long would the same engine last if it were installed in a well-maintained street-legal car? The answer depends on a number of variables, but it should last considerably longer.

The reason is load versus time. The higher the load, the shorter the life span of the engine. Because the loads are considerably lighter, an engine in a street-driven car should last longer than the same engine in a car driven to a world land speed record at Bonneville or in a one-ton truck pulling a 10,000-pound boat up Pike's Peak at 60 miles per hour.

Street-driven performance cars are exposed to short bursts of maximum power, usually covering less than a

Race-inspired Ford Boss 429 blocks were factory equipped with five four-bolt main caps. Most factory production, high-performance blocks fastened only the three center caps with four bolts. Rare race blocks are expensive and nearly bulletproof for the average street application.

Pistons are marked so they can be installed in their respective bores. An arrow shows the piston's orientation to the front of the block. Note two pairs of different-sized valve relief impressions. The large "eyebrow" is designed to accommodate the larger-diameter intake valve, while the smaller is for the exhaust valve.

mile. Driving the same car at wide-open throttle in a straight line for 100 miles would be similar to a sustained load imposed by a dynamometer. In terms of stress, chasing a lower elapsed time at the local drag strip would be somewhere in between. Eliminating tire slippage by bolting on a pair of slicks will also increase the stress factor because increased traction transfers additional load to the drivetrain.

You must understand that there is a finite life for all engines, high

Fontana Automotive's Clevor block combines the best qualities of Ford's canted-valve 335-Series Cleveland and wedge-head 351 Windsor engines—hence the "Clevor" nickname. The 115-pound block is equipped with iron "dry" cylinder sleeves and ductile iron four-bolt main caps.

performance or otherwise. The key is to satisfy your performance needs and balance them with the knowledge that the total amount of stress on your engine is a combination of its durability and the sheer volume of stress put on it—a combination of hours of operation and level of operation. What you must figure out is how to meet your power needs while exposing your engine to the least amount of stress possible.

NASCAR and Pro Stock drag race engines typically last for one race before they are rebuilt or "refreshed."

Engines built for lower classes of drag racing, circle track racing, and road racing can survive an entire season. In this case, time is dictated by load, which is supported by money. In other words, you can go as fast as you want for as long as you can afford it.

All Engines Are Balanced and Blueprinted

Balancing and blueprinting are relative terms. If engineered and assembled properly, all engines are balanced and blueprinted to some degree of precision. The variation of tolerance

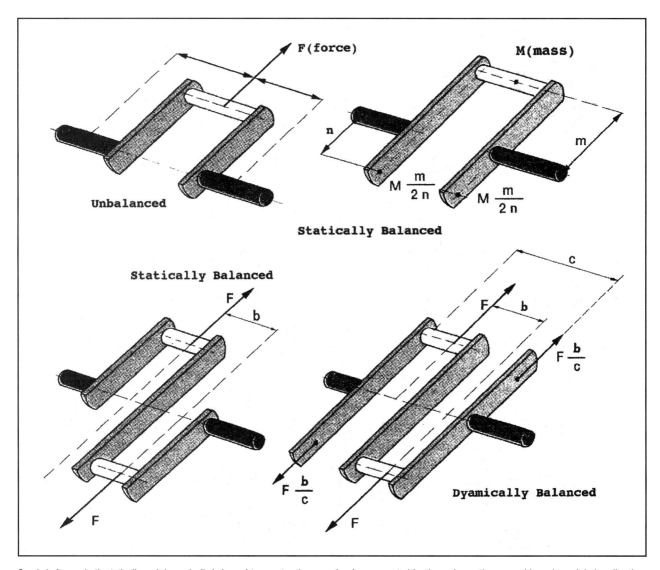

Crankshafts are both statically and dynamically balanced to counter the opposing forces created by the reciprocating assembly and to minimize vibration. Essentially, opposing inertial forces must be canceled as completely and efficiently as possible, or the slide-hammer effect would destroy the engine if it were accelerated to any purposeful speed.

or level of precision is at issue here. Think of a V-8 engine as 8 single-cylinder engines tied to a common crankshaft. The closer all 8 single-cylinder engines are matched, the more efficient the results.

When we think of balancing, we think of tires. A perfectly balanced tire rolls straight and true. A tire that is out of balance will vibrate or bounce, sometimes violently. An engine rotating assembly, the flywheel, crankshaft, and harmonic balancer, is much the same. Vibration will convert a rotating mass into an oscillating hammer. The faster the mass rotates, the more violent the hammering. Simply put, dynamic balancing minimizes vibrations and the stresses they cause. The reciprocating assembly, the connecting rods, wrist pins, and pistons, propel the rotating assembly in an engine. Balancing and blueprinting these components further reduces negative opposing forces that can diminish durability.

Blueprinting is essentially holding all measurements to a standard defined by an engineering blueprint. That means if the blueprint calls for a particular measurement to be 5.001 inches, with a tolerance of plus or minus (+/-) .003-inch, then the measurement must be between 5.004 and 4.998 inches to be acceptable, while the ideal measurement remains 5.001 inches. Thus, when blueprinting a particular component measurement, such as connecting rod length, all the rods must be 5.001 inches long within a tolerance of +/- .003 inch. The more precise the blueprint value, the smaller the acceptable range of tolerance. A value of 5.001 inches +/- 0 calls for zero tolerance, which means the measurement must be exactly 5.001-inches. Precision blueprinting adjusts all measurements as close as possible to the ideal value.

Balancing a reciprocating assembly is also a part of blueprinting. In this case, the weight and dimension of each component is matched to the others and to a given blueprint value.

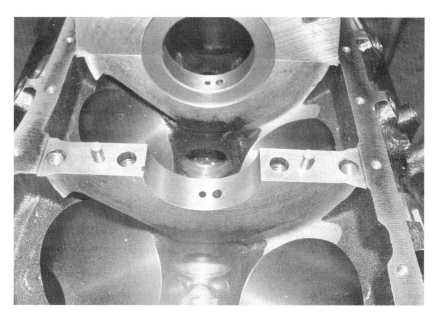

Racing blocks such as this Ford Motorsport 385-Series casting offer extra thick main webs, decks, and cylinders. Any four-bolt or two-bolt main cap can be enhanced with hardened-steel dowel pins, provided there is enough material to accommodate them. Dowel pin holes can actually weaken a stock block, so proceed with caution.

Holes are drilled in a counterweight to reduce its mass. Conversely, a high-density alloy called "heavy metal" is pressed into properly sized holes drilled into a counterweight to add mass to a rotating assembly (shown). Heavy metal is extremely dense, which means square inch for square inch, heavy metal is much heavier than iron.

Main bearing bores are checked to ensure that they are round and true. Align-honing a block straightens and aligns the main bearing bores, but it also removes material. If oversize OD bearings are not available, the main caps must be cut down to reduce the overall diameter of the holes. The bores are then honed round.

The art of balancing and blueprinting evolved from necessity. Factory tolerances are good, but they are not great. Original-equipment engines are assembled from mass-produced components, which are manufactured and machined to "acceptable tolerances." The definition of "acceptable tolerances" varies from one component to another. Not to berate car makers: today's factory tolerances are, well, tolerable, and they are getting better. Expensive, high-tech machines can hold tight tolerance values through an extended product run better than in the past. The proof is in the making. Newer engines last considerably longer today compared to their ancestral counterparts.

At times master engine builders take liberties with blueprinted values. Experienced high-performance engine engineers might increase or decrease the main or rod bearing clearance, for example, depending on the application. Each scenario has its advantages and disadvantages. Bearing clearance is the difference between the outer diameter (OD) of the crank journal and the inner diameter (ID) of the installed bearings. The value becomes the operating clearance, which is pressure fed with lubricating oil. Reducing bearing clearance increases friction while decreasing the amount of lubricating oil available to the bearing surfaces. A comparatively large bearing clearance will reduce friction and improve oiling. Bearing clearances that exceed acceptable limits will invoke the slide hammer effect. The greater the load on the engine, the more aggressive the pounding. Aside from the destructive potential, excessive clearances anywhere makes for a noisy engine. Too little operating clearance promotes excessive wear, and under extreme loads can cause the bearing to weld itself to the crank journal.

Each engine component is subject to blueprinting. The smaller the range of tolerance, the greater the assembly's precision. Expert balancing and blueprinting minimizes stress, which further promotes durability and efficiency. To make the point, a Ford engineer pulled the stock 5.0-liter HO engine out of a new 1994 Mustang GT and bolted it to a dynamometer. A dozen wide-open throttle, full-power passes were averaged to produce credible baseline torque and horsepower numbers. The engine was then dismantled, balanced, and blueprinted using acceptable racing values, then reassembled. No parts were replaced or upgraded. Follow-up dynamometer passes indicated a 12 horsepower gain. Why? Because internal stresses were minimized.

Common balancing and blueprinting procedures for a typical V-8 cam-in-block engine include, but are not limited to, the following checks and procedures:

Cylinder Block
Decks
- Machining head gasket surface(s) flat, smooth, and parallel to the crankshaft centerline
- Square (combined with decking)
- Machining decks to the proper angle in relationship to each other

Cylinders
- Diameter (bore size)
- Surface finish (RMS)

Canted-valve arrangements can generate excessive lateral pressure on the lifters and lifter bores. Excessive wear in this area can cause a number of problems, from premature cam failure to a reduction in oil pressure. Blocks can be renewed or enhanced by machining the lifter bores to accept bronze bushings.

- Out-or-round limit
- Taper limit
- Perpendicular to crankshaft centerline
- Bore spacing (center-to-center)

Lifter Bores
- Diameter (bore size)
- True (eliminate taper)
- Perpendicular with camshaft
- Overbore for bronze bushings (optional)

Bell Housing Boss (mating surface)
- Perpendicular to crankshaft centerline

Main Bearing Bores
- Align hone ensures centerline is straight and true
- Main bearing bore diameter
- Out-of-round limit

Camshaft Bearing Bores
- Out-of-round limit
- Distributor shaft bearing bore diameter

Engine Systems in Tucker, Georgia, machines hand-picked 460 blocks to accept four-bolt tongue-in-groove billet steel main caps. Main bearing webs are machined, drilled, and tapped for splayed bolts, and a tang is sized to fit into a groove in the cap. An Engine Systems stock block assembly will generate 900 horsepower—and live.

Crankshaft and Flywheel
Main Bearing Journal
- Diameter
- True (parallel with crankshaft centerline)
- Out-of-round limit
- Taper limit (per inch)
- Journal runout limit
- Surface finish (RMS)
- Correct radius

Main and rod journal diameters are checked with an outside micrometer. Journals must be round (runout) and true (taper). The diameter should fall within the blueprinted tolerance. Journals ground undersized require oversized bearings to make up the difference. It is common to undersize journals in .010-inch steps.

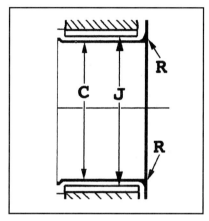

A small radius between the journal surfaces and the counterweights eliminates a starting point for stress fractures. In most applications, the larger the radius the better. Under no circumstances should the radius be machined away completely. The amount of radius (degrees of arc) can vary from one model to another.

Any machined surface on a crankshaft is subject to blueprinting. This machinist is using a telescoping gauge to measure the distance between the thrust surfaces. Once locked in place, the spring-loaded gauge is measured with a micrometer. Subtracting this measurement from the width of the thrust bearing will indicate the amount of crankshaft endplay.

Thrust Bearing Journal
- Correct length

Connecting Rod Journals
- Diameter
- Out-of-round limit (per inch)
- Taper limit
- Surface finish (RMS)
- Correct radius
- Indexed (centerline of crank pins are positioned at the correct angle)

Crankshaft technology could be considered a science unto its own, because materials and manufacturing procedures are continuously evolving. Materials range from cast-iron to nodular iron to various grades of steel. Crankshafts can be classified under one of three simple categories—stock, high-performance, and race.

Main Bearing Thrust Face
- Surface finish (RMS)
- Runout limit

Flywheel and Clutch Face
- Runout limit (TIR)
- Ring gear lateral runout (TIR)

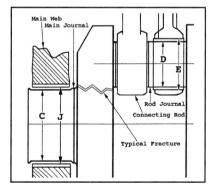

Forced induction increases the stress imposed on the reciprocating assembly. Grinding an iron crank compromises its integrity in two ways— it weakens the shaft, and it reduces the thickness of its durable "case hardened" outer layer. The weakest part of a crankshaft is the transition between the crank throws and the main bearing journals.

The smoothness of the bearing surface is equally important. Smoothness is given a numeric RMS value. Polishing cast-iron crank journals reduces friction and improves bearing life. The journals on this stock 5.0-liter crankshaft were polished with a motorized belt sander loaded with fine emery cloth.

Crankshaft Free End Play
Crankshaft Runout to Rear Face of Block (TIR max)
Connecting Rod Bearings
- Clearance to crankshaft journal
- Bearing wall thickness

Main Bearings
- Clearance to crankshaft journal
- Bearing wall thickness

Dynamic Balance
- Add or remove weight to ensure balanced high-speed rotation.

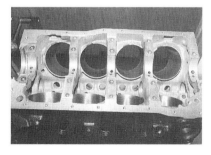

Oversized bores and a long stroke can convert a small-block into a big-block without changing the outside dimensions of the engine, but a stroked crank requires extra clearance. The cylinders and pan rail of this Motorsport A4 block have been notched to clear the rods. "There is no replacement for displacement."

Connecting Rods
Length (measure center-to-center of holes)
Piston Pin Bore Diameter

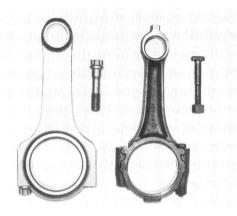

Connecting rods also run the gamut of sizes, weights, and durability. The strength of a connecting rod is determined more by rpm than power output in a street application. And because we are promoting low-rpm power by force-feeding the engine a dense mixture of air and fuel, peak rpm can be held to a more manageable range.

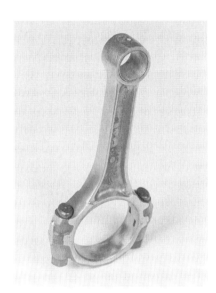

Stock iron connecting rods can be strengthened to some degree by shot-peening and deburring. Shot-peening reduces stress in the metal, and removing burrs eliminates or helps minimize areas that may allow a crack to form. Installing bronze bushings and converting to full floating wrist pins reduces stress and minimizes friction.

Crankshaft Bearing
Bore Diameter
- Out-of-round limit
- Taper limit
- Alignment (maximum
  bore-to-bore differential
  -Twist
  -Bend

Side Clearance (assembled to crank)
Balanced—weight matched

A race-prepared stock two-bolt block will easily handle 300 to 500 horsepower (depending on the make, model, and year) in a street application. Consistently hammering the engine at the drag strip will shorten its useful life. This stock block has been blueprinted, and all nonmachined surfaces have been deburred and polished.

Pistons
Diameter
Piston-to-Bore Clearance
Pin Bore Diameter
Ring Groove Width
- Compression (top)
- Compression (second)
- Oil

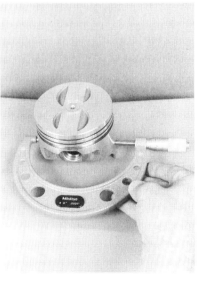

Pistons are barrel shaped, making it necessary to take several measurements perpendicular to the wrist pin halfway from the crown to the skirt. Use the largest measurement to set piston-to-wall clearance. Measure all of the pistons, then finish-hone each cylinder to allow for the blueprinted tolerance.

The compression height of the piston plus the length (center-to-center) of the connecting rod plus the length of the crank throw should equal the deck height of the block (the distance from the crankshaft centerline to the head gasket surface). The top of the piston should come flush with the gasket surface at top dead center (TDC).

Piston Pin
- Length
- Diameter
  -Pin-to-piston clearance
  -Pin-to-rod clearance

Custom pistons are a marvel of modern engineering and manufacturing techniques. This example features an oversized dish, exacting valve divots, a short wrist pin for weight savings, spiral pin locks, minimal skirt area, and a comparatively short compression height to accommodate a long connecting rod and/or a long (stroked) crank throw.

- Piston Ring Width
  -Top
  -Second
- Side Clearance
  (ring-to-ring groove)
  -Top
  -Second
- Oil

Ring end gap
 • Top
 • Second
 • Oil ring steel rail

The deck(s) must be perfectly flat, smooth, and parallel to the crankshaft centerline. Squaring a block means making sure the decks are parallel to each other and that they are planed to the correct angle. For example, the deck surfaces will be 90 degrees in relationship to each other on a 90-degree V-8.

Camshaft, Journals, and Bearings
Lobe Lift
 • Intake
 • Exhaust

Forged steel, roller-tipped rocker arms are more durable than stock components, but because the ball-in-socket fulcrum remains a high friction area, do little to eliminate friction. They are considerably better than stock, but not as good as rockers that incorporate a needle-bearing fulcrum.

Theoretical Valve Lift @ Zero Lash
 • Intake
 • Exhaust

Bearing Inside Diameter
Journal-to-Bearing Clearance

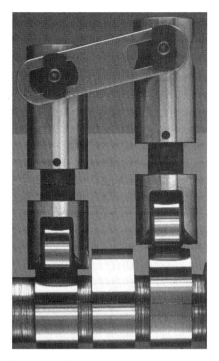

Roller cams eliminate a tremendous amount of internal friction. Plus, by the nature of their design, roller cams extend the profile range beyond the mechanical limitations imposed by a flat tappet design. The benefits outweigh the cost, and that's why nearly all OEMs have converted to roller cams, lifters, and cam followers in recent years. *Competition Cams*

Journal Diameter
 • Runout limit
 • Out-of-round limit
Valve Timing (each cylinder)
End Play

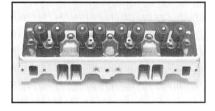

Cylinder heads are very intricate components, encompassing the combustion chamber, spark plug entry, valve assemblies, water passages, the intake and exhaust runners, and other related hardware. If it is an overhead cam arrangement, the head will also include the camshaft(s) and accompanying valve train components. Finding room for everything is a problem.

Cylinder Head and Valve Train
Combustion Chamber Volume (cc)
 • Match all
  -Intake runner volume
  -Exhaust runner volume

The valve train is the weakest assembly in any cam-in-block engine. As a general rule, factory hardware offers minimal durability, while imposing excessively high frictional losses. Crane's needle bearing, roller-tipped aluminum alloy rocker arms are lightweight, and they provide increased durability–all at an affordable price.

High-quality springs, retainers, locks, guide plates, studs, and valve stem seals are the rule, not the exception. Valve train hardware takes a beating. The higher the spring pressure, the more severe the abuse. Because we are encouraging low-rpm operating, ultrahigh spring pressures are unnecessary.

Valve Guide Bore Diameter
Valve Seats
 • Width intake and exhaust
 • Angle (1, 2 & 3)
 • Runout (TIR)

Valve Stem-to-Guide Clearance
Valve Head Diameter
Valve Face Runout Limit
Valve Face Angle
Valve Stem Diameter
Valve Spring Pressure
  (pounds @ specified length)
 • Closed
 • Open
Coil Bind (distance between coils @ full open)

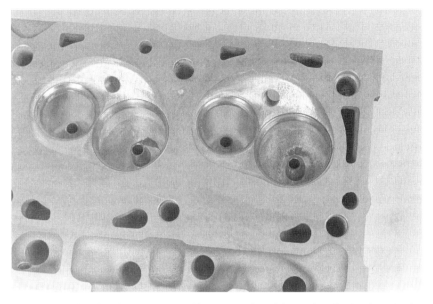

Valve seats and angles deserve a reasonable amount of special attention. Hardened steel valve seats are required for aluminum castings and are a recommended option for cast-iron heads. Likewise, back cutting the valves and seats with at least three complementary angles should be considered SOP.

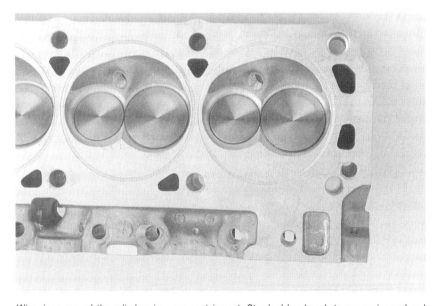

Wire rings around the cylinders improve containment. Standard head gaskets are engineered and designed to work well in naturally aspirated applications with stock compression ratios. Original-equipment and aftermarket high-performance gaskets are able to withstand higher cylinder pressures, and wire ring gaskets provide even better containment.

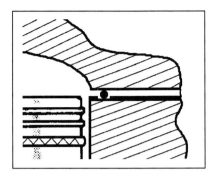

A cross-sectional illustration of an O-ringed cylinder shows how a wire encircling the bore is crushed into a relief, or groove, that has been cut into the block or head. A large-diameter wire ring extends beyond the thickness of the head gasket.

Oil Pump

Relief Valve Spring Tension
(pounds @ specified length)
Drive Shaft-to-Housing Bearing
Clearance
Relief Valve-to-Bore Clearance
Gear or Rotor End Clearance
(assembled)
Gear or Outer Race-to-Housing
Clearance

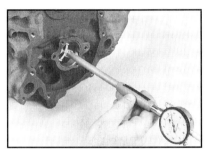

Camshaft bores and bearings are checked in much the same manner as the main bearings. Oversized OD bearings are installed to bring a honed bore back to spec.

Crate Engines

Crate engines are a good value, and many are assembled using high-quality components. Few, however, are balanced and blueprinted to a high level of precision. Many crate engines are mass-produced. In fact, some original-equipment crate engines are production passenger car engines that were simply plucked off the assembly line.

Gun makers first perfected the concept of mass-produced interchangeable parts over 100 years ago, and Henry Ford first applied the concept to automobiles. The practice is simple enough: components are mass-produced in large numbers within a given tolerance. Each is identical within that tolerance, for example + or -0.001 inch, and those parts whose size difference is greater than 0.001 inch, either bigger or smaller, are rejected.

From a manufacturing point of view, the tighter the tolerance, the more difficult the task. Machines that make engine parts must be constantly checked and adjusted to ensure that each part falls within the acceptable tolerance. Pistons, rods, cranks, and blocks are assembled from a seemingly endless supply of "bulk" components.

Any particular component is combined with any other component in random order. Engines are then assembled on an assembly line with little or no regard to mixing and matching components for optimum fit. The random selection of components of varying tolerances gives way to the possibility that a number of parts with extreme values will be combined together.

Let's say a particular connecting rod, piston, and bearing all measure at the minimum range of acceptable toler-

OEM and aftermarket crate engines are available in a wide variety of displacements, configurations, and performance ranges. Most off-the-shelf crate engines are relatively inexpensive compared to custom, hand-assembled powerplants.

ance, such as .001 inch below standard. Now let's say this piston-and- rod combination are combined with a minimum- spec crank journal and a maximum- spec bore. The result is a very loose assembly, because the tolerances "stacked up," each part's deviation from ideal size exacerbating the variance of the other part's. Although each individual component falls within its spe-

cific tolerance, the stack-up of extreme tolerances results in a noisy engine and affects its durability and longevity.

A stack-up of extreme tolerances can occur with factory production balance or blueprinted specifications. Precision blueprinting and balancing eliminates the problem, since each component is adjusted to fall within a very small range of tolerance.

Chapter Four
Superchargers

Superchargers can be loosely described as progressive air compressors, partly because their output varies with speed, increasing as speed increases up to the supercharger's design limitations. If the supercharger is run beyond its limits, efficiency suffers. At that point the blower becomes more of a heater than a compressor. When the overrevved supercharger heats the air-charge, its air density decreases and causes performance to level off.

Many engineering factors dictate the range of performance as well as the level of efficiency; therefore, it is extremely important that the supercharger be sized properly for the application. In this instance, "size" refers to the supercharger's performance capabilities, not necessarily its physical size.

Typically, superchargers are mechanically driven, although a few engineers have experienced limited success driving a small supercharger with an electric motor. All of the superchargers covered in this book are belt-driven off the engine.

As stated in chapter 1, superchargers fall into one of three categories: centrifugal, positive-displacement (rotary), or sliding vane. Beyond the mechanism used to drive them, each is unique in design and function. Because sliding vane compressors are not widely used for automotive applications, they will not be covered beyond the brief description offered in the first chapter.

Centrifugal Superchargers

In a way, centrifugal superchargers are mechanically driven turbochargers. Their compressor wheels and conical housings are similar in form and function. Basically, centrifugal blowers accelerate the speed of the incoming air. Slow-speed air enters the housing near the center of the compressor wheel and exits at its outermost edge at a much greater speed, thanks in part to centrifugal force.

Due to packaging limitations, the compressor wheel, called the impeller, must be driven at a much higher speed than the engine turns. This is accomplished by using different- sized pulleys or gears—similar to the way different-sized sprockets on a bicycle allow you to turn the rear wheel much more quickly than pedaling speed. The crank pulley overdrives the blower pulley, and a gearbox (or belt arrangement) then overdrives the impeller. Overdriving the compressor 7 to 7.5 times is common. Typical maximum impeller speeds range from 40,000 to 60,000 rpm. Without gear multiplication, the crank pulley would need to be very large, otherwise the compressor wheel would not spin fast enough to be effective. Vortech, Powerdyne, Paxton, and ProCharger all build centrifugal superchargers.

Positive-Displacement Superchargers

Positive-displacement superchargers consist of a pair of contoured, overlapping rotors or screws that rotate inside a unique housing. Air trapped between the rotors (or screws) and the housing is moved toward the outlet port. The size of the air space, or displacement, remains consistent and defines the size of the supercharger as well as its output potential. Air exiting the outlet or discharge port is packed into a comparatively small space. These air pulses generate a lot of noise and exert nonuniform torque on the rotors. Positive-displacement compressors are best suited for applications requiring relatively small pressure ratios. In addition, compared to a centrifugal compressor, the performance range of a positive-displacement blower is not limited by surge and choking. Its major disadvantages are its high noise level, poor efficiency, and large physical size.

The volumetric efficiency of a positive-displacement compressor depends on the running clearances of the rotors, the length of the rotors, their rotational speed, and the pressure ratio. Because these blowers displace a fixed volume of air, they operate at slower speeds than centrifugal superchargers.

As a general rule, the larger the physical size of the blower the greater its output potential. The total power to be gained from a supercharger may therefore be limited by the available space around the engine. As you will see, centrifugal blowers have a need for speed. Eaton, Kenne Bell, and Blower Drive Service market positive-displacement blowers.

Adiabatic Efficiency

It should be painfully obvious by now that to match an existing supercharger to any given application (as opposed to engineering a supercharger for a specific application), a "shopper" must evaluate numerous variables in an attempt to zero in on the optimum combination. Physical size and shape are very important factors, as are the drive requirements. Airflow requirements, pressure ratio, and drive speed must also fit within a comfortable range. And because heat greatly influences the overall effectiveness of a compressor, the amount of heat a compressor generates (an unavoidable byproduct of compressing air) should be given a high degree of priority. The value that defines the amount of heat a particular compressor generates is called its adiabatic efficiency.

When a volume of gas is compressed and cannot escape, pressure rises in proportion to the degree of compression. Further, we know from practical experience, as well as from theory, that the temperature of the gas rises too. However, the temperature of the gas does not rise in strict proportion, because although the gas is physically trapped, heat is not. An adiabatic operation is one in which no gain or loss of heat to or from external sources occurs. In practice, when the air-charge is compressed in the cylinder it reaches an appreciably higher temperature than it would in a truly adiabatic process. The measure of efficiency of a compressor is how close it comes to the true adiabatic state. For example, a compressor rated at 50 percent adiabatic efficiency will deliver compressed gas at a temperature twice that of a true adiabatic compression. The extra heat corresponds to losses due to the low pumping efficiency. Unfortunately, heat is an enemy of forced induction.

The density of a gas at any given pressure is inversely proportional to its temperature. In other words, the heat effectively reduces the rate of charge. Ultimately, it is the weight of the charge that will determine how much energy can be extracted during the combustion process and converted into useful work. Therefore, lowering the temperature of the charge increases its density and a denser charge will generate more work.

A more efficient compressor generates a lower air-charge temperature. For example, let's assume a compressor with a 50 percent adiabatic efficiency takes in air at an ambient temperature of 68 degrees Fahrenheit and delivers it at a pressure of 1.5 atmospheres (22 psi): The delivery temperature will be 194 degrees Fahrenheit. If the efficiency of the compressor were 75 percent, the outlet temperature would only be 153.1 degrees Fahrenheit. Even though the pressure is the same, the 153.1 degree air-charge is denser and will therefore support a greater power output.

The adiabatic efficiency becomes a more important factor as the ambient air temperature rises. When it's 100 degrees outside, the temperature of the air entering the supercharger will be 100 degrees or more. Adiabatic efficiency becomes critical at this point unless you plan your driving around the weather. Simply put, the higher the adiabatic efficiency the better.

Choosing the Right Charger

Because of their physical differences, positive-displacement and centrifugal blowers move air at different rates and at varying levels of efficiency. Neither system is perfect, but each has advantages to counter its disadvantages. Following are some features for each type:

-Positive-displacement superchargers can generate a high level of boost at relatively low engine speeds. Centrifugal superchargers generate a comparatively small amount of boost early in the rpm range.

-Typically, the output of a centrifugal blower will continue to increase gradually with engine speed. For that reason, positive-displacement blowers usually generate larger amounts of low-rpm torque compared to centrifugal chargers.

This illustration shows a typical installation of a 1FA212-41I ProCharger on a 1986–1993 5.0-liter HO Mustang. The machined-aluminum double-crank pulley replaces the stock single pulley. The larger-diameter outer groove drives the supercharger.

SUPERCHARGER SPECIFICATIONS

	P600B	P-1SC	P-1SCH	D-1SC	D-1	D-2	D-3C	D-3M
Compressor Housing Diameter	9"	9"	9"	9"	9"	10.5"	12"	12"
Inlet Hose Diameter	3.75"	3.75"	3.75"	3.75"	3.75"	4.5"	5"	5"
Inducer Diameter	3.37"	3.37"	3.37"	3.37"	3.37"	4.25"	4.7"	4.7"
Impeller Exducer Diameter	6.25"	6.25"	5.75"	6.25"	6.25"	6.25"	7"	7"
Outlet Hose Diameter	3"	3"	3"	3"	3"	3.5"	4"	4"
Outlet I.D.	2.62"	2.62"	2.62"	2.62"	2.62"	3.15"	3.59"	3.59"
Max RPM (Impeller)	60,000	65,000	65,000	65,000	65,000	63,000	57,000	56,000
Max Flow (CFM)	1200	1200	1200	1400	1400	2200	2700	2900
HP Usage (typical max)	775	825	825	925	925	1275	1500	1650
Internal Step-Up	3.36:1	4.10:1	4.10:1	4.10:1	4.44:1	4.44:1	4.44:1	4.44:1
Max Boost (psi)	27	30	30	32	32	32	34	36

Notes: • The stated figures are not absolutes, and may actually be higher depending upon the specific application.
• These figures are based on stated peak airflows; actual obtainable power levels may be higher in well prepared engines.
• All helixed ProCharger impellers operate with peak efficiencies of 72-77%, as defined by SAE J1723.
• When comparing supercharger adiabatic efficiencies, subtract approximately 4-5 percentage points for competitors' compressor housings with 90° outlets.
• Engine intake air temperature is the most relevant thermal measure (not SAE J1723) for a supercharger installed on a vehicle, especially when intercooled;
  SAE J1723 does not address the impact of engine dynamics, engine compartment heat transfer, intercooling or deficiencies caused by supercharger location.

ACCESSIBLE TECHNOLOGIES, INC. · WWW.PROCHARGER.COM
14801 WEST 114TH TERRACE · LENEXA, KS 66215 · TEL 913 338-2886 · FAX 913 338-2879

ATI's Supercharger Specifications matrix lists ProCharger's maximum parameters. The "HP Usage" illustrates power potential based on the supercharger's stated peak airflow output. All helix ProCharger impellers reportedly operate at peak efficiency between 72 and 75 percent.

-Heavier, underpowered vehicles respond well to positive-displacement blowers, while lighter, overpowered vehicles favor centrifugal chargers.

-Positive-displacement blowers are typically limited to smaller compression ratios (Delta P across the blower—P1 versus P2, i.e., Delta P is P1 versus, or compared to, P2). That is, a small-displacement blower will deliver a small amount of boost. A large amount of boost requires a large-displacement blower. To increase volume, it is necessary to increase the physical size of the blower. Looking at it another way, the displacement of the blower must be proportional to the displacement of the engine. Further, increasing the size of the blower adds weight to the engine assembly. A Roots supercharger capable of blowing 20 pounds of boost into a 400-cubic-inch engine would be both large and heavy. Typical original-equipment superchargers are sized to generate less than 10 pounds of boost.

-Centrifugal superchargers can deliver a comparatively large amount of boost from a considerably smaller package (the physical size of the blower assembly). The speed and shape of the impeller, as well as its size, dictate the output of a centrifugal supercharger.

This comparison assumes both superchargers are properly sized for a passenger car or light-truck engine utilizing a normal operating speed range from 1,000 to 6,500 rpm.

Selecting the right supercharger for your particular application starts and ends with research.

ATI/ProChargers

Accessible Technologies Inc. (ATI) manufacturers 8 different centrifugal superchargers appropriately called ProCharger. ATI is also one, if not the only, manufacturer that includes a properly sized air-to-air intercooler in its kits. A typical

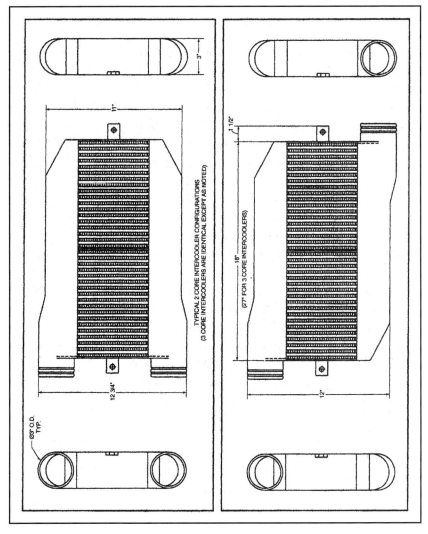

ATI air-to-air intercooler configuration is available in four sizes and two materials—aluminum or sheet metal. A Delta T value was reported to be classified information by an ATI spokesperson.

assembly includes the supercharger, brackets, and hardware needed to attach the blower to the engine: an air intake system including a high-flow air filter, a belt-drive system, an air-to-air intercooler, and all the tubes and fittings needed to connect the components together.

Installing an intercooler obviously requires additional time and effort, so be prepared. To be effective, the cooler must be positioned in the fresh-air stream entering the grille or front air dam. Be assured the extra work is worth the investment.

Technical features include CNC-machined billet impellers manufac-tured from 7075 T-6 aluminum, A356 aluminum volutes, transmission covers and backing plates, and billet gears hardened to 62 Rockwell C. The D-Series ProCharger uses a Duplex Support Bearing System that positions two specially machined bearings directly behind the impeller for added support. A Targeted Direct Bearing Oiling System ensures the bearings receive adequate lubrication.

ATI's latest and greatest is a quiet, self-lubricating ProCharger identified as P-1SC. A proprietary, patented gear design is credited for eliminating the typical blower whine. An internal oil pump distributes lubricant to the gears

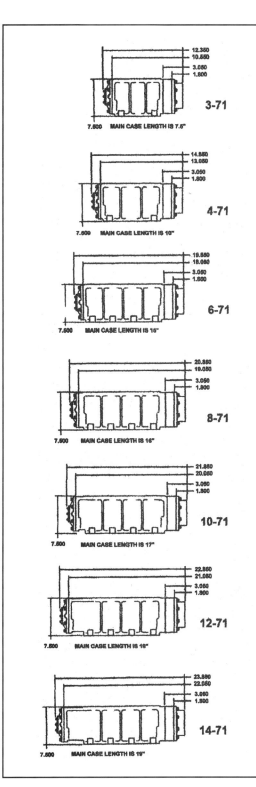

Industrial Roots 71-Series blowers were sized to the displacement of a particular diesel engine. The length of the blower housing and rotors dictate its potential output. All other dimensions remain unchanged. Given these parameters, a 14-71 was designed to feed a 994-cid diesel engine. *Blower Drive Service*

When most automotive enthusiasts think of a blower, this is the image they see. A Roots/GMC blower nestled between the heads of an American V-8 symbolizes the upper end of hotrodding's economic scale. It is big, it is bold, and it makes a statement. Its girth is also its most limiting feature.

Air/fuel mixture requirements are different for full-load, wide-open throttle and light-load, part-throttle operation. Mechanical fuel injection systems such as this can deliver a large volume of fuel to accommodate a large amount of boost, although their range of effectiveness is limited to a comparatively narrow rpm band.

Original Roots/GMC blowers were very inefficient, in part because they were designed to be more of a low-speed fan rather than a high-volume air compressor. Today's blowers use aircraft aluminum, superhard steel alloys, industrial-grade sealed bearings, and high-temperature seals.

and bearings. Oil in the self-contained gearbox should be changed every 6,000 miles. P-1SC is available with either a radial or helix impeller and is warrantied for up to three years.

ATI also offers a listing of blow-through supercharger systems for small-block Chevrolet engines. These systems use an energy-saving serpentine drive belt with a billet spring-loaded tensioner. Eight blow-through kits range from high output to race, and the CX100-D2I includes a universal intercooler and tubing kit that is nonapplication

specific. A stock 350 crate engine with a 9:1 compression ratio equipped with a P600B ProCharger delivering 10 pounds of boost reportedly gained 127 horsepower running on 93-octane pump gas. The same engine equipped with a Summit 292 hydraulic camshaft generated 209 horsepower, and a pair of Airflow Research cylinder heads added another 34 horsepower.

Roots, GMC, BDS

Roots defines both a particular blower design and the name of the original manufacturer. For this reason Roots should always be capitalized.

In 1859, Philander and Francis Roots of Connersville, Indiana, developed a device to pump water. When it proved a commercial failure, they applied the same device to moving air in a foundry. This Roots "blower" worked well, and they received a patent on it in 1860.

Auto manufacturers, including Gottlieb Daimler and Louis Renault, seized upon the air pump idea as a way of making engines more powerful. By 1909, Lee Chadwick was supercharging competition cars in the United States. Len Zengle won the inaugural 10-mile race in Indianapolis in one of Chadwick's supercharged creations.

Aero-engine designers also saw the blower's benefits as a means to fly higher and faster. The thin air at higher altitudes limits the amount of

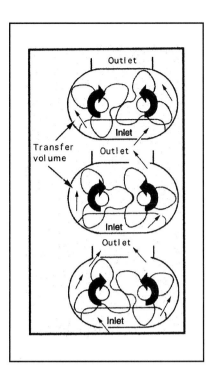

The volume of air "displaced" by a positive-displacement blower is proportional to the size of the blower in the same way that displacement defines the size of an engine, (i.e., a 300ci engine displaces 300ci of air every 720 degrees of crankshaft rotation). *Eaton Corporation, Supercharger Division*

This "basic" blown 460 Ford generates 609 horsepower at 5,600 rpm and 630 lbs-ft of torque with help from 8 pounds of boost. The reworked heads and race-prepared block and crankshaft are all that remain of the stock motor. Dished TRW pistons lower the factory compression ratio to a manageable 8:1.

Very few blower cars are driven daily in the truest sense of the word. More often, performance and efficiency run a distant second behind aesthetics. Typical Root/GMC blowers emit a distinguishable whine that can be maddening at specific rpm points. Still, they make horsepower and they look great.

In the world of street rods, carburetors are the metering device of choice partly because they are affordable and easy to understand, but mostly because they are nostalgic. Programmable electronic fuel injection systems are considerably more efficient, but few street rods are built for economy.

power a piston engine can generate. Stuffing more air into the engine was the fix. Supercharged aircraft engines were researched during World War I and put into widespread use during World War II.

The most common Roots blower adapted to automotive applications was mass-produced by General Motors, hence the GMC connection. Mass production made the blowers affordable to cash-impaired hot rodders. The Roots/GMC blower was originally designed to blow fresh air into a GM two-stroke industrial diesel engine. The displacement was too large for the cylinders to scavenge without help. A Roots blower was adapted to blow a high volume of low-pressure air into a cavity cast into the block. The exhaust valves opened near the end of the power stroke at about the same time the piston exposed the air holes on its way to BDC, its lowest

FINAL COMPRESSION RATIO CHART

BLOWER BOOST

COMP RATIO	2	4	6	8	10	12	14	16	18	20	22	24
6.5	7.4	8.3	9.2	10	10.9	11.8	12.7	13.6	14.5	15.3	16.2	17.0
7	8	8.9	9.9	10.8	11.8	12.7	13.6	14.5	15.3	16.2	17.0	17.9
7.5	8.5	9.5	10.6	11.6	12.6	13.6	14.6	15.7	16.7	17.8	18.6	19.5
8	9.1	10.2	11.3	12.4	13.4	14.5	15.6	16.7	17.8	18.9	19.8	20.9
8.5	9.7	10.8	12	13.1	14.3	15.4	16.6	17.8	18.9	19.8	20.9	21.9
9	10.2	11.4	12.7	13.9	15.1	16.3	17.6	18.8	20	21.2	22.4	23.6
9.5	10.8	12.1	13.4	14.7	16	17.3	18.5	19.8	21.1	22.4	23.6	24.8
10	11.4	12.7	14.1	15.4	16.8	18.2	19.5	20.9	22.2	23.6	24.8	26
10.5	11.9	13.4	14.8	16.2	17.6	19.1	20.5	21.9	23.4	24.8	26.2	27.6
11	12.5	14.0	15.5	17.0	18.5	20.0	21.5	22.9	24.5	26.0	27.5	28.9

This chart converts boost pressure into simulated compression ratios. The X-axis represents the computed static compression ratio. The Y-axis is calibrated in pounds per square inch of boost pressure. The corresponding vectors indicate the simulated compression ratio at full boost. *Blower Drive Service*

BOOST CHARTS ARE FOR "BDS" STAGE ONE BLOWERS ONLY

671 BLOWER (SMALL BORE)

Cubic Inches	-20%	-15%	-10%	-5%	1:1	+5%	+10%	+15%	+20%	+25%	+30%	+35%	+40%
289	5lbs	7lbs	11lbs	13lbs	17lbs	19lbs	21lbs	23lbs	26lbs				
327	3lbs	5lbs	7lbs	9lbs	11lbs	12lbs	14lbs	17lbs	21lbs	24lbs			
350	1lbs	3lbs	5lbs	7lbs	9lbs	11lbs	13lbs	15lbs	18lbs	21lbs	24lbs		
400		1lbs	3lbs	4lbs	6lbs	8lbs	10lbs	12lbs	15lbs	18lbs	20lbs	23lbs	
427			2lbs	3lbs	5lbs	7lbs	9lbs	11lbs	13lbs	15lbs	17lbs	20lbs	23lbs
454				2lbs	4lbs	6lbs	8lbs	10lbs	12lbs	14lbs	16lbs	18lbs	20lbs
500						2lbs	4lbs	6lbs	8lbs	10lbs	14lbs	16lbs	18lbs

This blower drive matrix best illustrates how a 671 BDS blower will respond to engine displacement and drive ratio. The numbers across the top of the chart represent percentage of blower speed, that is, −20 percent is 20 percent underdriven, +20 percent is 20 percent overdriven, and so on. *Blower Drive Service*

point in the cylinder. Forced air entering the bottom of the cylinder blew the exhaust out through the exhaust ports at the top. GM added standardized cylinders to make inline 3-, 4-, and 6-cylinder engines as well as V-4, V-6, V-8, V-12, and V-14 engines. The size of the blower was matched to the number of cylinders.

Vortech Engineering Inc.

Although Vortech superchargers appear similar, subtle changes to the compressor wheel, the size of the volute (compressor housing), the gears, and the bearings provide an effective adjustable range. Units can be fine-tuned to fit a variety of specific engine makes, models, and sizes in a number of different applications.

Vortech superchargers are available in six configurations: the V-1, V2 SQ, V-4, V-5, V-7, and V-9.

The V-1 platform includes the A-, R-, S-, SC-, and T-Trim superchargers.

V-1 chargers use straight-cut gears and are the coolest-running superchargers on the market, according to company literature. All Vortech street-legal kits built prior to January

---

Final Compression Ratio (FCR) = [(Boost ÷ 14.7) + 1] x CR		
Boost	=	Maximum blower boost
14.7	=	psi at sea level
CR	=	engine compression ratio
Corrected Compression Ratio = FCR - [(altitude / 1000) x 0.2]		

Use this formula to compute the final compression ratio. Premium 91-octane pump gas will support approximately 10:1 compression at an ideal 14.7 air/fuel mixture ratio. Richer air/fuel mixture ratios will support slightly higher compression. Use the formula on the bottom line to correct for altitude. *Blower Drive Service*

A Roots/GMC blower manifold is both an adapter and a plenum. This is a fabricated one-off blower manifold for a 500ci Cadillac engine. The discharge side of the blower is flat and considerably wider than it would be if it had been designed for a passenger car engine.

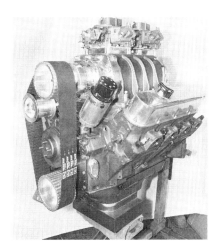

Some Root/GMC blowers double the overall height of the engine. This particular Cadillac engine should deliver between 900 and 1,000 horsepower. The owner plans to install it in a street-driven Ford F-100 pickup.

V-1 superchargers have been tested extensively throughout the years, both on and off the track. Blowing an extra 100 horsepower out of a stock Ford 5.0-liter HO engine with an A-Trim supercharger is a given. Intake manifold, cylinder head, camshaft, and exhaust enhancements can add another 40 to 80 horsepower.

VORTECH SUPERCHARGER SYSTEM APPLICATION GUIDE

FORD MUSTANG SUPERCHARGER SYSTEMS

P/N	Vehicle	Years	S/C Trim	Boost (PSIG)	HP/Torque Stock	HP/Torque Vortech	Crank Pulley/Rib	S/C Pulley/Rib	Belt Tensioner	Bypass Valve	Computer Add-Ons	Ignition	FMU	Fuel Pump (LPH)	Install Hours	Ship Weight (Lbs)	SC/Belt P/N	Accessory Belt P/N	Air Filter P/N	Flex Hose P/N 7U035-001
4FA218-010	Mustang 5.0-standard	`86-`93	V-1 A	5	205/276	275/344	6.0"/6	3.33"/6	Manual	No	Stock	Stock	12:1	Stock	4-5	45	2A046-527	N/A	8H040-010	3.5" x 12"
4FA218-030S	Mustang 5.0-Cobra	`93	V-2 SQ-S	8-10	235/285	376/400	6.875"/8	3.33"/8	Manual	Yes	Stock	MSD BTM	10:1	T-Rex	7-9	54	2A048-525	N/A	8H040-010	3.5" x 12"
4FA218-030T	Mustang 5.0-Cobra	`93	V-1 T	8-10	235/285	376/400	6.875"/8	3.33"/8	Manual	Yes	Stock	MSD BTM	10:1	T-Rex	7-9	54	2A048-525	N/A	8H040-010	3.5" x 12"
4FA218-040S	Mustang 5.0-HO	`86-`93	V-2 SQ-S	8-10	205/275	331/385	6.875"/8	3.33"/8	Manual	Yes	Stock	MSD BTM	12:1	T-Rex	7-9	54	2A048-525	N/A	8H040-010	3.5" x 12"
4FA218-040T	Mustang 5.0-HO	`86-`93	V-1 T	8-10	205/275	331/385	6.875"/8	3.33"/8	Manual	Yes	Stock	MSD BTM	12:1	T-Rex	7-9	54	2A048-525	N/A	8H040-010	3.5" x 12"
4FA218-070S	Mustang 5.0-HO with cooler	`86-`93	V-2 SQ-S	8-10	205/275	360/400	6.875"/8	3.33"/8	Manual	Yes	Stock	Stock	12:1	T-Rex	14-16	54	2A048-525	N/A	8H040-010	3.5" x 12"
4FA218-080S	Mustang 5.0-Cobra with cooler	`93	V-2 SQ-S	8-10	235/285	405/420	6.875"/8	3.33"/8	Manual	Yes	Stock	Stock	10:1	T-Rex	14-16	61	2A048-525	N/A	8H040-010	3.5" x 12"
4FF218-010S	Mustang 3.8 V6	`94-`98	V-2 SQ-S	8	150/215	215/259	Stock	3.33"/6	Stock	Yes	Stock	Stock	8:1	155	8-10	45	2A046-114	N/A	8H040-030	3.5" x 1.33 Ft.
4FG218-020S	Mustang 5.0-GT	`94-`95	V-2 SQ-S	6-8	215/285	319/370	6.875"/8	3.33"/8	Manual	Yes	Stock	MSD BTM	12:1 HO/10:1 Cobra	T-Rex	9-10	51	2A048-575	2A046-031	8H040-030	3.5" x 10"
4FH218-010S	Mustang 4.6-GT	`96-`97	V-2 SQ-S-CCW	6-8	215/265	290/345	Stock	3.60"/6	Stock	Yes	Stock	Stock	10:1	T-Rex	6-8	48	2A046-114	N/A	8H040-090	3.5" x 10"
4FH218-050S	Mustang 4.6-HO with cooler	`96-`98	V-2 SQ-S-CCW	10	215/265	323/365	Stock	3.33"/6	Stock	Yes	Stock	Stock	8:1	T-Rex	10-12	75	2A046-114	N/A	8H040-090	3.5" x 10"
4FH218-070S	Mustang 4.6-GT	`98	V-2 SQ-S-CCW	6-8	215/265	290/345	Stock	3.60"/6	Stock	Yes	Stock	Stock	10:1	155	6-8	48	2A046-114	N/A	8H040-090	3.5" x 10"
4FK218-010S	Mustang 4.6-Cobra	`96-`97	V-2 SQ SC-CCW	6-8	306/285	442/390	Stock	3.60"/6	Stock	Yes	Custom	Stock	8:1	T-Rex	8-10	51	2A046-113	N/A	8H040-090	3.5" x 12"
4FK218-050S	Mustang 4.6-Cobra HO with cooler	`96-`98	V-2 SQ-S-CCW	10	306/285	484/423	Stock	3.60"/6	Stock	Yes	Custom	Stock	8:1	T-Rex	12-14	78	2A046-113	N/A	8H040-090	3.5" x 12"
4FK218-080S	Mustang 4.6-Cobra	`98	V-2 SQ SC-CCW	6-8	305/285	442/390	Stock	3.60"/6	Stock	Yes	Custom	Stock	8:1	155	8-10	51	2A046-113	N/A	8H040-090	3.5" x 12"
4FL218-010S	Mustang 4.6-GT[5]	`99	V-2 SQ-S-CCW	6-8	260/302	398/393	Stock	3.60"/6	Stock	Yes	Custom	Stock	(8) 30 lbs/hr Inj.	None	6-8	48	2A046-114	N/A	8H040-090	3.5" x 10"

FORD TRUCK SUPERCHARGER SYSTEMS

4FB218-040S	F-Series/SUV 7.5[4]	`87-`97	V-2 SQ-S	4-5	230/385	311/450	6.50"/6	2.87"/6	Manual	No	Stock	MSD BTM	12:1	155	6-8	38	2A046-698	N/A	8H040-120	N/A
4FC218-030S	F-Series/SUV 5.8	`87-`96	V-2 SQ-S	5	200/300	281/371	6.50"/6	2.87"/6	Manual	No	Stock	MSD BTM	12:1	155	6-8	54	2A046-580	N/A	8H040-120	3.5" x 20"
4FC218-040S	Lightning 5.8	`93-`95	V-2 SQ-S	5	245/360	345/440	6.50"/6	2.87"/6	Manual	Yes	Stock	Hi-6 TR	12:1	155	6-8	60	2A046-580	N/A	8H040-120	3.5" x 20"
4FD218-050S	Ranger/Explorer 4.0	`91-`94	V-2 SQ-S	4-5	160/224	237/312	Stock	2.87"/6	Stock	No	Stock	Stock	12:1	155	6-8	48	2A046-103	N/A	8H040-130	N/A
4FE218-070S	F-Series/SUV 5.0	`87-`96	V-2 SQ-S	5	185/270	260/344	6.50"/6	3.125"/6	Manual	No	Stock	MSD BTM	12:1	155	6-8	42	2A046-580	N/A	8H040-120	3.5" x 20"
4FM218-010S	F-150, F-250 LD, Expedition/Navigator 4.6[3]	`97-`99	V-2 SQ-S	6-7	210/290	284/377	6.70"/6	3.60"/6	Manual	Yes	Stock	Stock	8:1	155	6-8	59	2A046-725	N/A	8H040-045	3.5" X 15"
4FM218-020S	F-150, F-250 LD, Expedition/Navigator 5.4 2-V[5]	`97-`99	V-2 SQ-S	6-7	230/325	322/420	6.875"/8	3.33"/8	Automatic	Yes	Stock	Stock	8:1	155	6-8	59	2A046-725	N/A	8H040-045	3.5" X 15"

GM F-BODY AND CORVETTE SUPERCHARGER SYSTEMS

4GF218-060S	F-Body 5.0/5.7 TPI	`88-`92	V-2 SQ-S	6-8	245/345	340/430	7.5"/6	3.48"/6	Manual	No	Stock	MSD BTM	8:1	155	9-10	56	2A046-605	2A046-988	8H040-030	3.5" x 14"
4GH218-050S	F-Body 5.7 LT1	`93	V-2 SQ-S	6	275/330	409/415	6.00"/8	3.33"/8	Automatic	Yes	Stock	Hi-6 TR	10:1 & 8 Inj.	T-Rex	12-13	67	2A046-408	N/A	8H040-030	3.5" x 17"
4GH218-050T	F-Body 5.7 LT1	`93	V-1 T	6	275/330	409/415	6.00"/8	3.33"/8	Automatic	Yes	Stock	Hi-6 TR	10:1 & 8 Inj.	T-Rex	12-13	67	2A046-408	N/A	8H040-030	3.5" x 17"
4GH218-060S	F-Body 5.7 LT1[1,2]	`94-`97	V-2 SQ-S	6	275/330	409/415	6.00"/8	3.33"/8	Automatic	Yes	Stock	Hi-6 TR	8:1	T-Rex	10-12	64	2A046-408	N/A	8H040-030	3.5" x 17"
4GH218-060T	F-Body 5.7 LT1[1,2]	`94-`97	V-1 T	6	275/330	409/415	6.00"/8	3.33"/8	Automatic	Yes	Stock	Hi-6 TR	8:1	T-Rex	10-12	64	2A046-408	N/A	8H040-030	3.5" x 17"
4GH218-080S	F-Body 5.7 LT1 with cooler[1,3]	`93	V-2 SQ-S	6	275/330	409/415	6.00"/8	3.33"/8	Automatic	Yes	Stock	Hi-6 TR	10:1	T-Rex	12-13	104	2A046-408	N/A	8H040-030	3.5" x 17"
4GH218-090S	F-Body 5.7 LT1 with cooler[1,3]	`93-`97	V-2 SQ-S	6	275/330	409/415	6.00"/8	3.33"/8	Automatic	Yes	Stock	Hi-6 TR	8:1	T-Rex	10-12	101	2A046-408	N/A	8H040-030	3.5" x 17"
4GV218-078S	Corvette 5.7 LT1	`92-`93	V-2 SQ-S-CCW	6-8	300/340	425/433	Stock	3.125"/8	Automatic	Yes	Stock	Hi-6 TR	10:1 & 8 Inj.	200	20-24	73	2A046-510	N/A	8H040-030	N/A
4GV218-088S	Corvette 5.7 LT1[1]	`94-`96	V-2 SQ-S-CCW	6-8	300/340	425/433	Stock	3.125"/8	Automatic	Yes	Stock	Hi-6 TR	10:1	200	19-23	70	2A046-510	N/A	8H040-030	N/A

GM TRUCK SUPERCHARGER SYSTEMS

4GB218-050S	Chevy Full Size/SUV 5.7 TBI	`90-`95	V-2 SQ-S	5-6	210/300	295/375	7.5"/6	3.125"/6	Manual	Yes	Stock	Stock	Suppl. Fuel Sys.	155	9-10	58	2A046-605	2A046-980	8H040-040	3.5" x 14"
4GC218-090S	Chevy Full Size/SUV/SS 7.4 TBI	`88-`93	V-2 SQ-S	5-6	230/385	315/465	7.5"/6	2.875"/6	Manual	Yes	Stock	Stock	Suppl. Fuel Sys.	155	9-10	57	2A046-598	N/A	8H040-040	3.5" x 10"
4GD218-050S	S-10, Blazer, Sonoma, Jimmy 4.3[5]	`96-`99	V-2 SQ-S	8	170/240	243/304	Stock	3.12"/6	Automatic	Yes	Stock	Hi-6 TR	Special	200	10-12	TBD	2A046-102	N/A	8H040-085	3.5" x 12"
4GG218-090S	Chevy Full Size/SUV 7.4 TBI	`94-`95	V-2 SQ-S	5-6	230/385	315/465	7.5"/6	2.875"/6	Manual	Yes	Stock	Stock	Suppl. Fuel Sys.	155	9-10	66	2A046-598	N/A	8H040-030	3.5" x 12"
4GM218-050S	Chevy Full Size/SUV 5.7 Vortec[4]	`96-`99	V-2 SQ-S	6-7	250/335	359/410	7.5"/6	3.60"/6	Stock	Yes	Stock	Stock	8:1	155	9-10	58	2A046-605	2A046-980	8H040-010	3.5" x 6"

DODGE AND JEEP TRUCK SUPERCHARGER SYSTEMS

4CB218-060S	Dodge Dakota 5.2	`91-`93	V-2 SQ-S	5	220/300	309/365	Stock	3.125"/7	Stock	Yes	Stock	Stock	12:1	155	5-6	45	2A047-113	N/A	8H040-040	N/A
4CD218-030S	Dodge Dakota/Ram 5.2/5.9	`94-`96	V-2 SQ-S	5	220/300	309/365	Stock	3.125"/7	Stock	Yes	Stock	Hi-6 TR	12:1	155	7-9	43	2A047-113	N/A	8H040-040	N/A
4CE218-010S	Dodge Durango/Dakota 5.9[4,5]	`97-`99	V-2 SQ-S	8	250/335	345/405	Stock	3.125"/7	Stock	Yes	Stock	Hi-6 TR	Suppl. Fuel Sys.	Stock	7-9	57	2A047-113	N/A	8H040-040	3.5" x 12"
4CJ218-010S	Jeep Cherokee/SUV 5.2	`93-`95	V-2 SQ-S	5	220/300	309/365	Stock	3.125"/7	Stock	Yes	Stock	Hi-6 TR	12:1	200	7-9	57	2A047-104	N/A	8H040-040	N/A
4CJ218-020S	Jeep Cherokee/SUV 5.2[3]	`96	V-2 SQ-S	5	220/300	309/365	Stock	3.125"/7	Stock	Yes	Stock	Hi-6 TR	12:1	200	7-9	57	2A047-104	N/A	8H040-040	N/A

Unless otherwise noted, all supercharger systems are CARB approved under EO #D-213-16 and include an exclusive standard 3-year limited warranty. NOTE: Install times listed are a general estimate, actual installation time may vary. System boost estimates are based on a stock engine at the stock rev limit at sea level. HP and torque numbers are at the crank. Polished systems available (add $200.00) except Corvette systems. All parts, descriptions, specifications, and estimated performance numbers are subject to change without notice. CW = clockwise, CCW = counterclockwise, LPH = liters per hour, TBD = to be determined. 1 = 1995-97 LT1 Camaros and Firebirds with traction control will require the purchase of a traction control relocation kit (available from Vortech at an additional charge), aftercooler system will not fit vehicles with traction control. 2 = 1996-97 LT1 Camaros, Firebirds and 1996 LT1 Corvettes may require the purchase of a mass air sensor massager P/N 4GM020-030 (available from Vortech at an additional charge). 3 = 1996-97 Models, 4 = 1997 Models, and 5 = 1999 Models (CARB approval is pending and not yet received for systems designated 3, 4, or 5). NOTE: The V-2 SQ will officially be available January 3, 2000. Until this time, these systems will include the V-1 S-Trim supercharger. Calculating belt length by part number: The last three digits of most belt part numbers is the belt length in inches example: P/N 2A046-535, belt length is 53.5"). PRODUCT DISCLAIMER: All specifications in the application guide are based upon the latest product information available at the time of printing. Vortech Engineering, Inc. reserves the right to make changes at any time, without prior notice, to colors, materials, specifications, part numbers, prices, and to discontinue products or product components.

VORTECH ENGINEERING, INC., 1650 PACIFIC AVENUE, CHANNEL ISLANDS, CA 93033 (805) 247-0226 PHONE, (805) 247-0669 FAX, WWW.VORTECHSUPERCHARGERS.COM

Vortech's Supercharger System Applications Guide provides a statistical overview of all preassembled kits to date. Along with the technical specifications, the guide also lists the model of the supercharger included in any given kit, as well as the maximum amount of boost it generates. *Vortech*

A 1996–1997 4.6-liter Cobra will typically gain 85 horsepower and 38 lbs-ft of torque with a base Vortech 4FK218-018S blower kit and no other modifications. According to Vortech's spokesperson, Bob Roese, a blown 4.6 Cobra will deliver 178 horsepower to the rear wheels when equipped with an aftercooler.

3, 2000, include a V-1 supercharger.

Vortech's V-1 A-Trim could be considered its entry-level supercharger for 1986 to 1993 5.0-liter Mustangs. The more popular S- and SC-Trim up the performance potential of the A-Trim, and the R- and T-Trim are used primarily for racing.

The V-2 SQ is an upgraded version of the V-1. Optimized helical-cut 3.6:1 ratio gears provide superquiet operation as indicated by the "SQ." A new low-friction impeller seal improves efficiency, and the mating surface of the compressor housing is sealed with an O-ring. V-2 SQ S-Trim and SC-Trim superchargers will support 680 horsepower. The new V-2 SQ is interchangeable with,

VORTECH SUPERCHARGER SPECIFICATION CHART

	Type	Rotation	Finish	Air Inlet Opening (Hose Diameter)	Air Inlet Opening (Inducer Diameter)	Air Discharge (Hose Diameter)	Air Discharge (Inside Diameter)	Impeller Speed (Efficient Max)	Impeller Speed (Absolute Max)	Performance @ Absolute Speed (Max PSIG*)	Performance @ Absolute Speed (Max Flow CFM*)	Performance @ Absolute Speed (Horsepower Range**)	Adiabatic Efficiency
Supercharger													
V-1 A-Trim	STD	Clockwise	Satin	3.50"	2.50"	2.75"	2.38"	40,000	45,000	10	720	480	66%
V-1 R-Trim	HD	Clockwise or Counterclockwise	Satin or Polished	3.75"	3.29"	2.75"	2.38"	55,000	58,000	24	1,100	750	74%
V-1 SC-Trim	STD/HD	Clockwise or Counterclockwise	Satin or Polished	3.50"	3.10"	2.75"	2.38"	50,000	53,000	20	1,000	680	75%
V-1 S-Trim	STD/HD	Clockwise or Counterclockwise	Satin or Polished	3.50"	3.10"	2.75"	2.38"	45,000	50,000	20	1,000	680	72%
V-1 T-Trim	HD	Clockwise or Counterclockwise	Satin or Polished	3.75"	3.29"	2.75"	2.38"	52,000	55,000	26	1,200	825	73%
V-2 SQ SC-Trim	STD/HD	Counterclockwise	Satin or Polished	3.50"	3.10"	2.75"	2.38"	50,000	53,000	20	1,000	680	75%
V-2 SQ S-Trim	STD/HD	Clockwise or Counterclockwise	Satin or Polished	3.50"	3.10"	2.75"	2.38"	45,000	50,000	20	1,000	680	72%
V-4 J-Trim	HD	Clockwise	Satin or Polished	5.00"	3.50"	3.50"	3.06"	50,000	58,000	28	1,600	1,100	74%
V-4 X-Trim	HD	Clockwise	Satin or Polished	5.00"	3.90"	3.50"	3.06"	55,000	58,000	29	1,700	1,300	79%
V-4 XX-Trim	HD	Clockwise	Satin	5.00"	3.90"	3.50"	3.06"	58,000	64,000	29	1,850	1,400+	78%
V-5 G-Trim	STD/HD	Clockwise or Counterclockwise	Satin or Polished	3.50"	3.125"	2.50"	2.06"	62,000	65,000	25	800	575	73%
V-7 YS-Trim	HD	Clockwise	Satin or Polished	4.0"	3.64"	3.0"	2.64"	60,000	65,000	29	1,500	1,000	74%
V-9 F-Trim	STD	Clockwise or Counterclockwise	Satin or Polished	3.50"	2.874"	2.50"	2.10"	60,000	65,000	20	800	575	72%
V-9 G-Trim	STD	Clockwise or Counterclockwise	Satin or Polished	3.625"	3.125"	2.50"	2.10"	60,000	65,000	20	800	575	72%

SPECIAL NOTES: * Pressure and flow performance data was acquired in the Vortech Engineering, Inc. test cell to SAE J1723 standards. To see details on SAE J1723 test procedures, go to www.sae.org/prodserv/stds/J1723_199508.htm. Superchargers are not rated for flow or pressure at efficiencies below 60%. ** Horsepower data resulted from engine dyno tests and/or extrapolated from compressor map data. Due to our rating system, horsepower figures are a relative guide and not an absolute maximum. Superchargers exceeding 6PSIG require a Vortech standard bypass valve or a Vortech Maxflow racing bypass valve. Superchargers exceeding 10PSIG require a Vortech Maxflow Mondo or Maxflow racing bypass valve. Cog belt drive systems are recommended for all heavy duty superchargers.
Calculating Impeller Speed (Serpentine Pulley Applications): Crank Pulley Diameter x 3.45 x Engine RPM at Shift = Impeller Speed
Supercharger Pulley Diameter
Calculating Impeller Speed (Cog Pulley Applications): # of Crank Pulley Teeth x 3.45 x Engine RPM at Shift = Impeller Speed
# of Cog Supercharger Pulley Teeth

VORTECH ENGINEERING, INC., 1650 PACIFIC AVENUE, CHANNEL ISLANDS, CA 93033 (805) 247-0226 PHONE, (805) 247-0669 FAX, WWW.VORTECHSUPERCHARGERS.COM

The Supercharger Specification Chart illustrates the engineering differences between different models. The "Impeller Speed (Absolute Max)" listed for each charger is an extremely important value. Driving the impeller beyond its absolute maximum speed is not recommended. Impeller speeds above the "Efficient Max" value can damage the supercharger. *Vortech*

and replaces, the V-1 S-Trim in Vortech street-legal kits built after January 3, 2000.

The V-4 format includes the J-, X-, and XX-Trim superchargers. V-4 superchargers are engineered for all-out competition, and the V-5 was designed for four- and six-cylinder engines with a displacement between 1.6 and 4.0 liters. The V-7 YS-Trim offers V-4 performance in a compact package that is compatible with most existing brackets. The V-9 F-Trim and G-Trim are high-pressure, subcompact superchargers designed to fit in the tightest engine compartments. V-9 chargers blow 800 cfm (cubic feet per minute) at 65,000 rpm and will support 575 horsepower.

Standard V-1 S-Trim chargers can be upgraded with a high-efficiency

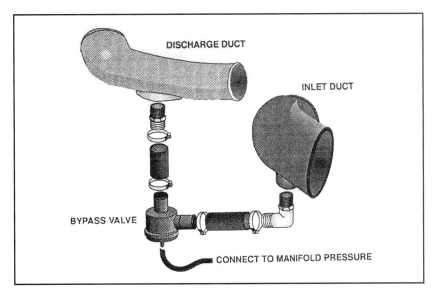

Compressor surge occurs when there is not enough airflow to support a specific pressure on the outlet side of the impeller. For example, quick deceleration after a high-speed run, when the throttle is closed, but the compressor is still at high speed. An idle bypass valve is used to combat compressor surge. *Vortech*

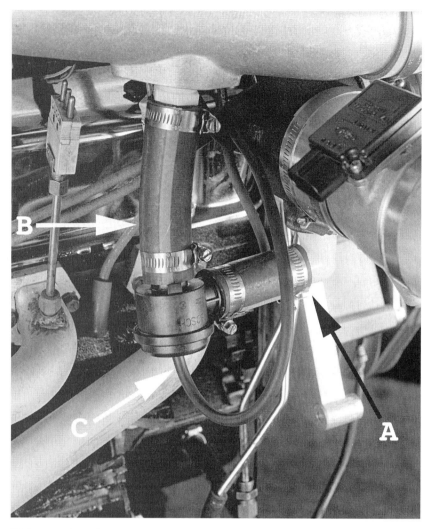

Idle bypass valves eliminate compressor surge by venting discharge air back to the inlet side of the compressor (A). The pressure on the discharge side of the supercharger (B) and the inlet side are then equalized. A pressure sensor hose (C) ported to the intake manifold controls the diaphragm.

A 4:1 ratio FMU increases the fuel pressure 4 psi for each pound of boost; a 6:1 ratio increases fuel pressure 6 psi for each pound of boost and so on. Vortech offers five fixed (non-adjustable) FMUs ranging from 4:1 to 12:1 ratio. The FMU ratio is a critical factor. *Vortech*

Vortech's optional Super FMUs can be adjusted to optimize the fuel curve through a selection of stepped internal spacers and a number of external adjustments. To obtain optimum results, monitor the exhaust with a quality air/fuel ratio meter. *Vortech*

curved-blade impeller, which is high-speed balanced to racing specifications, and with a new S-Trim compressor housing. Enhancements include all-new bearings and seals, new select-fit impeller spacer and nut, and new compressor retainers. The new assembly is inspected and fully balanced.

An HD V-1 S-Trim can be factory upgraded to a T-Trim with a high-speed, precision-balanced, curved-blade T-Trim impeller and T-Trim compressor housing. The hardware package that includes the new bearings and seals listed above is also part of this upgrade.

Vortech can also convert an HD V-1 R-Trim into a T-Trim by machining the gearbox to accept a new high-flow, high-efficiency T-Trim impeller. Again, the hardware package and services listed above are included in this in-house procedure.

Although a large number of Vortech superchargers are installed on "competition only" vehicles, the company is devoted to engineering and marketing bolt-on supercharger kits designed for specific cars, trucks, and SUVs. Vortech supercharger kits contain all the necessary brackets, fittings, hoses, and fasteners to complete the modification.

Kits are engineered to accommodate all factory accessory drive components, including the air pump and air conditioning compressor if the vehicle is so equipped. All assemblies include some type of fuel management system, and an additional fuel pump is supplied if the application calls for one. Some kits contain an ignition retard system, and all wiring incorporates factory connectors wherever necessary. To better explain the installation procedure, complete diagrams, photographs, and computer-generated images are used to illustrate their instruction manuals. Most kits can be installed in approximately 7 to 10 hours using conventional hand tools. Except for drilling a few holes, no extensive modification or cutting is necessary.

All Vortech superchargers use engine oil to lubricate and cool the bearings and gears. Engine oil is plumbed from a pressure source to a metered orifice threaded into the gearbox. A return hose attached to the bottom of the gearbox allows the oil to drain back into the crankcase. Some systems drain into the valve cover and some directly into the oil pan. In either case, it is necessary to drill or punch (depending on the application) a hole to accommodate a fitting. Oil pan drain holes must be tapped to accept a threaded fitting. Needless to say, an ample supply of clean, fresh lubricating oil is essential. The brand of oil used isn't nearly as important as the change interval.

Installing a smaller blower pulley or a larger crank pulley will increase impeller speed, which in some cases will increase the output of the supercharger. Some Vortech superchargers can be overdriven, others cannot. Confirm the effectiveness of any modification with Vortech Engineering before implementing a change, particularly if the modification includes increasing impeller speed. Vortech blower kits are engineered to deliver optimum performance out of the box. Reasonable safety factors are dialed into the system as well. Unreasonable modifications can damage the blower and the engine. Overspeeding any supercharger can compromise efficiency and durability. Use the following formulas to calculate maximum impeller speed:

Crank Pulley Diameter (in inches)1 x 3.452 x engine rpm @ shift divided by the Supercharger Pulley Diameter (in inches) equals Impeller Speed.

Example with Serpentine Pulley:

7.0 inches x 3.45 x 6,000 = 43,514 rpm
3.33inches   (Impeller Speed)

Using a compressed air source to simulate boost is a fast, efficient way to "dial in" a Super FMU baseline. Use an adjustable air pressure regulator to pressurize the manifold sensor port on the FMU in one-pound increments, then activate the fuel pump(s) to obtain a fuel pressure reading.

Example with Cog Pulley:

73-teeth x 3.45 x 7,500 = 55,555 rpm
34-teeth   (Impeller Speed)

* When measuring pulley diameters, measure at the top of the ribs where the serpentine belt rides. For cog pulleys, substitute the number of teeth for the diameter.

** 3.45 denotes the internal overdrive ratio inside the supercharger gearbox. Substitute 3.60 when computing the impeller speed of a V-2 SQ charger

.

Progressive Dynamometer Tests

There is nothing more interesting to an automotive engineer than validating research in a controlled environment. This exercise involves a series of dynamometer tests illustrating a progressive forced induction buildup from a naturally aspirated baseline. Although dynamometer testing is not necessarily representative of "real-world" performance, the results can be applied to a number of practical applications.

These tests are representative of a typical buildup on a street-driven car by a do-it-yourself performance enthusiast. After installing an off-the-shelf blower kit, the search for more performance includes a certain amount of

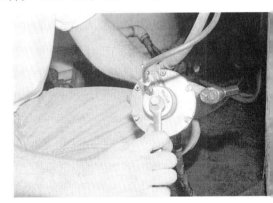

Install the proper shim pack and/or change the adjusting screws to adjust the fuel pressure settings. Plotting the readings will produce a visual fuel delivery curve (fuel pressure versus boost pressure versus engine rpm). *Always* adjust the air/fuel ratio *from* rich *toward* lean.

Vortech kits are engineered to bolt on with minimal effort. The installation procedure has been researched, well thought out, and documented. Factory components are utilized wherever possible to keep the installation neat and clean.

Maximum Effort Equals Maximum Results

This exercise shows what can be accomplished when the correct, off-the-shelf high-performance parts are assembled by a team of professional engine builders.

Engine Builder: Kuntz & Company
Displacement: 427ci
Block: Stock Ford 9.500-inch deck 351 Windsor
Heads: Pro-Wedge Wil-Bert/TFS aluminum, diamond-honed bronze guide liners, one-piece swirl-polished stainless-steel valves, hardened steel rocker studs and guide plates, competition springs matched to the camshaft, and 10-degree hardened steel locks and retainers
Pistons: Forged Venolia custom machined to Kuntz & Company engineering specifications. 1/16-, 1/16-, 1/8-inch ring pack positioned .252 inch below the fire dome
Rings: Childs and Albert Dura-Moly
Rods: Eagle steel H-beam
Crank: Stock Ford Stock iron crankshaft, shot-peened, magnafluxed and deburred, indexed, computer balanced. 4.187-inch stroke
Cam: 1.025-inch base circle, hydraulic roller, 114-degree centerline, .612/.640-inch valve lift, 244/252 degrees of duration, 20-degrees of overlap (at .050-inch tappet lift)
Rocker Arms: Competition Cams 1.6 ratio, extruded-aluminum, needle-bearing fulcrum, roller tip
Compression: 10.8:1 naturally aspirated/10.3:1 supercharged
Fuel: 112 octane Sunoco no-lead racing fuel
Intake Manifold: Naturally aspirated: GT-40 w/ported lower Supercharged: Ported GT-40 lower, port-matched Bennett Racing upper plenum
Throttle Body: 70-mm BBK/Edelbrock
Mass Air Meter: 80-mm C&L
Fuel Injectors: R&E Racing 36 lb/hr
Fuel Pumps: Two Accel in-line electric
Fuel Pressure: 45 psig idle/110 psig @ full boost
Supercharger: Vortech R-Trim w/2.5-inch pulley
Maximum Boost: 12 pounds
Electronic Engine Control: Stock EEC-IV w/Crane Interceptor II*

Performance:
Naturally aspirated: 508.1 horsepower @ 5,300 rpm and 536.1 lbs-ft of torque @ 4,600 rpm
Supercharged: 782.0 horsepower @ 5,900 rpm/733.6 lbs-ft. of torque @ 5,000 rpm

* Crane no longer makes the Interceptor II.

This experiment was conducted specifically to illustrate the benefits of a sound blower engine buildup. All components were professionally prepared and assembled. The naturally aspirated SEFI 427 Ford engine generated an impressive 508.1 horsepower at 5,300 rpm and 536.1 lbs-ft of torque at 4,600 rpm.

After lowering the compression ratio from 10.8 to 10.3, an R-Trim Vortech supercharger was installed along with a port-matched Bennett Racing upper plenum. Boost was limited to a serviceable 12 pounds per square inch. After fuel and timing were optimized, power increased to 782.0 horsepower at 5,900 rpm/733.6 lbs-ft of torque at 5,000 rpm.

trial and error, due largely to the arrant number of variables.

Baseline values were extracted from a stock Ford Sequential Electronic Fuel Injection (SEFI) 5.0-liter long-block equipped with a pair of Hooker equal-length, short-tube headers, and two 3-foot exhaust pipes dumping into low-restriction Borla mufflers.

Test 1: Baseline

Baseline values leveled off at 252.0 horsepower at 4,900 rpm and 314.4 lbs-ft of torque at 3,500 rpm after fuel pressure and timing were optimized.

Test 2

Conversion to forced induction was accomplished by installing a Vortech 4FA218-010 supercharger kit with standard A-Trim blower, Vortech's own 73-millimeter Max Flow mass air meter, a 65-millimeter throttle body, 36 lb./hr injectors, and an adjustable FMU. Fuel pressure and timing were optimized to complement the modifications, and the mass air meter was calibrated to recognize the larger injectors. The system generated 10 psi of boost with the optional 8E020-295 2.95-inch compressor pulley. Power output leaped to 370 horsepower at 5,200 rpm and 389.4 lbs-ft torque at 4,600 rpm.

Test 3

Test 3 began by replacing the 2.95-inch compressor pulley with a smaller 2.75-inch pulley (part number 8E020-275). A 7.3 percent overdrive increased impeller speed from 48,200 rpm to 51,700 rpm. Boost jumped from 10 psi to 11 psi. Early pulls indicated the air/fuel mixture was rich. Overdriving the compressor beyond its engineered limits reduces its efficiency and superheats the incoming air-charge. Any potential performance gain can be compromised by superheating the air-charge.

The mass air meter was recalibrated in an attempt to correct the problem. The overly simple modification increased performance to 382.7 horsepower at 5,200 rpm and 411.6 lbs-ft of torque at 4,600 rpm with a safe 10:1 air/fuel mixture ratio.

Although a performance gain was realized, driving the supercharger beyond its design limits is not recommended. Overspeeding the impeller compromises the mechanical efficiency of the supercharger. Modifications that increase the airflow through the engine or upgrading the supercharger are better choices.

Test 4

The standard A-Trim supercharger was replaced with a larger B-Trim equipped with a 2.95-inch pulley for test four. Air-charge temperature dropped dramatically, illustrating the B-Trim's improved efficiency. Boost pressure receded slightly and the meager horsepower gain fell into the dynamometer's repeatable error factor. Interestingly, torque diminished dramatically in response to the change. Clearly the larger B-Trim was oversized for the application. Performance values peaked at 385.1 horsepower at 5,800 rpm and 392.3 lbs-ft of torque at 4,400 rpm.

Test 5

A 2.75-inch compressor pulley was installed in place of the 2.95-inch pulley to increase impeller speed, and the 73-millimeter mass airflow sensor was replaced by an 80-millimeter unit in an effort to increase airflow through the engine. The combination generated 412.5 horsepower at 5,400 rpm and 417.4 lbs-ft of torque with a single T-Rex inline fuel pump. So far the dynamometer tests indicated a 160.5 horsepower and 103 lbs-ft of torque gain over the naturally aspirated baseline of 252 horsepower at 4,900 rpm and 314.4 lbs-ft of torque at 3,500 rpm.

Further testing indicated the engine's inability to process more air. The intake, heads, and cam were simply restricting airflow.

Illustrating the impact on the horsepower is the best way to demonstrate the outcome. Forced induction dramatically improved power, of course, from the baseline 252 peak horsepower. However, the horsepower increase is only a small portion of the total data collected. The output of a centrifugal supercharger increases as the speed of the impeller (and engine) increase, as evidenced by the meager power gain at the beginning of each pull. Maximum gain at 2,500 rpm was 18.1 horsepower, and the minimum gain was 9.3 horsepower. Forced induction pushed the power peak higher in the rpm range (from 4,900 rpm to 5,400 rpm), albeit in a gradual arch, while the forced induction ramped to a peak. Usable horsepower throughout the entire operating range is far more important than any peak number. Summarizing all of the data, it's easy to see why a centrifugal supercharger is a good wide-open throttle, high-rpm power adder.

Torque is just as important, if not more important, as horsepower. The forced induction graph lines indicate two impressive improvements over the stock torque values: torque is considerably higher throughout the entire rpm range, and the bulk of the improvement occurs near the middle of the rpm band, not at the end. The area under the curves represents usable power. It's also interesting to note that the progressive modifications did not produce progressively higher results. Test 3 (A-Trim supercharger) generated more torque from 4,000 rpm to 5,500 rpm than Test 4 (B-Trim supercharger), but Test 4 and 5 produced more torque than Tests 2 and 3 above 5,300 rpm. Once again, that's more usable power spread over a longer duration of time.

The boost (residual pressure) further indicated a centrifugal supercharger's need for speed. Test 3 begins to wane slightly above 4,800 rpm because the supercharger was pushed beyond its engineered maximum effi-

ciency threshold.

An undesirable byproduct of compressing air is heat. As boost increases, so does the temperature of the compressed air. During these tests, the average ambient air temperature was 80 degrees Fahrenheit, which means the air-charge ingested by the naturally aspirated engine was approximately 80 degrees. After passing through the supercharger, the air temperature increased to 259 degrees Fahrenheit at the end of the pull. This data represents the average temperature of all five tests. High air-charge temperature hurts performance and promotes detonation. The more efficient the compressor, the lower the air-charge temperature. Driving the impeller past its maximum efficient speed threshold superheats the air-charge. On an exceptionally hot day, air-charge temperatures can easily top 350 degrees Fahrenheit.

Eaton Corporation, Supercharger Division

In 1949, Eaton built a prototype 75ci helical rotor supercharger but never put it into production. The assembly was set aside temporarily because at the time, improved performance was achieved through larger-displacement engines. The late 1970s spurred new interest in supercharging, in part because gasoline

Eaton currently manufactures five supercharger models: the new M20, M-45, M-62, M-90, and M-112. The M-45 displaces .75 liters of air per revolution; the M-62, 1.00 liters; the M-90, 1.50 liters; and the larger 112, 1.84 liters.

Some Eaton-based aftermarket manufacturers adapt production designs to a particular engine with specialized manifolds and ductwork, which keeps costs low. A single supercharger model or design can then be adapted to a large number of varying applications.

prices were driven up by the energy crisis.

In 1984, Eaton began working with Ford Motor Company to design a supercharger for the 3.8-liter V-6 engine. Their combined effort produced the 1989 Thunderbird SC—the first production supercharged vehicle built since 1957.

Today, Eaton Corporation does not manufacturer do-it-yourself supercharger kits. Rather, Eaton's Supercharger Division engineers positive-displacement superchargers for original-equipment manufacturers such as Jaguar, Mercedes Benz, General

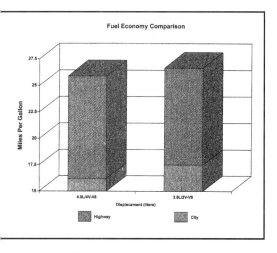

Studying this chart lends a better understanding of the diverse advantages to forced induction. Extracting more power from a smaller engine provides the best performance and economy. *Eaton*

Jackson Racing Supercharger Applications

Acura

Year	Model	Engine	Part Number
1094–up	Integra GSR	B18C1	989-500
1994–up	Integra Non-VTEC	B18B1	989-510
1997–up	Integra Type R	B18C5	989-600

Honda

Year	Model	Engine	Part Number
1988–91	Civic, CRX Si Only	D16A6	989-000
1992–95	Civic, Del Sol	D16Z6/D15B7	989-100
1996–98	Civic EX, Del Sol Si	D16Y8	989-200
1999–00	Civic EX	D16Y8	989-201
1996–00	Civic CX, DX, LX	D16Y7	989-210
1997–up	CRV	B20B4/B20Z2	989-705
1997–up	Prelude	H22A	989-650
1197–up	Prelude SH	H22A	989-655
1999–up	Civic Si	B16A2	989-250
All	Any	ZC	989-110

Miata

Year	Notes	Engine	Part Number
1990–93	PS, AC	1.6L	999-000
1990–93	No AC	1.6L	999-005
1990–93	No Ps, No AC	1.6L	999-010
1990–93	AC, No PS	1.6L	999-015
1990–93	RH Drive, PS, AC	1.6L	999-025
1990–93	RH Drive, PS, No AC	1.6L	999-085
1990–93	RH Drive, No PS, No AC	1.6L	999-090
1990–93	RH Drive, AC, No PS	1.6L	999-095
1994–97	PS, AC	1.8L	999-100
1994–97	PS, No AC	1.8L	999-105
1994–97	No Ps, No AC	1.8L	999-110
1994–97	AC, No PS	1.8L	999-125
1994–97	RH Drive, AC, PS	1.8L	999-130
1994–97	RH Drive, PS, No AC	1.8L	999-140
1994–97	RH Drive, No PS, No AC	1.8L	999-145
1994–97	RH Drive, AC, No PS	1.8L	999-155
1999–up	PS, AC, No AT	1.8L	999-200
1999–up	PS, No AC, No AT	1.8L	999-205
1999–up	No PS, No AC	1.8L	999-210
1999–up	AC, No PS, No AT	1.8L	999-215
1999–up	RH Drive, AC, PS	1.8L	999-250
1999–up	RH Drive, PS, No AC	1.8L	999-255
1999–up	No PS, No AC	1.8L	999-260
1999–up	RH Drive, AC, No PS	1.8L	999-265

Motors, and Ford Motor Company. To be successful in the original-equipment arena, any component or assembly must be quiet, very efficient, and extremely durable. The fact that Eaton superchargers are widely used by a number of car makers is testimony to their engineering prowess.

To build a superior supercharger, Eaton engineers first added a third lobe to the traditional twin-lobed, Roots-type blower. Then each lobe was given a 60-degree helical twist. The helix design reduces noise and improves efficiency. Precision manufacturing techniques further enhance proficiency and ensure prolonged durability. For example, the performance output of a conventional positive- displacement blower is limited in part by the large clearances between the rotors and the stationary housing. Large tolerances allow air to leak past the rotors. Eaton was successful in minimizing these operating tolerances, which enabled the company to produce a smaller, more powerful supercharger. Eaton superchargers are the smallest, most efficient positive- displacement blowers on the market today.

Studying the inlet and outlet port designs using prototypes and computer modeling led to modifications that reduced noise and improved efficiency even further. Engineers learned that lengthening the time it takes for the supercharger to compress the air improved its pumping action, while dampening the audible frequencies generated by the spinning rotors. Helical rotors and an axial inlet also lengthened the supercharger's useful rpm range. An Eaton blower offers improved efficiency up to 14,000 rpm.

Power on demand has economic advantages as well. During typical driving conditions, the engine is under boost only about 5 percent of the time. The best possible fuel economy is achieved the other 95 percent of the time, when the engine is naturally aspirated.

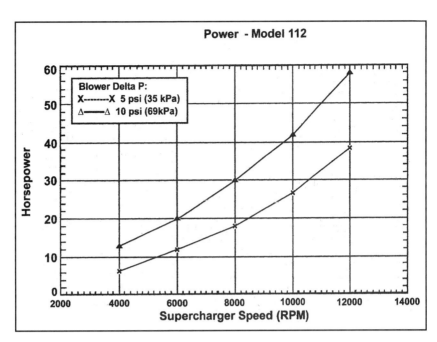

This graph illustrates the "more boost equals more power" principle of forced induction. It's important to note that doubling the amount of boost does not double the power output of the engine. The amount of air entering (and exiting) the engine involves quite a large number of variables. *Eaton*

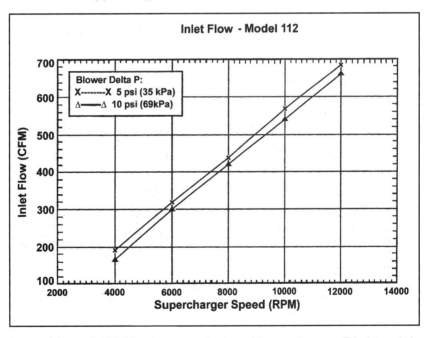

As you might expect, inlet airflow increases as the demand for power increases. This data could be extracted from a mass airflow meter. Notice how doubling the amount of boost produces a comparatively small increase in inlet airflow. Higher pressure does not equate to more volume. *Eaton*

The Eaton family of superchargers is compatible with virtually all passenger car and light-truck engines, regardless of the number of valves per cylinder or the type of fuel used. Typical power improvements range from 25 percent to 50 percent, depending on the model blower used and the application.

Factory-installed Eaton superchargers have met every customer durability test imposed by original-equipment manufacturers. Numerous Eaton-equipped

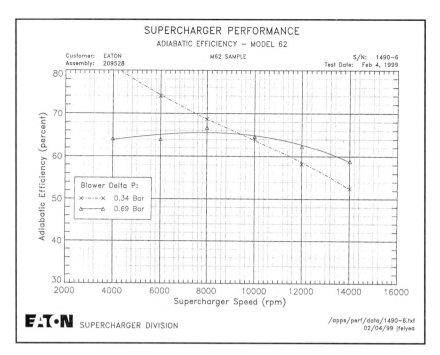

The gauge used to compare one supercharger to another is adiabatic efficiency. Given the nature of the machine, it's difficult to mass produce a positive-displacement supercharger with an adiabatic efficiency much above 60 percent. Minimizing the clearance between the rotors and the housing minimizes leakage, which in turn improves efficiency. *Eaton*

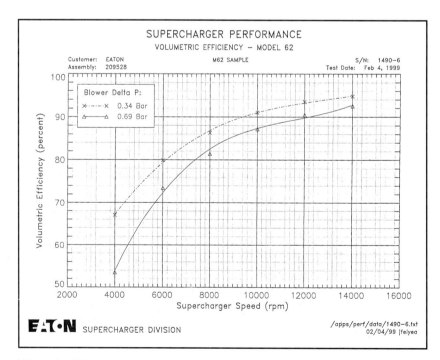

Volumetric efficiency represents the supercharger's ability to gulp air. The VE of a typical Roots charger will peak, then fall off slightly as speed increases, but Eaton's VE will climb steadily throughout the entire rpm range. Eaton's fourth-generation supercharger is one of the most efficient positive-displacement blowers available. *Eaton*

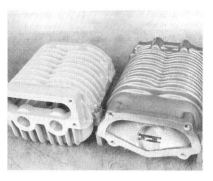

Magnuson/Eaton fourth-generation supercharger housings (right) feature an integrated bypass valve that allows the pressures across the blower to equalize during low-power, part-throttle operation. The valve essentially eliminates parasitic power loss by taking the blower off-line. Eaton's third-generation blower is shown on the left.

vehicles have successfully completed the required 100,000-mile vehicle durability test. In the real world outside the test facility, Eaton superchargers will typically run 200,000-plus maintenance-free miles. All Eaton superchargers have a self-contained oiling system that does not require a fluid change for the life of the unit.

A truly advanced positive-displacement supercharger must be both compact and efficient, given that the overall size of the compressor is a detriment. Eaton's excellent ratio of airflow capacity to package size is a plus, given the limited amount of available space in a modern-day engine compartment.

Several aftermarket manufacturers, such as Magnuson Products and Jackson Racing, offer Eaton-based supercharger kits for a variety of passenger cars, light trucks, and sport utility vehicles.

To date, Eaton-based supercharger kits are available for:

- GM 5.3, pickup/SUV
- Chevrolet pickups, Tahoe, Yukon, and Suburban with 5.7-liter Vortech engine
- Ford trucks with 5.4- and 4.6-liter engines
- Ford Explorer with 5.0-liter engine

The bypass portal is cast into the blower housing to simplify packaging and ensure durability. The actuator can be mounted on either side of the blower and indexed in one of 12 possible locations (6 per side) around the shaft.

- Land Rover Discover/Defender
- Lexus LX-450
- Range Rover SUV with 4.0-liter engine
- Toyota 4 Runner, Tacoma, and T100 with 3.4-liter engine
- Acura Integra GSR and 1997–1998 Integra Type R
- Honda Civic/CRX, Civic/Del Sol, and CRV
- Mazda Miata
- Audi/Volkswagen with 2.8-liter (30-valve) and 1.8-liter (30-valve) engines
- BMW 318 and Z3
- Ford Mustang and Thunderbird
- Porsche Boxter
- Harley Davidson motorcycles

Toyota Racing Division and Eaton Superchargers

Toyota Racing Division (TRD) is into Eaton superchargers in a big way, mainly because of Eaton and Magnuson Products manufacturer systems that meet or exceed original-equipment quality and durability standards. TRD markets, installs, and warranties Eaton-based supercharger kits at its dealerships. A Toyota customer can drive away in a new supercharged vehicle from any of Toyota's factory-authorized sales and service facilities, and a do-it-yourself tuner can purchase the very same kit and do the installation himself.

Holley/Weiand Superchargers-Roots

It only seems natural that the world's largest carburetor manufac-

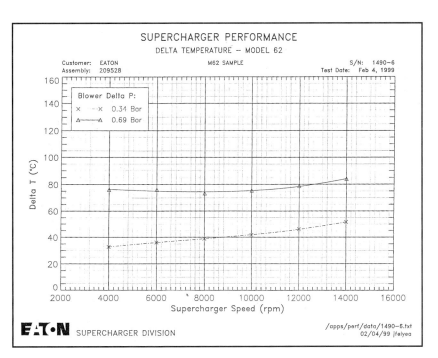

The higher-pressure ratio of the compressor, the higher the Delta T. Increasing the air-charge temperature 80 degrees Celsius (176 degrees Fahrenheit) at 10 psi of pressure may seem like a lot, but in reality, is quite low by comparison. The temperature variation for an Eaton M62 is less than 10 degrees from 4,000 to 14,000 rpm. *Eaton*

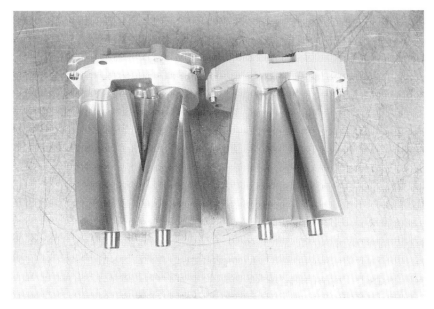

The fourth-generation's discharge port extends into the gearbox housing to minimize the overall length of the new housing. The lengths of the rotors (and the displacement of the supercharger) remain unchanged.

turer would market a line of Roots-type superchargers kits and accessories. Holley/Weiand superchargers are basically refined Roots-type GMC blowers. However, each component is unique to Holley/Weiand—that is, Weiand and GMC/Roots components are not interchangeable. Also, Weiand assemblies are built to scale, unlike GMC blowers, which were originally sized for a specific two-stroke industrial diesel engine. Weiand superchargers

Input shaft assemblies are available in a variety of different lengths to accommodate virtually any application. The blower housing can be rotated in any position around the input shaft centerline—it will discharge up, down, to either side, or anywhere in between.

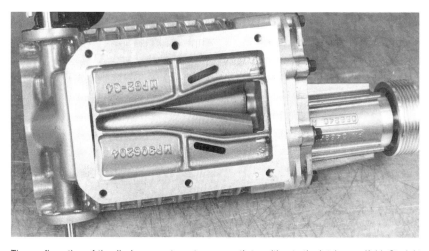

The configuration of the discharge port creates a smooth transition to the intake manifold. Straight rotor Roots blowers generate a lot of noise, in part because each discharge event creates an audible pulse. These blowers pound the air into the engine. Eaton superchargers squeeze air into the engine, eliminating undesirable noise.

Assemblies are lightweight, compact, and durable. Sealed bearings support the input shaft, and the gearbox requires no maintenance.

are designed to be compatible with OEM small- and big-block V-8 engines. Appendix 1 contains a complete list of Holley/Weiand superchargers and accessories.

Paxton Automotive Corporation

Paxton Corporation is one of the oldest supercharger manufacturers in the United States. During the 1960s Paxton superchargers were available as a cost option on Ford Thunderbirds, Shelby GT350s, and Studebaker Avanti. To date, Paxton manufactures six supercharger configurations—SN 2000, Novi 1000RR, Novi 1000, Novi 2000RR, Novi 2000, and Novi 3000.

The SN Series, incorporating a unique 4.4 :1 ratio planetary ball-drive mechanism, dates back to the 1960s. The SN 2000 is a modern version of the original design. The company boasts of its ultraquiet operation and deems it perfect for applications requiring no more than 6 pounds of boost.

SN superchargers feature self-contained oiling; this oil must be changed every 3,000 miles. Paxton recommends replacing the Type-F automatic transmission oil in the supercharger gearbox, and the engine oil, at the same interval to simplify the service routine.

Novi chargers use billet steel, helical-cut gears to transfer power from the drive belt to the compressor. The drive multiplication is 3.54:1, and the gearbox uses engine oil to cool and lubricate the gears.

The Novi 1000 and 1000RR Series superchargers were engineered for small-displacement engines. The "RR" designation means Reverse Rotation. The 1000's range of operation will accommodate four-, six- and small 8-cylinder engines.

Novi 2000 is Paxton's mainstay because of its exceptionally broad operating range. Typical automotive applications in kit form are engineered to deliver 8 pounds of boost when coupled to a stock small-block engine.

Paxton's Novi 3000 is a monster blower capable of supporting 1,400 horsepower, according to industry specifications. The volute (compressor housing) on the 3000 is 40 percent larger than that of the Novi 2000, and its interior surface is reported to be "abrasive flow machined" to maximize flow potential. Its inlet diameter measures 5 inches and the discharge nozzle is 3.5 inches across. To further enhance durability, the helical-cut steel-billet gears and the 8-inch 201 alloy cast-aluminum impeller are cryogenically treated.

Powerdyne Automotive Products

Powerdyne centrifugal superchargers use a belt drive assembly

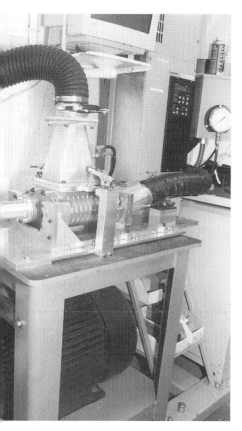

Magna Charger 1996–2000 5.7-liter Vortec kits include an Eaton MP90 supercharger. All Magna Charger kits are 50-state emissions legal and are guaranteed for a full three years or 36,000 miles. Applications include 1996–2000 Chevrolet and GMC 1500/2500/3500 pickups, Chevrolet Tahoe, Chevrolet and GMC Suburban, GMC Yukon, Cadillac Escalade, and GMC Denali.

In addition to its line of aftermarket Magna Charger supercharger kits, Magnuson Products in Ventura, California, houses the only Eaton remanufacturing facility on the West Coast. All new and remanufactured superchargers are bench-tested on one of two computer-controlled test stations before they are installed or shipped.

instead of gears to transfer power from the input shaft to the impeller. There is no direct metal-to-metal contact between the two shafts. As a result, Powerdyne superchargers are relatively quiet, compared to other centrifugal chargers. Gear-driven chargers produce a noticeable whine, particularly at slow speeds. The noise is less detectable at higher speeds but it is always present when the engine is running. Except for the typical whistle produced by the impeller, Powerdyne superchargers emit very little noise. Drivers who want to make a statement regarding their performance capabilities may find the gear noise desirable. Those who would prefer the silent approach, or performance enthusiasts who drive luxury

The 5.7 Vortec kit is one of the simplest forced induction kits to install because no oil lines are needed. A plug-in frequency modifier delivers a recalibrated mass air meter signal to the stock CPU when the engine is under boost. The CPU then richens the fuel using the stock injectors.

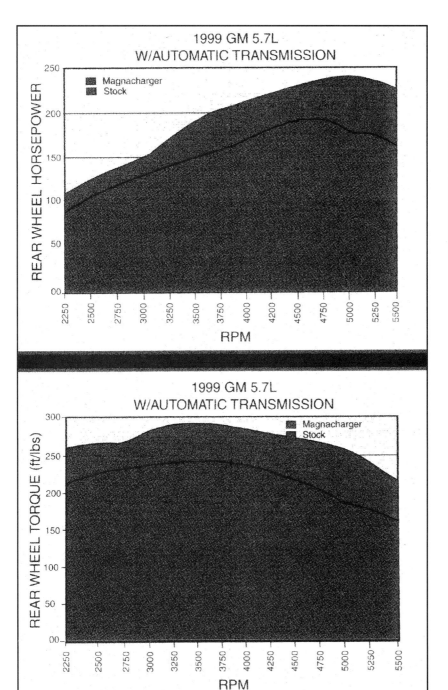

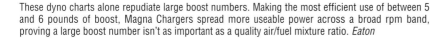

These dyno charts alone repudiate large boost numbers. Making the most efficient use of between 5 and 6 pounds of boost, Magna Chargers spread more useable power across a broad rpm band, proving a large boost number isn't as important as a quality air/fuel mixture ratio. *Eaton*

Magnuson's GM 5.3-liter Magna Charger kit is equally impressive. The self-adjusting single serpentine belt arrangement further reduces installation time. All MC kits are complete, including illustrated installation instructions. Applications include 1999–2000 Chevrolet Silverado, 2000 Chevrolet Tahoe, 2000 Chevrolet Suburban, 1999–2000 GMC Sierra, 2000 GMC Yukon, and 2000 GMC Yukon LX.

vehicles, might find an audible announcement annoying. Further, because the belt arrangement does not require any form of lubrication, Powerdyne superchargers are somewhat easier to install. No pressurized oil supply or return line is required.

Powerdyne rates its kits by the amount of boost each generates when installed on a stock engine- i.e., a 4.5-pound kit, a 6-pound kit, a 9-pound kit, and so on. Currently the 6-pound kits are "street-legal"; the 9-pound kits are not.

Complete kits include a fuel enrichment system and some, but not all, use a powerchip to electronically recalibrate fuel delivery. Installation will take between four and 8 hours, depending on the application and the mechanical abilities of the installer. All Powerdyne kits can be installed using basic hand tools.

Opcon Autorotor AB/Kenne Bell

Autorotor AB, a subsidiary of Opcon AB in Nacka, Sweden, manufactures an extremely efficient twin-screw, positive-displacement supercharger. The Opcon Group of automotive-related companies opened the facility and began producing superchargers in 1990. Opcon Autorotor AB is also working with a number of leading automotive manufacturers to develop fuel cell– driven vehicles. Several car makers plan to market vehicles propelled by zero-emission fuel cells in 2003.

Like Eaton Corporation's Supercharger Division, Opcon AB does not manufacture aftermarket blower systems, but works closely with companies

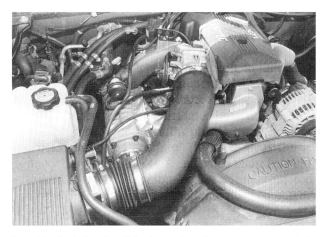

Everything is designed to fit in the stock engine compartment, and the entire kit can be installed using standard hand tools. A 5.3-liter kit consists of less than 10 components, not counting clips, clamps, and fasteners.

Magna Charger's Ford 4.6- and 5.4-liter kits tuck the supercharger beneath a two-piece intake manifold. Air enters the back of the supercharger and is forced up into the bottom of the intake. MC 4.6- and 5.4-liter kits are engineered to fit all 1997–2000 F150, Expedition, and Navigator vehicles with SOHC engines.

Ford 4.6- and 5.4-liter kits come equipped with an integrated air-to-water heat exchanger. The intercooler core is positioned over the supercharger discharge port. A pump circulates coolant to a water-to-air heat exchanger located behind the grille area.

The supercharger resides in the valley between the cylinder heads. The three tubes are the intercooler supply and return ports. This system will blow an extra 50 to 60 horsepower out of a 5.4, but more importantly, the engine will generate approximately 200 lbs-ft of additional torque from 1,000 to 4,000 rpm.

that do. Kenne Bell is one such supplier. Kenne Bell headquarters are located in Rancho Cucamonga, California.

Autorotor AB and Eaton superchargers are similar in that both ingest air through the end of the rotor housing (opposite the drive end) and expel it out the side or bottom, depending on the orientation of the unit. The inlet and outlet must be adapted to accommodate a given application. Autorotor superchargers will work in either a blow-through or draw-through configuration.

Kenne Bell specializes in V-8– and V-10–powered Ford cars and trucks, Dodge trucks, and Jeeps. Cast-aluminum manifolds and adapters provide a place to mount the compressor as well as direct the airflow from the air filter to the engine.

Fuel and timing enhancement is managed in a number of different ways, depending on the kit and the application. Some kits come with a fuel management unit (FMU) while others depend on a computer chip. A piggyback processor called an "optimizer module" is standard with some kits and optional for others. The optimizer module works in conjunction with the factory computer to recalibrate fuel and timing curves, and it alters the transmission shift points. Kenne Bell computer management systems are preprogrammed at the factory.

Certain kits include an application-specific switch chip to optimize fuel, timing, and electronic transmission shift points (providing the vehicle is equipped with an electronic transmission). Application-specific switch chips are designed to operate the factory computer. The driver can select either of two preprogrammed performance maps. Features and options include the following:

This is a Magnuson Products preproduction kit for the 2.4-liter Cavalier and Sunbird. Other offerings still on the drawing board include a kit for Volkswagen's 2.0-liter engine, Ford Focus, and Chrysler's PT Cruiser. A kit for the 3.4-liter V-6 Grand Am is also in the works.

The third-generation kit is a two-piece assembly that uses this application-specific cast-aluminum manifold to adapt a generic Eaton supercharger to the intake manifold. This system works very well, but it is not quite as compact as the fourth-generation assembly. The displacement of the superchargers remains unchanged.

To enhance aesthetics and durability, the fourth-generation TRD 3.4-liter I-6 kit for the 4Runner integrates the supercharger into the upper plenum. This space-saving feature also greatly simplifies the installation procedure. This is truly a "bolt-on" supercharger kit. The 3.0-liter I-6 kit for the Camry is similar in appearance.

TRD's 4.7-liter V-8 kit for the Tundra is under development and very near completion. Early performance numbers are very impressive—280 horsepower to the rear wheels and more tuning is planned. The supercharger is nestled beneath the intake manifold. Production assemblies will incorporate an integrated intercooler.

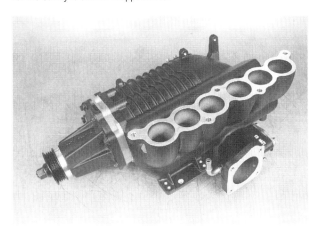

The air inlet, supercharger housing, and upper plenum are cast together. Besides conserving space, an integrated system positions the supercharger in the most efficient location and it helps hold costs down by eliminating the need for additional ductwork, brackets, and hardware.

A similar system is planned for Toyota's 4.0-liter marine engine. This kit is still in the early stages of development. Plans are also in the works to build a supercharger kit for the Toyota 4.5-liter I-6 Landcruiser.

This stock 3.0-liter 2000 Solara equipped with a TRD supercharger kit cranks out 250 horsepower. The kit is designed around Eaton's fourth-generation M62 charger and includes integrated architecture.

This cutaway provides a look at a Novi 2000's 3.54:1 gear multiplication and the precision tolerances between the impeller and the volute. Aircraft-grade, high-speed bearings hold the input and output shafts in perfect alignment as the impeller accelerates to speeds over 45,000 rpm.

Paxton's Novi 3000 is designed and engineered for racing. For that reason, Novi 3000 is not available in kit form for street applications. The 3000's volute measures 13.5 inches across, and the intake opening is 4.25 inches in diameter. Paxton advertises that a 3000 will push 2,900 cubic feet of air per minute.

Novi 2000 is the most versatile and, understandably, the most popular supercharger in Paxton's lineup. A 2000 will blow 1,700 cfm of air at maximum speed, which will support 980 horsepower, according to company reports. The power number is computed based on naturally aspirated airflow data.

- Raises the rpm limit to 7,000
- Available for positive-displacement or centrifugal superchargers
- Specific calibration for nitrous oxide injection
- Can implement calibration written for 5.0 Cobra without replacing the computer
- Reprograms the fan limits to improve cooling
- Available for naturally aspirated or forced induction applications
- Upgradeable to accommodate different power adders (cost option)
- Custom chips are also available

Switch chips are designed for Ford vehicles equipped with either EEC-IV or EEC-V. Blower kits engineered for Dodge trucks rely on a pre-programmed piggyback "optimizer module." Fuel and timing "maps" are optimized for full- and part-throttle operation on Kenne Bell's in-house DynoJet chassis dynamometer.

Paxton kits are equipped with 6-, 8-, or 10-rib pulleys. Obviously, the wider the belt, the better. Some applications can be upgraded to accept a wider belt, others cannot. Placement of the supercharger and available space are the two main conditions. The same applies for cog pulleys.

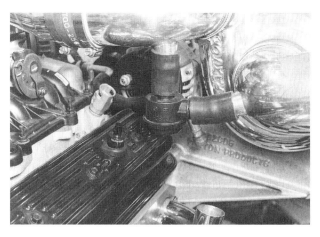

Some applications require an idle bypass valve, others do not. The purpose and function of an idle bypass valve is discussed at great length earlier in this chapter. Upgrading almost any system to include an idle bypass valve will normally enhance drivability and prolong durability, particularly during aggressive driving conditions.

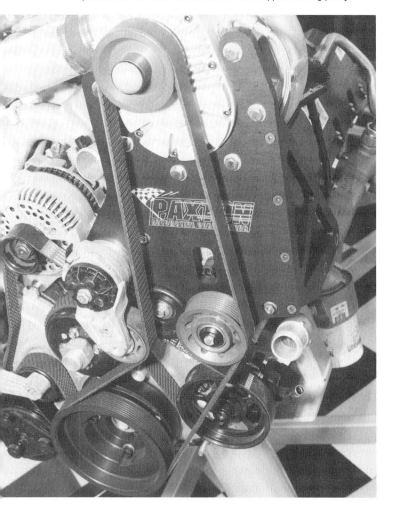

This shot illustrates the intricacies of a Paxton 1001814 4.6-liter Cobra kit. The reverse-direction Novi 2000 attaches to the front of the engine using a series of spacers. Keeping the blower low and close to the engine block simplifies the installation and eliminates any possibility of flexion.

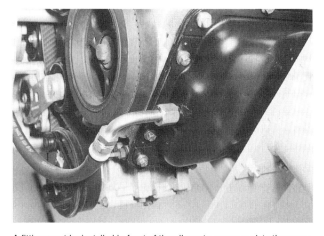

Alignment and flexion are the two most common drive belt problems. They are also the two best reasons to purchase an application-specific kit. Alignment addresses the position of the blower pulley in relation to the crank pulley. The centerlines must be parallel and on the same plane to provide perfect alignment.

A fitting must be installed in front of the oil pan to accommodate the supercharger oil return hose. Because the oil return relies on gravity, the port to sump must be lower than the bottom of the gearbox.

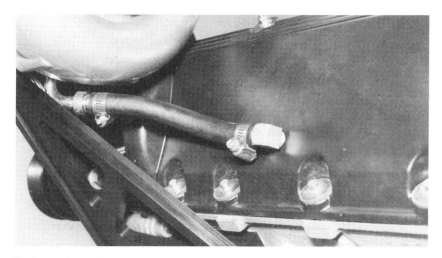

The Paxton Ford 5.4-liter truck kit mounts the blower above the engine, so the oil is returned to the driver's-side valve cover. Oil return should be as simple as the architecture will allow. The oil return hose should always follow a descending path to the sump.

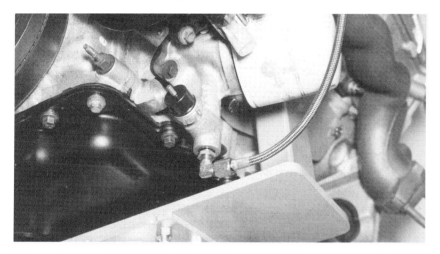

Novi superchargers are lubricated with engine oil. Paxton uses an existing pressure port to simplify the installation. As with the oil return, the oil supply system should be as simple as possible; but unlike the oil return, the source of pressurized engine oil can be anywhere above or below the supercharger.

Oil is supplied through a braided stainless-steel hose with a threaded fitting at each end. A special fitting needed to adapt the supply hose to the inlet port meters the flow of oil entering the gearbox. Only a small amount of oil is needed to cool and lubricate the gears.

Both switch chip and optimizers are OBDII compliant and, because they supplement the factory computer, drivability, fuel mileage, and emission controls remain intact and unaffected during cruise (low power) conditions. Likewise, fuel pressure and volume are increased when necessary by using various methods and devices. In some cases, the factory fuel pump must be upgraded or an auxiliary pump added. Some kits include an electronic enhancement called a "Boost-A-Pump" that can increase the output of any factory electric fuel pump by controlling the voltage to the motor.

BMW Z3 Roadster Intercooled Supercharger Kit

Imagine a BMW Z3 with an additional 60 horsepower and a large torque increase at all engine speeds. A Bell Engineering Group, Inc., BMW Z3 supercharger kit will make it happen without compromising drivability or sacrificing durability.

The Supercharger

The BEGI Z3 kit was designed around a belt-driven Autorotor AB (Type OA 2076) twin-screw (Lysholm principle) supercharger displacing 0.76 liters per revolution. An Autorotor supercharger was chosen in part because it delivers greater low-rpm boost, higher volumetric efficiency, and reduced parasitic load, all with a lower discharge temperature. To further the point, this kit will increase the air-charge temperature less than 90 degrees Fahrenheit at full boost.

The Intercooler

An intercooler is required for a supercharger system configured to deliver 7psi boost on an engine that has a 10:1 (or higher) compression ratio. In this application, the temperature reduction and increased air-charge density will produce a 10.5 percent horsepower gain.

A Paxton-enhanced Mustang 4.6-liter Cobra will deliver just shy of 400 horsepower to the rear wheels. Paxton's standard "street" kits are engineered to generate from 7 to 8 pounds of boost when installed on a stock engine.

General Layout

It is necessary to replace the massive BMW intake manifold to create a compact, uncluttered system. The Autorotor supercharger and cast-aluminum blower manifold replace the original intake manifold. The manifold also serves as the upper mount for the compressor. Fuel injectors retain their stock location. An intermediate sliding plate allows fore and aft adjustment to facilitate proper pulley alignment.

The compressor is also supported at the lower face of the engine mount and a third mount loops the drive extension. Packaging allows easy access to all engine service items. This centralized location provides a very rigid, vibration-free mounting for the supercharger and drive. The intercooler is sized for a 200-horsepower

Paxton's 1101109-M and 1101112-M Chevy Impala SS kits exemplify modern forced induction engineering at its best. Paxton designed these kits around the super-quiet SN 2000 supercharger. A LT1 will generate 40 percent more horsepower on 92-octane pump gas when stimulated with 5 pounds of boost.

Paxton offers blow-through kits for some GM engines that are equipped with central fuel injection. This overly simple application replaces the stock air cleaner with an enclosed top hat. Auxiliary fuel injectors in the hat provide fuel enhancement under boost conditions.

The dual-purpose manifold is installed in place of the factory dipstick. Oil is drawn from the bottom of the gearbox and returned to the top.

PAXTON SUPERCHARGER COMPARISON

	NOVI 3000	NOVI 2000	NOVI 2000RR	NOVI 1000	NOVI 1000RR	SN 2000
CFM	2900	1700	1700	850	850	650
Max Horsepower	1500	980	980	500	500	350
Internal Drive						
Helical Cut Gear	x	x	x	x	x	
Planetary Ball						x
Scroll Rotation						
Clockwise	x	x		x		
Counter-Clockwise			x		x	x
External Scroll Diameter	13.5"	10.0"	10.0"	9.0"	9.0"	9.0"
Front to Back Thickness	8"	7"	7"	6"	6"	7"
Intake Diameter						
External	5.0"	4.0"	4.0"	3.25"	3.25"	3.5"
Internal	4.25"	3.5"	3.5"	2.90"	2.90"	2.5"
Discharge Diameter						
External	3.5"	3.0"	3.0"	3.0"	3.0"	2.75"
Internal	3.1"	2.6"	2.6"	2.6"	2.6"	2.5"
Impeller Diameter	8.0"	6.5"	6.5"	5.0"	5.0"	5.75"
Straight Discharge	x	x	x	x	x	
Rear Discharge		x				x
Forward Discharge		x				

Paxton Automotive Corporation
1250 Calle Suerte • Camarillo, California 93012-805 • (805)987-8660 • Fax: (805)987-2985 www.paxtonautomotive.com

PAXTON
AUTOMOTIVE CORPORATION
SUPERCHARGERS

The variations of all six Paxton superchargers are shown in this comparison chart. After the maximum horsepower requirement is determined, the direction of rotation, the inlet and outlet configuration and dimensions, and the overall size of the blower will help determine the packaging parameters for a particular installation. *Paxton*

Phone: **(888)9-PAXTON**
Fax: **(805)987-2985**
www.paxtonautomotive.com

APPLICATION GUIDE

Part Number	Make	Model	Year	Engine	Injection	S/C Type	Description
1100900-M	Chevy	Camaro	1985-87	305/350	TPI	SN H/O	S/C KIT, High Output
1101100-M	Chevy	Camaro	1988-92	305/350	TPI	SN H/O	S/C KIT, High Output
1101106-M	Chevy	Camaro	1993-95	LT1	TPI	SN H/O	S/C KIT, High Output
1101107-M	Chevy	Camaro	1996-97	LT1	TPI	SN H/O	S/C KIT, High Output w/o Traction
1101109-M	Chevy	Impala	1994-95	LT1	TPI	SN H/O	S/C KIT, High Output
1101112-M	Chevy	Impala	1996	LT1	TPI	SN H/O	S/C KIT, High Output
1101901-M	Chevy	Truck	1988-93	350	TBI	SN H/O	S/C KIT, High Output
1101905-M	Chevy	Truck	1994-95	350	TBI	SN H/O	S/C KIT, High Output
1101910	Chevy	Truck	1996-99	350	CPI	NOVI	S/C KIT, NOVI 2000
1105010	Chevy	Truck	1996-98	454	CPI	NOVI	S/c KIT, NOVI 2000
1101700-M	Chevy	Early	Pre-84	350	CARB	SN H/O	S/C KIT, Spread Bore Carb Encl.
1100100-M	Chevy	Early	Pre-84	350	CARB	SN H/O	S/C KIT, Square Bore Carb Encl.
1215000-M	Pontiac	Firebird	1985-87	305/350	TPI	SN H/O	S/C KIT, High Output
1200600-M	Pontiac	Firebird	1988-92	305/350	TPI	SN H/O	S/C KIT, High Output
1101106-M	Pontiac	Firebird	1993-95	LT1	TPI	SN H/O	S/C KIT, High Output
1101107-M	Pontiac	Firebird	1996-97	LT1	TPI	SN H/O	S/C KIT, High Output w/o Traction
1201205-M	Dodge	Ram	1993-98	318/360	Port	SN H/O	S/C Kit, High Output
1201201-M	Dodge	Dakota	1996-96	318/360	Port	SN H/O	S/C Kit, High Output
1201211	Dodge	Ram	1993-98	318/360	Port	NOVI	S/C Kit, NOVI (coming soon)
1201210	Dodge	Ram	1995-00	V10	Port	NOVI	S/C Kit, NOVI 2000
1201204	Dodge	Ram	1997-99	318/360	Port	NOVI	S/C Kit, NOVI (coming soon)
1201202-M	Jeep	Grand Cherokee	1993-97	318	Port	SN H/O	S/C Kit, High Output
1000300-M	Ford	Mustang	1966-70	289/302	Carb	SN H/O	S/C Kit, High Output
1000702-M	Ford	Mustang	1983-85	302	Carb	SN H/O	S/C Kit, High Output
1001800-M	Ford	Mustang	1986-93	302	EFI	SN H/O	S/C Kit, High Output
1001803-M	Ford	Mustang	1994-95	302	EFI	SN H/O	S/C Kit, High Output
1001810	Ford	Mustang	1986-93	302	EFI	NOVI	S/C Kit, NOVI 2000
1001812	Ford	Mustang	1994-95	302	EFI	NOVI	S/C Kit, NOVI 2000
1001813	Ford	Mustang	1996-98	4.6L	EFI	NOVI	S/C Kit, Single Overhead Cam
1001814	Ford	Cobra	1996-98	4.6L	EFI	NOVI	S/C Kit, Dual Overhead Cam
1001815	Ford	Mustang	1999	4.6L	EFI	NOVI	S/C Kit, Single Overhead Cam
1001816	Ford	Cobra	1999	4.6L	EFI	NOVI	S/C Kit, Dual Overhead Cam
1001911	Ford	F-Series & Excursion	1988-99	V10	EFI	NOVI	S/C Kit, NOVI 2000
1001912	Ford	F-Series & SUV	1997-98	5.4L V8	EFI	NOVI	S/C Kit, NOVI 2000
1001913	Ford	F-Series & SUV	1999	5.4L V8	EFI	NOVI	S/C Kit, NOVI 2000
1001915	Ford	F-Series & SUV	1999-2000	4.6L	EFI	NOVI	S/C Kit, NOVI 2000 (coming soon)
1001912	Lincoln	Navigator	1997-98	5.4L	EFI	NOVI	S/C Kit, Single Overhead Cam
1001914	Lincoln	Navigator	1999	5.4L	EFI	NOVI	S/C Kit, Dual Overhead Cam

Paxton's application matrix offers a table-top view of its 38 systems. Each kit comes complete with all the brackets, piping, and hardware, as well as one of several different application-specific fuel-enhancement systems. Some kits may include an electronic timing retard computer. *Paxton*

Powerdyne engineers blower kits for a number of popular applications. Each can be installed in 8 hours or less in a home garage using standard hand tools. Of all the centrifugal superchargers, Powerdyne is the easiest to install, because the drive housing (gearbox on other chargers) does not use engine oil for lubrication. *Powerdyne*

The drive belt assembly—called SilentDrive— runs cooler and quieter than gear-driven superchargers. Under normal driving conditions, these belts typically last for 50,000 miles or more, according to Powerdyne's Web site. The engine will run naturally aspirated should the blower drive belt break. *Powerdyne*

application and is mounted behind the headlight assembly. The system also incorporates an idle bypass valve, which reduces parasitic drag to less than 0.5 horsepower during deceleration and cruise.

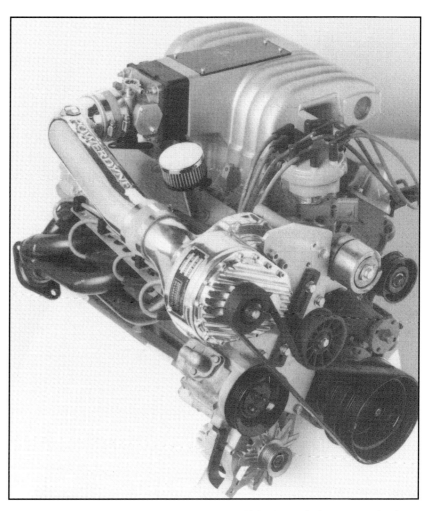

Typically a stock Ford 5.0-liter engine will generate an additional 75 to 85 horsepower when force-fed with 6 pounds of boost and upward of 100 horsepower with 8 pounds. Powerdyne kits are calibrated for stock engine applications. A typical system relies on an FMU to raise fuel pressure to overdrive the injectors. *Powerdyne*

Fuel System

A secondary regulator that reacts to boost pressure is added to the original Z3 fuel delivery system. Fuel pressure increases at a specific, progressive rate in relationship to boost, resulting in a constant air/fuel mixture ratio through the entire rpm range.

Power and Performance

A stock Z3 will deliver 109 horsepower to the rear wheels. BEGI's supercharger kit will boost output to 163 (approximately 190 horsepower at the flywheel). These power figures were measured with a stock exhaust system in place.

Emissions Equipment

All factory BMW emissions equipment remains in place and completely functional. BEGI reports an Autorotor BMW Z3 will easily pass any tailpipe emissions test in America. A CARB exemption order (EO) (see chapter 8) application is pending.

Installation

The BEGI Autorotor BMW system is a simple, straightforward kit that can be installed by a novice mechanic in 8 to 10 hours.

(continued on page 71)

Full load performance characteristics of Autorotor Supercharger Type OA 1032

Displacement: 0,32 l/rev. Built in press ratio: 1,3 Test condition: Discharge press: 2,0 bar abs.
Suction pressure: 1,0 bar abs. Suction temp: 20° C.

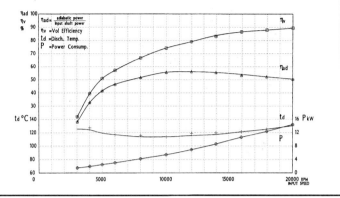

Full load performance characteristics of Autorotor Supercharger Type OA 2059

Displacement: 0,59 l/rev. Built in press ratio: 1,3 Test condition: Discharge press: 2,0 bar abs.
Suction pressure: 1,0 bar abs. Suction temp: 20° C.

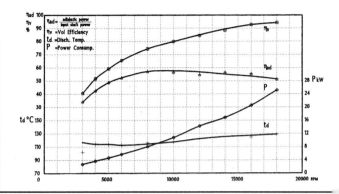

Full load performance characteristics of Autorotor Supercharger Type OA 1040

Displacement: 0,40 l/rev. Built in press ratio: 1,44 Test condition: Discharge press: 2,0 bar abs.
Suction pressure: 1,0 bar abs. Suction temp: 20° C.

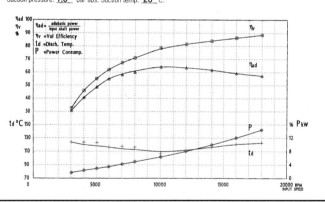

Full load performance characteristics of Autorotor Supercharger Type OA 2089

Displacement: 0,89 l/rev. Built in press ratio: 1,44 Test condition: Discharge press: 2,0 bar abs.
Suction pressure: 1,0 bar abs. Suction temp: 20° C.

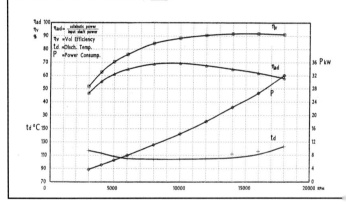

Full load performance characteristics of Autorotor Supercharger Type OA 1050

Displacement: 0,50 l/rev. Built in press ratio: 1,44 Test condition: Discharge press: 2,0 bar abs.
Suction pressure: 1,0 bar abs. Suction temp: 20° C.

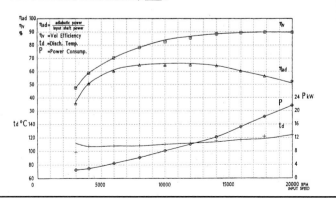

These three-part graphs illustrate Autorotor's high degree of efficiency. Adiabatic power compared to input shaft power (ad) and volumetric efficiency (v) are read using the 30-to-100 percentage scale at the top left of the graph. Discharge temperature (td) follows the Celsius (C) scale at the lower left, and power consumption (Pkw) is listed at the lower right of the graph. All are a product of compressor speed. Although all the information contained in these graphs illustrates efficiency, the volumetric efficiency and discharge temperature can be used for comparison. The vital statistics for 8 Autorotor superchargers ranging in size (displacement) from .32 to 1.5 liters per revolution are listed. Note that the discharge temperature remains relatively stable as volumetric efficiency increases. *AutoRotor*

Full load performance characteristics of Autorotor Supercharger Type OA 3116

Displacement: **1,16** l/rev. Built in press ratio: **1,4** Test condition: Discharge press: **2,0** bar abs.
Suction pressure: **1,0** bar abs. Suction temp: **20°** C.

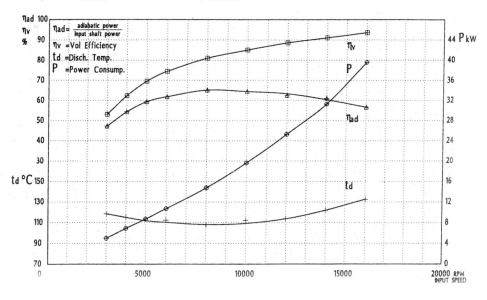

Full load performance characteristics of Autorotor Supercharger Type OA 3133

Displacement: **1,33** l/rev. Built in press ratio: **1,4** Test condition: Discharge press: **2,0** bar abs.
Suction pressure: **1,0** bar abs. Suction temp: **20°** C.

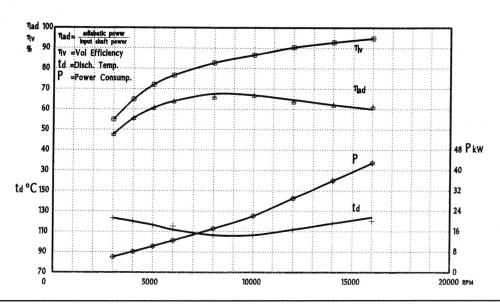

Autorotor
Member of the OPCON Group

SIZE RANGE 1: OTHER BUILT IN PRESSURE RATIOS AND DISPLACEMENTS ARE AVAILABLE ON REQUEST

STANDARD MODELS OF SR 1 MARCH 31 1999	PRODUCT ID NUMBER	SUPER-CHARGER TYPE	BUILT IN PRESSURE RATIO	DISPL.MENT LITRES/REV	DIMENSION			WEIGHT KGS	MAX SPEED RPM (CONT.)	MAX CAP. M³/MIN
					A	B	C			
	102001	OA 1032	1.3	0.32	163.5	0	46	3.8	18000	5.3
	102051	OA 1040	1.4	0.40	183	0	46	4.3	18000	6.6
	102101	OA 1050	1.4	0.50	214	50	61	4.8	18000	8.3

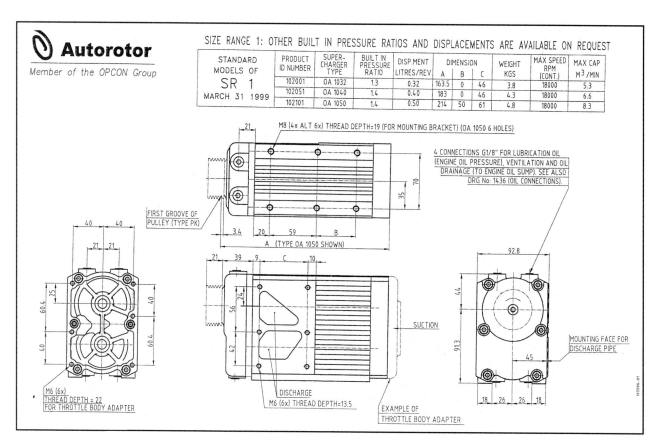

SIZE RANGE 2: OTHER BUILT IN PRESSURE RATIOS AND DISPLACEMENTS ARE AVAILABLE ON REQUEST

STANDARD MODELS OF SR 2 FOR EXTENDED DRIVE MARCH 31 1999	PRODUCT ID NUMBER	SUPER-CHARGER TYPE	BUILT IN PRESSURE RATIO	DISPL.MENT LITRES/REV	DIMENSION			WEIGHT KGS	MAX SPEED RPM (CONT.)	MAX CAP. M³/MIN
					A	B	C			
	101052	OA 2059	1.3	0.59	187	80	59	6.5	15000	8
	101151	OA 2076	1.6	0.76	217	55	59	7.3	15000	10.5
	101266	OA 2089	1.4	0.89	247.8	55	74	8.0	15000	12.3

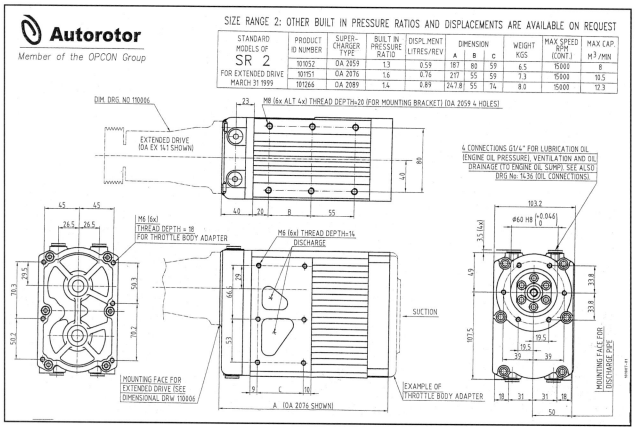

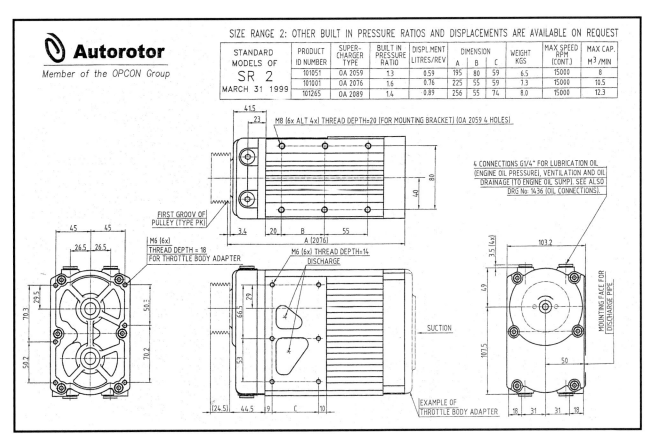

Autorotor

Member of the OPCON Group

SIZE RANGE 2: OTHER BUILT IN PRESSURE RATIOS AND DISPLACEMENTS ARE AVAILABLE ON REQUEST

STANDARD MODELS OF SR 2 MARCH 31 1999	PRODUCT ID NUMBER	SUPER-CHARGER TYPE	BUILT IN PRESSURE RATIO	DISPL.MENT LITRES/REV	DIMENSION			WEIGHT KGS	MAX SPEED RPM (CONT.)	MAX CAP. M³/MIN
					A	B	C			
	101051	OA 2059	1.3	0.59	195	80	59	6.5	15000	8
	101001	OA 2076	1.6	0.76	225	55	59	7.3	15000	10.5
	101265	OA 2089	1.4	0.89	256	55	74	8.0	15000	12.3

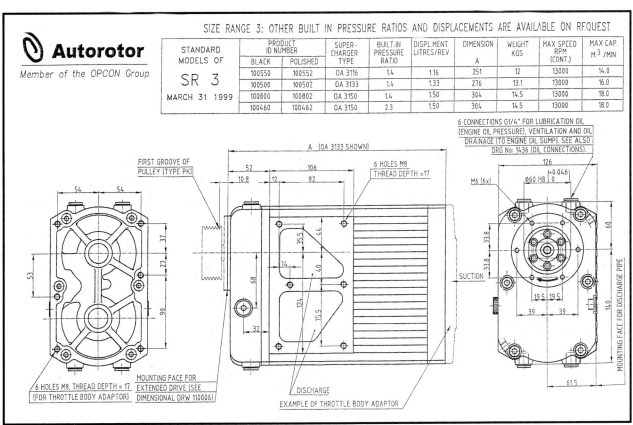

Autorotor

Member of the OPCON Group

SIZE RANGE 3: OTHER BUILT IN PRESSURE RATIOS AND DISPLACEMENTS ARE AVAILABLE ON REQUEST

STANDARD MODELS OF SR 3 MARCH 31 1999	PRODUCT ID NUMBER		SUPER-CHARGER TYPE	BUILT.IN PRESSURE RATIO	DISPL.MENT LITRES/REV	DIMENSION A	WEIGHT KGS	MAX SPEED RPM (CONT.)	MAX CAP. M³/MIN
	BLACK	POLISHED							
	100550	100552	OA 3116	1.4	1.16	251	12	13000	14.0
	100500	100502	OA 3133	1.4	1.33	276	13.1	13000	16.0
	100800	100802	OA 3150	1.4	1.50	304	14.5	13000	18.0
	100460	100462	OA 3150	2.3	1.50	304	14.5	13000	18.0

69

Autorotor
Member of the OPCON Group

STANDARD MODELS OF MX MARCH 31 1999	PRODUCT ID NUMBER		SUPER-CHARGER TYPE	BUILT IN PRESSURE RATIO	DISPL.MENT LITRES/REV	DIMENSION A	WEIGHT KGS	MAX SPEED RPM (CONT.)	MAX CAP. M³/MIN
	BLACK	POLISHED							
	104251	104252	OA 418	1.1	1.8	276	12.3	13000	22
	104351	104352	OA 422	1.2	2.2	304	13.3	13000	27

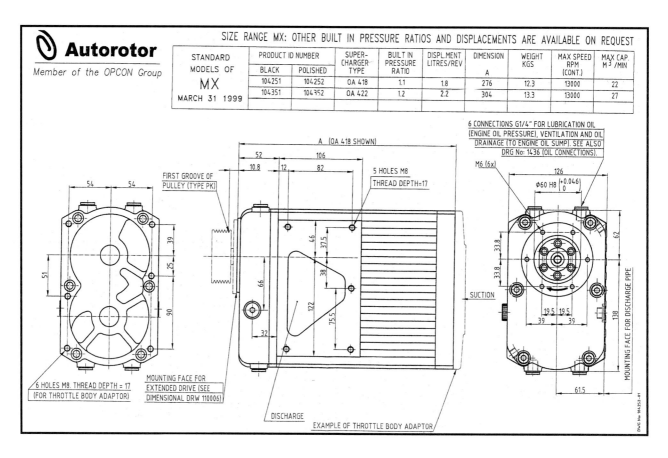

Autorotor
Member of the OPCON Group

STANDARD MODELS OF MX MARCH 31 1999	PRODUCT ID NUMBER		BUILT IN PRESSURE RATIO	SUPER-CHARGER TYPE	DISPL.MENT LITRES/REV	WEIGHT KGS A	MAX SPEED RPM (CONT.)	MAX CAP. M³/MIN
	BLACK	POLISHED						
	104201	104202	1.1	OA 426	2.6	14.7	13000	31

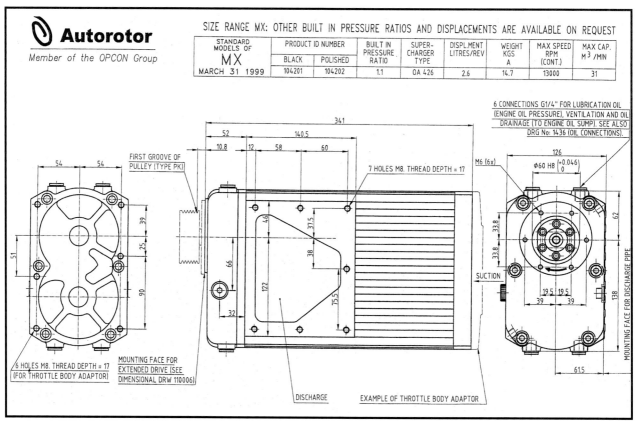

Illustrations on pages 68, 69, and 70
Besides providing the physical dimensions of all six Autorotor supercharger models, these drawings illustrate the way a positive-displacement blower must grow in size in response to horsepower demand. The largest MX model, OA 426, weighs just under 32.5 pounds and measures 13.4 inches long, 4.95 inches high, and 5.42 inches wide. It displaces 2.6 liters of air per revolution with a 1.1:1 pressure ratio. At 6.42 inches long, the smallest supercharger weighs just 8.37 pounds and displaces .32 liters per revolution. *AutoRotor*

(continued from page 65)

Fuel Economy

Though fuel economy is a function of driving habit, expect economy to drop approximately 3 miles per gallon in the city and 1 mile per gallon during highway driving after the supercharger kit has been installed.

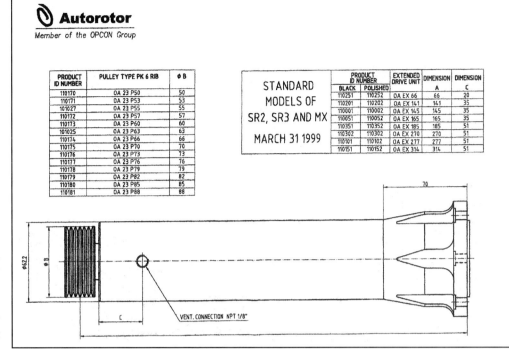

PRODUCT ID NUMBER	PULLEY TYPE PK 6 RIB	Ø B
110170	OA 23 P50	50
110171	OA 23 P53	53
101027	OA 23 P55	55
110172	OA 23 P57	57
110173	OA 23 P60	60
101025	OA 23 P63	63
110174	OA 23 P66	66
110175	OA 23 P70	70
110176	OA 23 P73	73
110177	OA 23 P76	76
110178	OA 23 P79	79
110179	OA 23 P82	82
110180	OA 23 P85	85
110181	OA 23 P88	88

STANDARD MODELS OF SR2, SR3 AND MX MARCH 31 1999

PRODUCT ID NUMBER BLACK	POLISHED	EXTENDED DRIVE UNIT	DIMENSION A	DIMENSION C
110251	110252	OA EX 66	66	20
110201	110202	OA EX 141	141	35
110001	110002	OA EX 145	145	35
110051	110052	OA EX 165	165	35
110351	110352	OA EX 185	185	51
110302	110302	OA EX 270	270	51
110101	110102	OA EX 277	277	51
110151	110152	OA EX 314	314	51

Eight blower extensions ranging from 66 to 314 millimeters in length allow the blower to be mounted at various distances from the crank pulley. Only the SR2, SR3, and MX blowers will accept an extension. *AutoRotor*

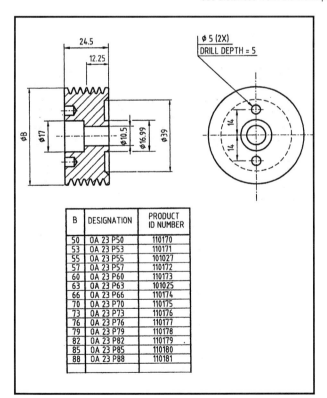

B	DESIGNATION	PRODUCT ID NUMBER
50	OA 23 P50	110170
53	OA 23 P53	110171
55	OA 23 P55	101027
57	OA 23 P57	110172
60	OA 23 P60	110173
63	OA 23 P63	101025
66	OA 23 P66	110174
70	OA 23 P70	110175
73	OA 23 P73	110176
76	OA 23 P76	110177
79	OA 23 P79	110178
82	OA 23 P82	110179
85	OA 23 P85	110180
88	OA 23 P88	110181

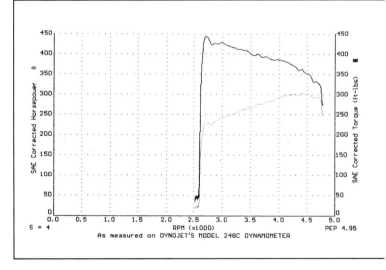

This stock 4.7-liter engine in a 1995 K2500 Suburban measured 305.1 horsepower at 4,400 rpm and 443.1 peak torque at 2,700 rpm at the rear wheels, after an Autorotor supercharger, a pair of Dart Merlin cylinder heads, and a stainless-steel Borla exhaust system were installed.

One of 14 pulleys ranging in size from 50 to 88 millimeters is used to match the speed of the blower to the application. While installing a smaller pulley will create a larger amount of boost earlier in the rpm range, it may also overspeed the supercharger at redline. *AutoRotor*

Chapter Five
Turbochargers

When properly sized and calibrated, a turbocharger will deliver outstanding performance while demanding few concessions. A turbocharger is more efficient than a supercharger, both thermally and mechanically. Capitalizing on the laws of thermodynamics, a turbocharger takes advantage of heat energy that would otherwise be wasted. From a purely mechanical point of view, a turbocharger reacts to load rather than engine speed, which means it does not impose a load penalty on the engine unless it is making boost. For these reasons, a turbocharged engine can deliver optimum fuel economy and pleasing drivability when operating in a naturally aspirated mode. It is any wonder more original-equipment manufacturers choose to turbo charge rather than supercharge?

Turbo Basics

Look at a turbocharger as a self-contained, motor-driven compressor. The compressor side consists of an impeller or compressor wheel and compressor housing. The turbine and housing is the motor that drives the compressor. They convert the potential energy stored in the hot exhaust gas into kinetic energy needed to drive the compressor wheel. The size and shape of the turbine wheel and housing will determine the effectiveness of the conversion process. Likewise, the size and shape of the impeller and housing will dictate the performance characteristics of the compressor.

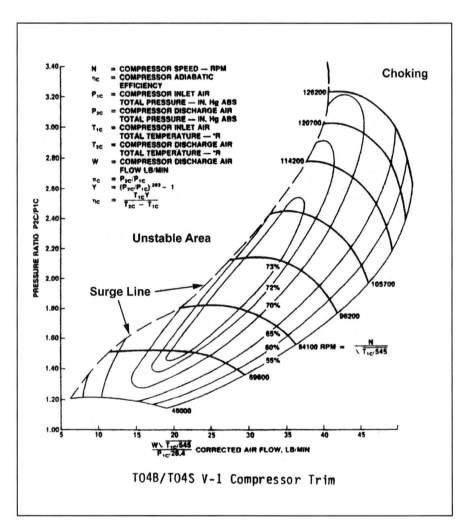

A compressor performance map consists of lines of constant compressor efficiency and constant corrected speed on a plot of pressure ratio (Delta P) against corrected mass flow. The islands in the center of the map represent the stable operating range. The unstable region on the left is the surge line. Local flow reversal eventually occurs in the boundary layer when mass flow is reduced at a constant pressure ratio. Reduction in mass flow will cause the flow to reverse completely, which will cause a drop in pressure. The process repeats when flow reestablishes itself. Compressors should not be operated in this unstable area. The choke line represents the limit of the stable operating regime on the right. The velocities increase as mass flow increases, and eventually the flow becomes sonic, indicated by this limiting area. Additional mass flow through the compressor can only be obtained by increasing its speed. When the diffuser is choked, the mass flow rate will be limited, even if the speed of the compressor is raised substantially. *Turbonetics*

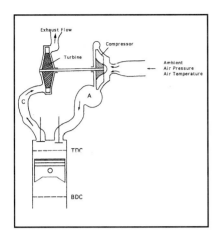

The compressor raises the density (and temperature) of the air at A. Exhaust gases, C, drive the turbine. Spent gases are then expelled to the atmosphere. The pressure differentials between the air inlet must be controlled at all times to produce a stable system.

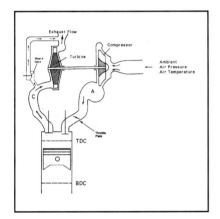

A wastegate controls the output of the compressor. When the pressure in the intake or exhaust manifold reaches a predetermined threshold, pressure in the bleed hose forces the actuator to open the wastegate against spring pressure, which allows a small amount of exhaust gas to bypass the turbine.

Proper sizing requires matching the performance characteristics of a particular compressor and turbine assembly to a given engine. These parameters dictate a range of optimum efficiency. Further, a turbocharger's range of efficiency falls within an effective rpm band (referring to the speed of the impeller, not engine speed). This efficient range of operation is displayed on a graph called a performance map.

Computing the performance of a turbine assembly is complex. The size (diameter) of the turbine wheel repre-

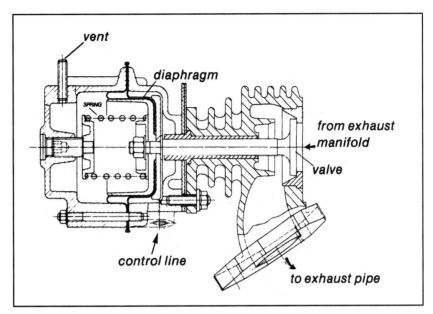

A properly controlled wastegate will regulate maximum boost pressure quickly and smoothly. The gate should open and close in precise increments to provide a smooth, calibrated transition. It should react quickly, but not abruptly, and without overcompensating. *Volkswagen of America, Inc.*

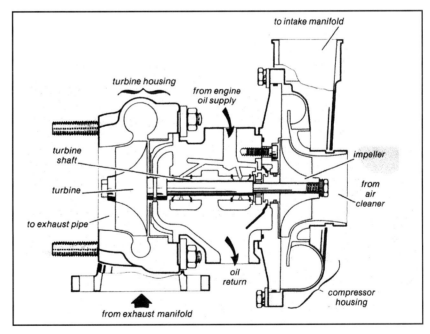

The configuration of the compressor housing and impeller will change the operating parameters, as will the turbine housing and the turbine. Within a range of conditions, housings and wheels can be mixed and matched to suit a particular application. Airflow, pressure ratio, and rpm requirements dictate some of the necessary parameters.

sents its ability to do work when acted upon by a given volume of exhaust flow. Without drowning the topic in a sea of mathematics, let's just say a larger wheel is slow but more powerful compared to smaller wheel, which is quicker and more agile.

Under the category of "no free lunch," the turbine assembly also offers some restriction to exhaust flow. The restriction causes back pressure in the exhaust manifold or header when the compressor is generating boost. Some back pressure in a turbo system

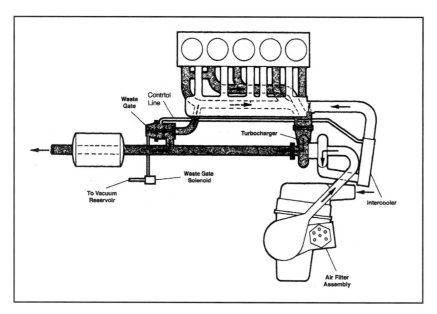

The EEC also electronically controls the wastegate on this Audi 5000S. Retarding the ignition timing incrementally up to 8 degrees controls detonation. Should the engine continue to knock, the EEC will open a solenoid valve that will apply vacuum to the wastegate vent tube, further limiting boost. *Volkswagen of America, Inc.*

These HKS external wastegates range from street to all-out competition. Standard 40-millimeter valves are recommended for street use, and the larger 50-millimeter valves are for racing applications. Different-sized springs, base flanges, gaskets, and flex outlet tubes are also available for custom installations. *HKS*

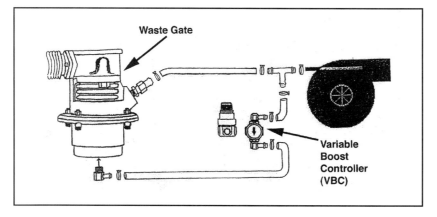

Applying boost pressure to both sides of the actuator will "dampen" valve action, improving control. Action or reaction can be calibrated by regulating the amount of pressure delivered to one side of the actuator using a HKS Variable Boost Controller (VBC) kit, which will work with either single- or dual-port wastegates. *HKS*

is unavoidable. Too much, however, can lead to severe problems and too little indicates an inefficient system. Excessive back pressure created by an undersized turbine can elevate the exhaust gas temperature (EGT) beyond safe limits. Assuming a worst-case scenario, extreme EGTs can damage valves and/or melt pistons. A minor infraction will cause the engine to detonate when under load.

Sizing a turbine assembly to the compressor and the engine is a compromise between power, speed, and efficiency. Airflow through the engine is a key factor. The output of the compressor must overcome the airflow demands of the engine at a given rpm. In effect, the compressor must force more air into the intake manifold than the engine can ingest. The disparity creates pressure.

Engineered Plumbing

In most cases, the ductwork needed to direct the airflow from a supercharger to the engine is minimal. The outlet of the supercharger need only be plumbed to the throttle body or intake manifold. If the outlet flange of the supercharger is mated directly to the intake manifold, only ductwork from the air filter to the inlet is needed. A stacked system that positions each component, one on top of the other, requires no actual plumbing at all, as in the case of a Roots blower sandwiched between the carburetor(s) and the intake manifold.

Turbocharger plumbing is somewhat complex by comparison because exhaust gases provide the power needed to drive the compressor wheel. To execute that task, turbochargers require additional plumbing to route exhaust gases through the turbine housing. The complexity is compounded somewhat because the turbine and compressor housings are in close proximity to each other.

Mounting the inlet of the turbine housing directly to the exhaust manifold or header simplifies the installation, but only to a point. It eliminates only one section of tubing, or two sections if it is a twin-turbo system.

Installing a turbocharger on a naturally aspirated engine usually requires plumbing from a remote air filter to the inlet of the compressor, high-pressure tubing connecting the outlet of the compressor to the inlet port of the engine, and enough tubing to route the exhaust through the turbine housing. Inline engines present fewer plumbing problems compared to V configurations, because routing exhaust from two manifolds requires even more piping.

Hot Turbochargers

Turbochargers also generate (or trap) an enormous amount of heat. Because the turbine restricts the exhaust flow, the manifold or header and the turbine housing absorb, and therefore radiate, a large portion of the heat generated by the combustion process. Exhaust temperatures can easily reach 1,500 degrees Fahrenheit. Needless to say, the air circulating through the engine compartment transforms the manifold, turbine housing, and exhaust pipe(s) into a convection oven. Wires, hoses, and in some cases, the paint on the hood can be reduced to ashes. A less obvious, but significant, problem is the temperature of the air-charge, which provides the best performance at the lowest temperature. Keeping the inlet air-charge as cool as possible is a difficult task, considering the act of compressing air produces heat as well. The fact that the compressor housing is located mere inches from the exhaust turbine housing further compounds the problem. Insulation is therefore an important part of the turbocharger system.

Pressure Variables

Controlling the pressure differentials throughout the system is a science unto itself. To cite an isolated example, pressure in the exhaust manifold increases (back pressure) as boost

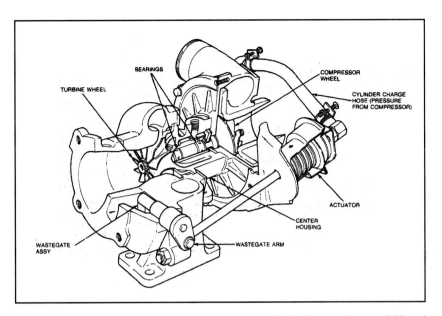

A number of OE manufacturers utilize an integrated wastegate design, because they are reliable and easy to service. An integrated wastegate is always sized properly for the application. Serious performance enthusiasts do not favor this design, because the calibration of the gate is somewhat fixed. *Ford Motor Company*

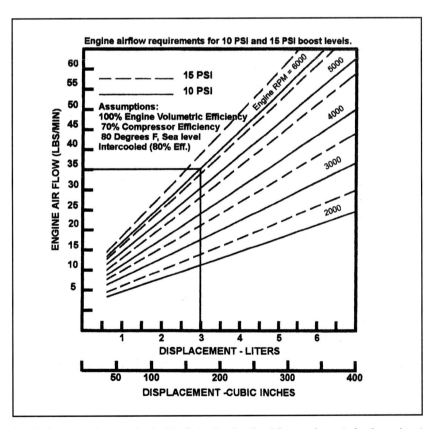

A turbocharger can be properly sized by first estimating the airflow requirements for the engine at varying rpm levels using this graph, circulated by Turbonetics. This chart covers high-performance engines that are capable of achieving 100 percent volumetric efficiency. The adiabatic efficiency for the compressor will be at least 70 percent, delivering either a 10- or 15-psi maximum boost pressure. *Turbonetics, Inc.*

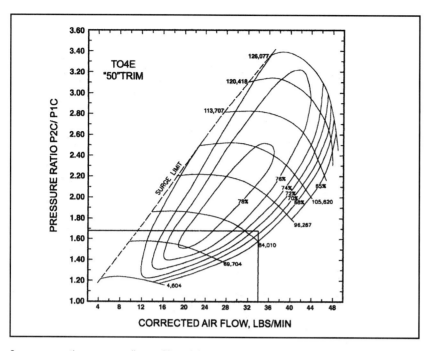

Compressor ratios corresponding to 10- and 15-pound boost levels are 1.68 and 2.02, respectively. Use the airflow data acquired from the previous graph to select the appropriate performance map that corresponds with a particular turbocharger. Plot the data on the map so the engine torque peak operating point is as close to the compressor peak efficiency island as possible, while maintaining the engine-rated speed point in the compressor within the 60 percent or higher efficiency region. *Turbonetics, Inc.*

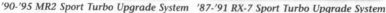

'90-'95 MR2 Sport Turbo Upgrade System   *'87-'91 RX-7 Sport Turbo Upgrade System*

TO4S Turbo   *T51S Turbo*

A number of manufacturers offer upgrades for factory turbocharged cars. These particular kits are marketed by HKS. Preengineered performance upgrades are a good investment, because most can provide a 10 to 25 percent power increase with very little effort and at minimal expense. These direct-replacement kits are more efficient, and they reduce the thermal load across the engine. *HKS*

increases. However, from an overall perspective, pressure within the system from the air filter to the tailpipe can vary greatly and change rapidly in response to load. These extreme pressure variations create a number of engineering problems. A turbo system can be very unruly or even self-destructive without complicated pressure controls. For these reasons, a variety of pressure and flow-control valves are needed to stabilize the system at various speeds and loads.

To illustrate a typical scenario, a turbocharger compressor assembly (the turbine and compressor wheels and the shaft) spinning at high speed will continue to spin at high speed (freewheel) for a period of time after the engine decelerates. Such is the case when a drag car driver cuts the throttle as soon as he crosses the finish line. Engine speed drops to idle and the transition from full power to no power occurs in a fraction of a second. But inertial forces keep the impeller spinning at high speed, which continues to compress air against a closed throttle plate. The resulting pressure differentials can impose severe uneven loads on the turbo and the engine.

Turbo lag is the most common problem associated with turbocharging.

Turbo lag occurs because the compressor assembly in a turbocharger cannot react as quickly as the engine. By comparison, the speed of a belt-driven supercharger coincides with the speed of the engine, which means the supercharger accelerates and decelerates at essentially the same speed as the crankshaft. The turbine and impeller in a turbocharger are not mechanically connected to the engine. For that reason, inertia becomes a formidable force. Because exhaust gases drive the turbine, airflow through the engine must increase to a sufficient volume before the turbocharger will react. Only then can the turbocharger gain enough speed (spool up) to generate boost. The time it takes a turbocharger to react (attain minimum

Turbonetics
Turbocharger Stats, Facts, Figures, and Formulas

Turbocharger Performance Calculations

Atmospheric pressure at sea level = 14.7 psi (absolute)

Standard temperature at sea level = 60 degrees Fahrenheit

Absolute Conditions

Absolute Pressure = boost pressure + 14.7psi = psi (absolute) = psia

Absolute Temperature + degrees Fahrenheit + 460 = degrees R

Air Density (weight of one cubic foot of air)

p = lbs/cubic foot = #/cu. ft. = 2.7 P/T

Where P = absolute air pressure (psia)

    Where T = absolute air temperature (degrees R)

Example: p @ sea level = 2.7(14.7)/(460 + 60) = .076 #/cu.ft.

Airflow (four-stroke engine):

V = cu.ft./minute = (CID/1,728) x (rpm /2) x Nv = Volumetric airflow

Where cid = engine displacement in cubic inches

    (Note: 1 liter = 61.02 cubic inches)

    Where rpm = engine speed in revolutions per minute

    Where Nv = volumetric efficiency of engine

    (Note: assume .85 for most production engines; highly modified engines approach 1.00)

    Where

    W = V x p = Mass flow (#/minute)

Where V = Volumetric airflow (cu.ft./minute)

    Where p = air density (#/cu.ft.)

Pressure Ratio (PR):

PR= Compressor discharge pressure (absolute)/ Compressor inlet pressure (absolute)

PR = P2c/P1c

Y = Calculation constant for air = $(P2c/P1c)^{.283} - 1$

Compressor Discharge Temperature (T2c):

ΔT = Temperature rise due to heat of compression = T1c x Y/Nc

Where T1c = Compressor inlet temperature (absolute)

    Where Y = Calculation constant for air

    Where Nc = Compressor efficiency (assume .7 for most applications)

T2c = T1c + ΔT = degrees R (absolute)

Air Density At Boost (p2):

p2 = 2.7 (boost pressure + 14.7)/(460 +T2c) = #/cu.ft.

Airflow at Boost (four-stroke engine):

V1 = V2 = Volumetric airflow (Volumetric airflow does not change)

W = V x p2 = Mass flow at boost (#/minute)

Horsepower Estimates:

For carbureted engines in ok condition:

  1 #/minute = 8 to 8.5 horsepower

For EFI engines in ok condition:

  1 #/minute = 8.5 to 9 horsepower

For performance EFI engines:

  1 #/minute = 9 to 11 horsepower

Turbine (Expansion) Discharge Temperature (T2t):

ΔT = T1t x Nt x Y/(1+Y) = Temperature decrease due to expansion (degrees Fahrenheit)

Where T1t = turbine inlet temperature (absolute)

    Where Nt = turbine efficiency (assume .7)

    Where $Y = (P1t/P2t)^{.283} - 1$

    Where P1t = turbine inlet pressure (absolute)

    Where P2t = turbine discharge pressure (absolute)

Therefore, turbine discharge temperature

(T2t) = T1t - ΔT = degrees R (absolute)

Energy Equations (for compressor or turbine):

Q = BTU/minute = W x Cp x ΔT

Where W = mass airflow (#/minute)

    Where Cp = specific heat of air = .24 BTU/#/degree F

    Where ΔT = actual temperature rise/fall during compression/expansion

Compressor example: For W = 50 #/minute: ΔT = 150 degrees

Q = 50 x .24 x 150 = 1,800 BTU/minute = 42.4 horsepower

Note: 1 horsepower (HP) = 42.44 BTU/minute

Definitions

Choke—Right-hand boundary of map, which would be formed if all speed lines were extended to the 1.0 pressure ratio. Represents the maximum flow capacity of the compressor.

Compressor map—A total plot of the performance of a compressor wheel in a specific housing. The vertical axis is always pressure ratio while the horizontal axis is usually mass flow, but may also be depicted as volumetric flow.

Efficiency "islands"—Shown as defined areas or "islands" on the compressor map, these boundaries represent the connected points of equal compressor efficiency as determined by calculation after a compressor is tested. Usually represented as a percentage.

Flow correction—See equation at bottom of map and altitude chart. Must be used when inlet conditions are significantly different from sea level conditions.

Pressure ratio—Usually referred to as PR, this ratio derived by dividing the absolute compressor discharge pressure by the absolute compressor inlet pressure (P2/P1).

Speed lines—Compressor performance is determined by spinning at a specific rotational rate (speed in rpm) and varying the discharge pressure to determine the resultant compressor flow. The combined plot of this performance is referred to as a "speed line." The speed used to generate a specific speed line is usually shown on a compressor map.

Surge—Left-hand boundary of compressor map that defines area of instability. The compressor cannot function to the left of this area.

ENGINE DISPLACEMENT	COMPRESSOR TRIM	TURBINE TRIM	TURBINE HOUSING
60-100 CID	T3-50 Trim	T3 Standard	.36/.48
100-150 CID	T3-Super 60	T3 Standard	.48/.63
150-200 CID	T3-Super 60	T3 Standard	.63/.82
200-250 CID	T4-S3 Trim	T4 "O" Trim	.58/.69
250-300 CID	T4-V1 Trim	T4 "P" Trim	.69/.81
300-350 CID	T4-V1 Trim	T4 "P" Trim	.81/.96
350-400 CID	T4-H3 Trim	T4 "P" Trim	.96/1.30
400-450 CID	T4-H3 Trim	T4 "P" Trim	1.30

Use this Turbonetics chart to make an initial selection for a typical single turbocharger street application supplying 10-psi boost. High-performance race engines will require turbine configurations based on specific requirements, which may vary considerably from these recommendations. Contact Turbonetics for additional information. *Turbonetics*

This Celica runs a 10.4-second quarter-mile at 137 miles per hour with help from a single inter-cooled T66 turbocharger and larger fuel injectors. Performance is more impressive considering the car with driver weighs 3,650 pounds. The twin overhead-cam 6 produces 675 horsepower and 650 lbs-ft of torque. The turbo spools up at 4,400 rpm.

operating speed) is called "turbo lag." As the name implies, turbo lag is the time it takes the speed of the turbo to catch up with the speed of the engine.

Turbo lag is unavoidable. It can be minimized to a large degree, or it can be pronounced. As a general rule, the larger the turbo (the mass of the turbine and compressor wheels and the shaft that connects them) in relationship to the size of the engine (displacement), the longer the turbo lag. The reason is simple: more energy is required to accelerate a larger mass. A large turbo will generate a higher level of boost but will be slower to react. A small turbo will react quicker but may be more limited in output. An acceptable arrangement is a compromise between the two.

In a real-world example, when the driver puts the pedal to the floor and the throttle is wide open, the engine gulps for air and the driver waits for the compressor to react. Exhaust pressure is low because engine speed is low. Natural aspiration forces air and fuel into the cylinders and the engine begins to accelerate. Exhaust flow increases in response to engine speed and the turbocharger spools up when airflow through the engine reaches a sufficient level. As the turbine and compressor wheels gain ample velocity, pressure in the intake manifold increases (boost). The reaction time (lag) can be measured in milliseconds if the turbo is well matched to the application or in whole seconds if the turbo is too large. A 5-second lag equates to an extremely long power delay.

Fuel and Ignition Timing

Maintaining an ideal timing lead and air/fuel mixture ratio throughout

Racing bypass valves typically vent to atmosphere. These adjustable, large-capacity valves react quickly during the heat of competition. Most racing valves, and some sophisticated street valves, are double acting, meaning pressures are available on both sides of the diaphragm.

the entire rpm range complicates the modification even further. This is a performance issue for all internal combustion engines, whether supercharged, turbocharged, or injected with nitrous oxide. Consider ignition timing and air/fuel ratio, along with air density, as ingredients in a chemical formula. Optimum power is on the other side of the equal sign (i.e., timing + air/fuel + air density = optimum power). Only the right amount of each component will produce optimum power. Fortunately, armed with the right knowledge, anyone can achieve good proportions of these power ingredients. Fuel and timing are covered in detail in chapter 8.

Don't be discouraged by all this techno-jargon. Turbochargers are extremely efficient, affordable, and very popular. Properly sized, a well-engineered turbo system can double the power output of almost any engine.

Turbocharger Manufacturers

Bell Engineering Group, Inc., and CarTech Racing are two quality turbocharger manufacturers. Following are some of their offerings.

5.0-Liter Mustang Kit

Few companies offer turbocharger kits for American V-8 engines because a complete, bolt-on system is both complex and expensive. Depending on the level of performance, the size of the engine, or the application, two smaller turbochargers are favored over one large turbocharger. CarTech Racing, a product line manufactured by Bell Engineering Group, Inc., in San Antonio, Texas, has been successfully promoting turbo power for 5.0-liter Mustangs for a number of years. The CarTech Mustang Street Sleeper Kit contains over 250 components, which include the folowing:

- A Garrett TO4 turbocharger
- A four-into-one turbo header
- A 3-inch-diameter down pipe

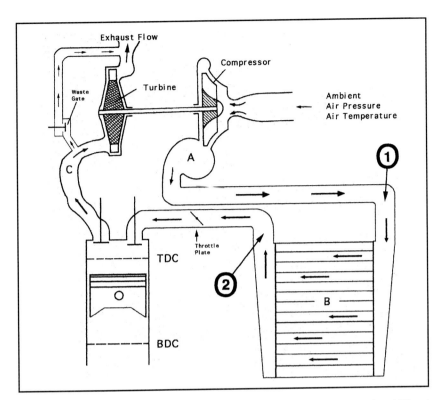

Delta (Δ) means difference or differential. The temperature differential or temperature drop (ΔT) and the pressure differential or pressure drop (ΔP) of an intercooler can be measured at 1 and 2. The ΔT equals T1 minus T2. The ΔP equals P1 minus P2.

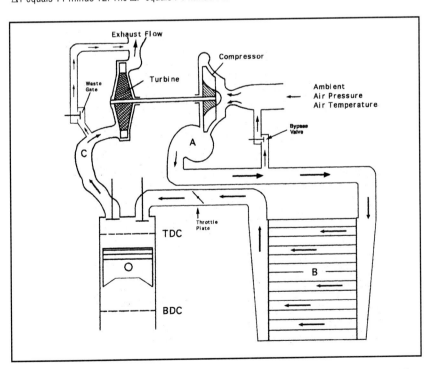

A bypass valve added to the discharge side of the turbocharger further regulates the pressure differentials within the system. Bypass valves unload, or vent, boost pressure without reducing compressor speed during deceleration and part-throttle, low-load operation. Like wastegates, they are activated by pressure changes in the intake manifold. Equalizing the pressure across the compressor enhances drivability and reduces uneven loads imposed on the turbocharger.

TYPICAL RACING BYPASS VALVE INSTALLATION

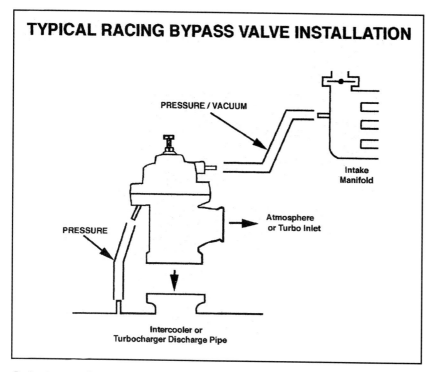

Racing bypass valves release boost pressure between shifts when the engine is not under load. Dual-port valves apply pressure to both sides of the actuator. Installing a heavier or lighter return spring will dial in a particular range of calibration. Fine-tuning is achieved by adjusting the screw on the top of the valve. *HKS*

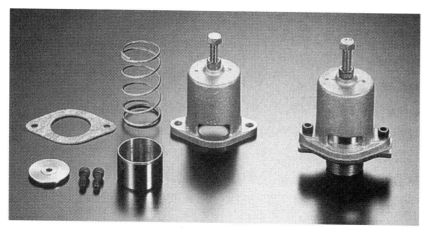

Pop-off valves add a level of protection in the event the wastegate malfunctions. These safety valves are positioned in the intake system and open only when intake manifold pressure exceeds a predetermined threshold. Like racing bypass valves, various-sized springs provide a range of calibration while the final setting is accomplished by turning the adjusting screw. *HKS*

- A crossover tube
- A Y-pipe
- An air filter
- A fuel management unit (FMU)
- A high-pressure fuel pump
- A choice of a low- or front-mounted air-to-air intercooler
- A racing wastegate with ultra-high-temperature diaphragm
- A CarTech boost gauge and mount
- All the hardware needed to install the system

This single-turbo kit is reportedly capable of generating up to 750 horsepower and can be driven on the street.

O-ringed heads and 7/16-inch ARP head studs are required if the system is adjusted to deliver over 10 pounds of boost. A competent mechanic can complete the installation in approximately 20 hours.

CarTech's Outlaw Kit is designed for drag racing only and should be installed on a race-prepared engine equipped with either World Products Dart or Trick Flow Specialties (TFS) heads. This kit will reportedly generate up to 1,000 horsepower when combined with the proper high-performance equipment. A base Outlaw Turbo Kit includes the following:

- A T-64E turbocharger (1,050 cfm)
- Optional T-70 compressor wheel (1,280 cfm)
- Optional T-72 compressor wheel (1,350 cfm)
- Optional T-76 compressor wheels (1,500+ cfm)
- 1- 3/4-inch ID 14-gauge, mandrel bent four-into-one turbo header
- 2.5-inch front crossover tube with flanges
- 1.25-inch valve wastegate
- 3-inch down pipe
- 2.5-inch black powder coated intercooler tubes
- Three-core, double-row air-to-air intercooler

If that's not enough power, the single turbo Outlaw Kit can be upgraded to a twin-turbo system with the following changes:

- Two TE-44 turbochargers with the option to upgrade
- Two 1-3/4-inch ID 14-gauge mandrel bent four-into-one turbo headers
- Two 3-inch down pipes
- Two 1-1/4-inch valve wastegate
- 5x8x31-inch air-to-air intercooler
- Black powder-coated tubes

Jeep Wrangler Turbocharger Kit

BEGI, also manufacturers a turbo system designed specifically for the Jeep Wrangler. The single turbo kit is reported to be perfectly drivable, simple, easy to service, easy to install, and easy to live with. The presence of the turbo is not detectable until the boost comes on. Additionally, there are no surges or flat spots, according to Corky Bell, BEGI's chief engineer.

Torque increases from 199 to 301 lbs-ft and rear-wheel horsepower, measured on a DynoJet chassis dynamometer, peaks at 222 compared to the 152 generated by the naturally aspirated engine. Boost begins at a comparatively low 1,800 rpm and levels off at 7 pounds.

An auxiliary electronic computer maintains the correct air/fuel mixture while the engine is under boost. Enough fuel is provided to achieve a maximum power ratio of 12.5:1.

BEGI's 250-base-horsepower Jeep Wrangler kit includes the following:

• An Airesearch T03 turbocharger with water-cooled housing and internal wastegate
• A compressor bypass valve
• A hand-fabricated, thick-walled turbo exhaust manifold
• An intercooler with cold air pickup
• A K & N air filter
• A boost gauge
• A complete fuel system
• Comprehensive installation instructions

Other than premium-octane pump fuel (no less than 92 octane), general tuning maintenance, and 2,500-mile oil change intervals, no other engine modifications are required. The oil change interval can be extended to 5,000 miles when quality synthetic oil is used.

Installation is well within the ability of the hobbyist mechanic, according to published reports. Assembly time is estimated between 10 and 16 hours using conventional hand tools. Some special tools are included in the kit.

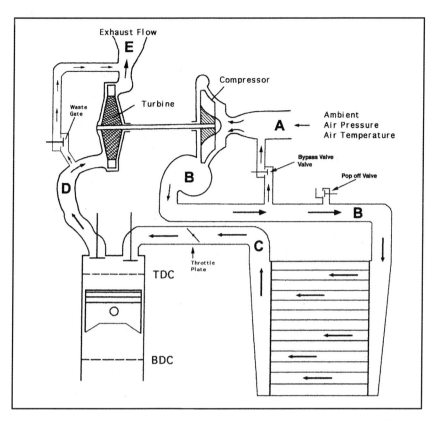

Controlling the ever-changing pressure differentials in a turbocharger system quickly and efficiently is difficult. Monitoring the pressure variables at A, B, C, D, and E during all phases of operation can provide invaluable diagnostic information.

CarTech systems are adaptable to a number of varying applications. This system positions the turbo above the front of the driver's-side valve cover, and the air filter is inside the engine compartment. The battery has been relocated to the passenger's side of the car, which means the total weight of the turbocharger and intercooler assemblies are added to the front axle. *CarTech*

The system is covered by a one-year warranty, including items that are warrantied by the original-equipment manufacturer.

Acura NSX Intercooled Twin-Turbocharger Kit

According to Corky Bell, an otherwise stock NSX equipped with a BEGI twin turbocharger kit will generate 390 base horsepower and 305 lbs-ft of torque.

Although any competent mechanic can install the system, BEGI offers expert in-house installation at its facility in San Antonio, Texas. Pickup and delivery is possible if the customer provides the cost of airfare and fuel to get the car to and from its facility.

BEGI also points out that the kit fits within the engine compartment and does not require any modifications to the body.

The fuel management system keeps the air/fuel mixture optimum under all operating conditions and does not alter the stock electronic controls in any way. Emission compliance, fuel economy, reliability, and factory drivability remain intact.

The BEGI NSX system includes an efficient intercooler that returns the compressed air at a temperature approximately 11 degrees F above ambient.

The performance values in the chart below were measured using a Vari-Com VC-200 analyzer.

CARB exemption order application is pending. The process is similar to applying for a patent in that the company has applied to CARB (not the U.S. government) for an exemption order (EO). CARB will review the product and issue an EO number certifying it does not increase the emissions output of the vehicle.

Mazda Miata Turbocharger Kit and Accessories

Bell Engineering Group, Inc., is offering four versions of its AERO-Max systems designed for the Mazda Miata.

AERO-Max EC is an entry-level turbocharger system for 1990–1997 Miatas. The kit generates from 4.5 to 5 pounds of boost and can be upgraded to a Stage 1, 2, or 3 trim level. This kit is not available for 1999 and later cars.

Their AERO-Max S1 turbocharger kit produces from 6 to 6.5 pounds of boost and includes the following components:

- Bypass valve
- High-pressure fuel pump
- Fuel pressure gauge
- MSD ignition retard
- Boost gauge with mounting cup

The S1 kit is available for both pre-1999 1.6- and 1.8-liter cars as well as 1999 and later versions. A stock 1.6-liter Miata is rated at 99 horsepower and 91 lbs-ft of torque. A 1.6 equipped with an S1 turbocharger kit will generate 144 horsepower and 133 lbs-ft of torque.

An AERO-Max S2 is considered a midlevel kit producing between 8 and 8.5 pounds of boost. The S2 kit adds a 13.5-inch intercooler and the accompanying piping and mounting hardware to the S1 kit.

BEGI's AERO-Max S3 kit produces from 10 to 10.5 pounds of boost and includes larger fuel injectors. S2 and S3 kits are available for pre-1999 1.6- and 1.8-liter cars. The company requests that you contact them before ordering either of these kits for a 1999 or later car.

All AERO-Max kits include an Aerocharger turbocharger that is billed as the world's only variable-geometry, self-contained, ball-bearing turbocharger. Aerocharger's Variable Area Turbine Nozzle (VATN) reportedly combines the low-speed torque benefits normally associated with supercharging with the superior high-speed horsepower attained with a turbocharger in a single unit.

Other benefits include the following:

- Aerocharger features an air-cooled bearing system, which requires no coolant lines.
- The Aerocharger also features a lubrication system that uses its own internal synthetic oil. The reservoir must be filled every 15,000 miles but never requires a change. No oil lines are needed.
- Ball bearings make it the fastest-responding turbocharger on the market. Properly sized for the application, there is minimal turbo lag.
- Full boost is available as low as 2,500 rpm compared to 4,000 rpm for a traditional turbocharger, which means asmoother, more linear power delivery.

BEGI Custom Components

BEGI also offers a line of individual components for racers and individuals interested in designing a custom system.

The model 20005 Rising Rate Fuel Pressure Regulator is used in all current BEGI supercharger and turbocharger kits. The 20005 allows the tuner to dial-in an optimal fuel curve by adjusting the rate of fuel pressure increase as well as the amount.

MSD Ignition Timing Control

This control (Att 8662—MSD Ignition Timing Retard) retards the

NSX Twin Turbo	BEGI	Stock
Horsepower	390	270
Torque: lbs-ft	305	225
0 to 60 mph (seconds)	4.4 to 4.8	5.9
1/4 Mile (seconds)	12.8	14.4
Velocity	113	99.0

GReddy turbocharger kits and accessories are extremely popular with front-wheel drive performance enthusiasts. Applications for Honda, Toyota, Nissan, and Mazda cover 11 models from 1987 through 1996.

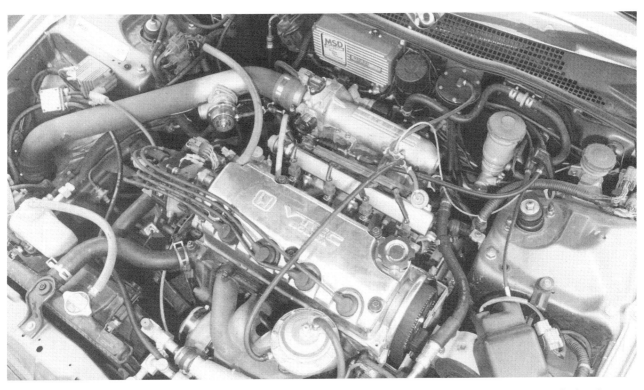

Accessories include intercooler kits, turbo timers, fuel management systems, boost control kits, fuel controls, wastegate valves, blow-off valves, boost-cut controllers, and turbo speed limiter cut controllers. See appendix 2 on page 155.

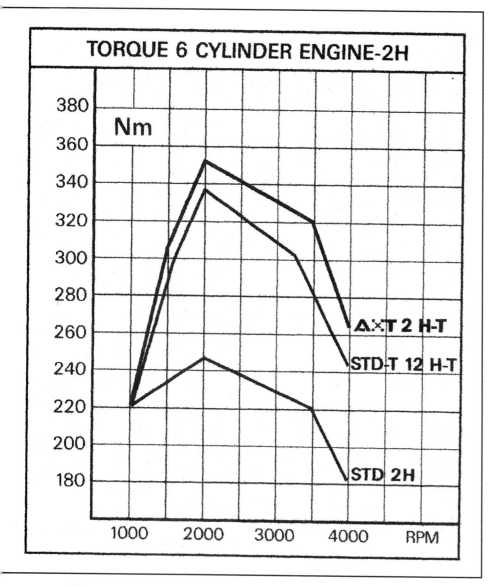

TORQUE 6 CYLINDER ENGINE-2H

Nm

AXT 2 H-T

STD-T 12 H-T

STD 2H

380 360 340 320 300 280 260 240 220 200 180

1000 2000 3000 4000 RPM

This graph illustrates the potential power gain with either of two (standard- T 12 H-T) Ray Hall turbocharger kits installed on a 2H inline 6-cylinder engine. *Ray Hall*

timing in relationship to boost pressure. Tests have shown midrange torque can be enhanced with a modest timing advance, while the unit retains ample retard function to control engine knock.

Intercooler Upgrades

The "Racer" intercooler is 50 percent larger than the standard cooler included in the BEGI supercharger and turbocharger systems, which will support power outputs up to 300 horsepower. Options include the following:

- Miata Intercooler 1.6- or 1.8-liter
- Miata Racer Intercooler (upgrade only)
- Racer Intercooler (not an upgrade)

Fuel Injectors

Boost pressure in excess of 8 psi requires larger injectors. A set of 250-cc/min injectors can be installed in place of the stock 215 cc/min injectors without recalibrating the system. The factory oxygen sensor and the CPU have enough latitude to compensate for the larger injectors when the

engine is not under boost. A 1.6-liter engine will accept 375-cc/min injectors with a small adjustment to the flow meter. BEGI injectors are available in 250-, 275-, 325-, 350-, and 375-cc/min sizes.

J&S Safeguard Knock Sensor

Safeguard, manufactured by J&S (Jse1004-J&S Knock Sensor), is an active detection and prevention system for detonation or preignition (engine knock or ping). Safeguard is a discretionary timing retard system in that it retards the ignition timing on the next cycle after detecting the first ping. The advantage is that full timing lead is available to the threshold of detonation. Safeguard also has the ability to retard the timing to only the cylinder that pings. Nondiscretionary timing retard systems pull timing at a preset rate responding to boost pressure whether or not detonation occurs.

Extended Reach Spark Plugs

The NGK ZFR6F-11 spark plugs show a consistent 4- to 5-horsepower increase over stock plugs (Nap4251 Extended Reach Spark Plugs).

Quick Change Boost Control

The QCBC permits in-cockpit boost change with the flip of a toggle switch. This turbocharger accessory can divide the maximum wastegate setting into two stages. For example, the lower stage can limit boost to 8 psi, while the higher setting will allow about 12 psi boost. A QCBC installs in about one hour and requires one adjustment (Car 10214 Quick Change Boost Control).

Coolant Radiator Upgrade

BEGI's fat-core radiator will provide additional cooling for forced induction applications (Car 29775 Coolant Radiator Upgrade).

GReddy Performance Products

GReddy's Honda Civic and Mazda Miata turbo systems, as well

as its Nissan and Mitsubishi twin-turbo upgrades, are designed around its massaged TD04 turbocharger. These systems are reported to deliver an optimized balance between peak horsepower, torque, and engine response. GReddy is one of the largest domestic manufacturers for imports and is known for its high-quality, innovative products. Its turbochargers are specifically designed and tested to achieve the best-sized turbo per application. Appendix 2 contains a complete list of GReddy turbo systems and upgrades.

Ray Hall Turbochargers

Can't locate a turbocharger kit for your vehicle? You are not alone.

Supercharger and turbocharger kit manufacturers and engineers target the most popular cars, trucks, and SUVs. Performance enthusiasts who drive one of the millions of vehicles that don't fall into the manufacturers' idea of popular must often resort to fabricating a one-off system. Occasionally, an application-specific kit can be easily adapted to fit another vehicle, provided the engine is the same make and model.

Ray Hall Turbocharging, Australia's largest turbocharger kit manufacturer, offers an impressive list of systems for some popular worldwide export vehicles. These vehicles may not be the most popular in countries other than Australia, but if you own one and have been searching for more power, Ray Hall is the place to call. Their Nakajima Advanced Engineering Group markets AXT Advanced 4X4 Turbo Systems.

Ray Hall Turbocharging manufactures kits for the following automobiles:
Mazda Bravo and Ford Courier four- cylinder, worldwide, 2.5-ltr. diesel;
Nissan QD32 four- cylinder, worldwide, Navara 3.2-liter diesel;
Toyota 5L, four-cylinder, worldwide, Hilux 3.0-liter diesel;
Toyota 2L/3L four-cylinder,

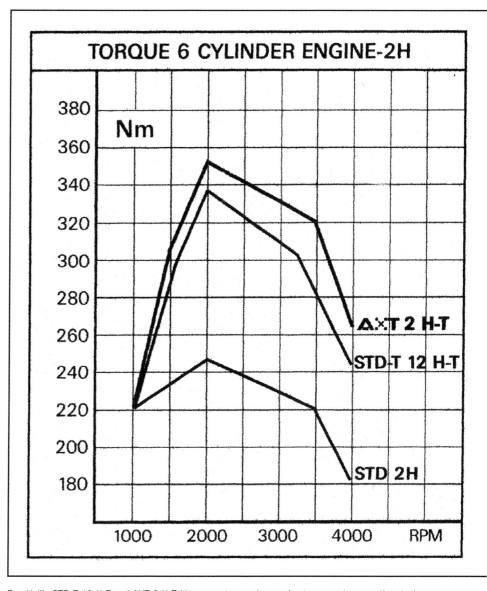

Ray Hall's STD-T 12 H-T and AXT 2 H-T kits generate very impressive torque gains over the stock naturally aspirated 2H as well. Keep in mind this is a production inline engine. *Ray Hall*

worldwide, Hilux/4 Runner/Surf 2.4-/2.8-liter diesel;
Nissan TD25/27 four-cylinder, worldwide, Navara 2.5-/2.7-liter diesel;
Toyota 1HZ six-cylinder, worldwide, Landcruiser 4.2-liter diesel;
Nissan TD42/Ford Maverick 6-cylinder, worldwide GQ Patrol 4.2-liter diesel;
Toyota 2H six-cylinder, worldwide, Landcruiser 4.0-liter diesel;
Toyota 3B four-cylinder, worldwide, Landcruiser 3.4-liter diesel.

All kits for the models listed include:
- A custom-built water-cooled turbocharger
- Either a one-piece or two-piece fully annealed ductile iron exhaust manifold
- A mandrel-bent exhaust pipe that accommodates the stock system
- Braided stainless-steel, Teflon-lined water and oil lines
- Stainless-steel hardware (clamps, studs, and so on)
- Cast-alloy air ducts

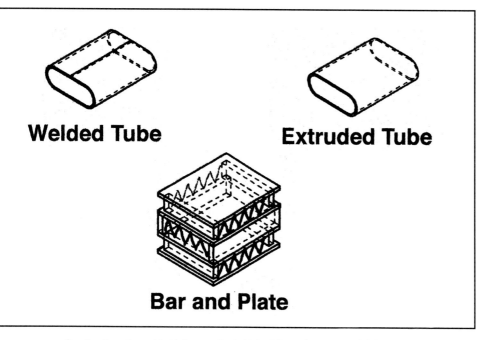

Welded Tube   **Extruded Tube**

Bar and Plate

Construction of a welded-tube or extruded-tube intercooler core sandwiches tubes between two header plates in rows. Cooling fins fill the spaces between the tubes. Bar and plate cores are constructed from fin and box wafers stacked one on top of the other. *SAE J1148—1997 Society of Automotive Engineers*

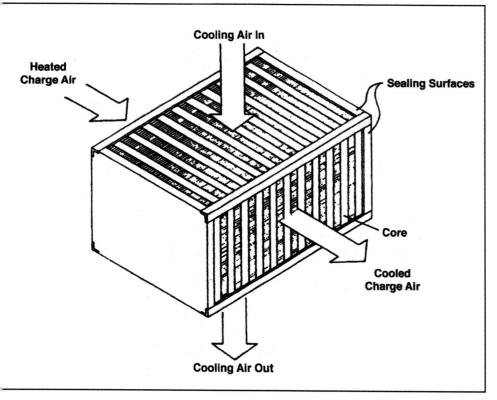

Heat is transferred from the charge air to the cooling air as both pass through the core. Normally the aspect ratio (width-to-height ratio) is close to a square, or slightly rectangular, with nearly the same width as height. This drawing was developed based on information taken from SAE J1148, 1997- Society of Automotive Engineers, Inc.

Optional accessories available with certain kits are an oil cooler kit, which provides maximum durability in ambient temperature conditions over 30 degrees Celsius, and includes the following:

- A larger-internal-diameter hose and fittings to minimize oil pressure drop
- High-temperature resistant hydraulic hoses
- Specific vehicle oil cooler mounting brackets
- Viton sealing O-rings
- Oil filter adapter mounting tube nut, manufactured to maintain original-equipment design characteristics

Also available for some kits is a fuel enrichment kit, which provides the most economical balance between power, economy, and smoke emissions. It matches original equipment in design and quality for technically correct air/fuel ratio management, prevents thermal stress caused by overflowing, and reduces both light-load fuel consumption and full-load smoke emissions.

Another optional accessory is an intercooler kit, which includes short, smooth-flowing cast-alloy ducts and a remote-mounted electric fan-cooled heat exchanger. The intercooler kit lowers thermal stress on the engine, while improving fuel economy and reducing smoke emissions.

Ray Hall also engineers and manufactures custom turbocharger systems, builds racing engines, designs fuel injection systems, and modifies and prepares ski boats.

Heat Exchangers

Heat is a byproduct of compression, and although a certain amount of heat is necessary for complete combustion, excessive heat can adversely affect performance. Although an extreme example, it is possible for the air-charge to gain an additional 300 degrees in temperature as a result of the compression

Exercise in Futility

Generally, car makers use sound engineering procedures to produce a marketable product. The success of that product has more to do with marketing, competition, and consumer buying habits than with the viability of the product itself. Case in point: Toyota spent millions of dollars in engineering labor to bring a factory twin-turbo Supra to market for the 1993 model year. The engine is strong, the electronic controls are cutting edge, and the two-stage turbocharger system is serviceable. The production 180ci engine generates a respectable 220 horsepower at 5,800 rpm and 210 lbs-ft of torque at 4,800.

Despite the relatively complex twin-turbo configuration, the car responds very well and is quite easy to drive—the true mark of a well-engineered production car.

The search for more power motivated Rob Smith to build a fire-breathing single-turbo system to replace the factory twin-turbo setup. Rob owns RPS Performance Products, Inc., which owns Turbo Clutch, a subsidiary that develops, manufactures, and markets racing clutches.

The single-turbo responded with predictable success. Low-speed drivability was slighted in favor of high-speed power. Most performance-minded enthusiasts would consider the compromise a worthwhile tradeoff. A stock 3,650-pound (with driver) Supra so equipped consumes the quarter-mile in 10.40 seconds at a top speed of 137 miles per hour. The engine delivers 675 horsepower and 650 lbs-ft of torque to the rear wheels. Aside from the T66 turbo, a custom tubular header, an intercooler, and larger injectors, the engine remains factory stock. Equally important, the big turbocharger spools up at 4,400 rpm at wide-open throttle.

The success of that project fueled Rob's longing to build and market an affordable twin-turbo upgrade that would deliver more power without compromising drivability. The goal was obtainable and the engineering sound, so the project was carried through to completion, but the results were less than optimum.

The moral if the story is, that it's not always easy to out-engineer factory engineers.

Toyota's twin-turbo system is actually a dual-stage arrangement in that one turbocharger spools up early in the rpm range to boost bottom-end power. At a predetermined threshold, a flapper valve brings the second

Toyota's twin-turbo system is actually a dual-stage arrangement, in that one turbocharger spools up early in the rpm range to boost bottom-end power. At a predetermined threshold, a flapper valve brings the second turbo online. Staging the turbocharger reduces turbo lag and pushes the power band lower in the rpm range.

turbo on line. Staging the turbocharger reduces turbo lag and pushes the power band lower in the rpm range, which promotes low-end performance. Durability becomes a problem when the small turbochargers are overdriven in an attempt to squeeze more power out of the engine.

Smith's twin-turbo kit was well thought out. Each T25/T28 Garrett hybrid would be driven simultaneously from its own three-cylinder header. Blending all three tubes into the turbo flange would improve efficiency and hasten turbo response. Ideally, the turbos would deliver full boost at 3,500 rpm.

(continued on page 88)

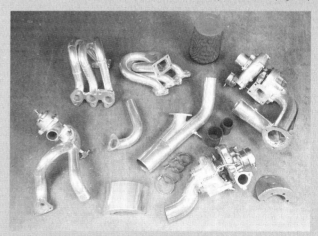

Smith's kit drives two T25/T28 Garretts simultaneously from their own three-cylinder header. Ideally, the turbos would deliver full boost at 3,500 rpm. Braided stainless-steel hoses were used to route engine oil from the original ports to the new turbos.

(continued from page 87)

Braided stainless-steel hoses were used to route engine oil from the original ports to the new turbos. Procedures to simplify the installation—such as dimpling some tubes and shortening studs to provide additional clearance for the header flange nuts—were worked through. A manifold was fabricated to accept braided stainless-steel oil return lines.

Each three-cylinder header was designed to fit within the available space. The kit was designed to bolt on without fabrication. Even the stock unmodified exhaust pipe remains in its original location.

The two-piece exhaust crossover mates the two turbochargers with the original down pipe. Indexing the compressor and exhaust housings is an important step, because all of the exhaust plumbing is manufactured from hard tubing. The exhaust crossover is outfitted with a flange to accept the original oxygen sensor.

The front header staggers the position of the second turbocharger. The design further simplifies the installation by allowing easy access to the exhaust and compressor discharge ports. The discharge manifold, designed to intersect with the factory ductwork, incorporates an HKS racing pop-off valve.

Packaging is precise and compact. The RPS Performance Products system will deliver 530 horsepower and 500 lbs-ft of torque to the rear wheels, but the larger turbos don't spool up until 4,200 rpm—a disappointing realization. Although the turbochargers will survive quite well in this environment, Smith is apprehensive about the cost-per-horsepower ratio. A second look at the numbers gave way to a clue—three cylinders totaling 90 cid could not deliver sufficient airflow to drive the larger turbos at low rpm. Ideally, maximum boost should occur at around 3,500 rpm.

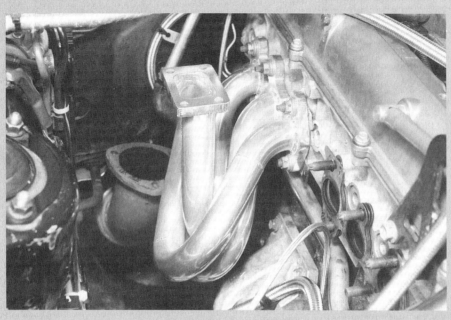

Each three-cylinder header was designed to fit within the available space. The kit was designed to "bolt-on" without fabrication. Even the stock unmodified exhaust pipe remains in its original location. A manifold was fabricated to accept braided stainless-steel oil return lines.

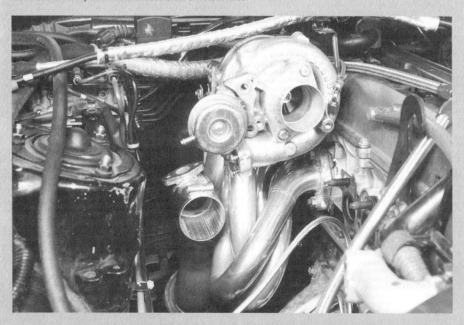

The two-piece exhaust crossover mates the two turbochargers with the original down pipe. Indexing the compressor and exhaust housings is an important step, because all of the exhaust plumbing is manufactured from hard tubing.

The front header staggers the position of the second turbocharger. The design further simplifies the installation by allowing easy access to the exhaust and compressor discharge ports. The discharge manifold is designed to intersect with the factory ductwork and incorporates an HKS racing pop-off valve.

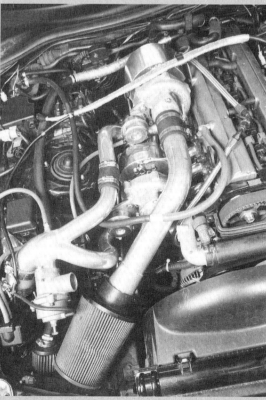

The RPS Performance Products system delivers 530 horsepower and 500 lbs-ft of torque to the rear wheels, but the larger turbos don't spool up until 4,200 rpm—a disappointing realization. Three cylinders totaling 90 cid could not deliver sufficient airflow to drive a larger turbo at low rpm. Ideally, maximum boost would occur around 3,500 rpm.

process. The higher the ambient (outdoor) air temperature, the worse the problem. In terms of performance, raising the air temperature of a dense air-charge is taking two steps forward and one back. The density of air diminishes with temperature; therefore 300-degree air is less dense than 100-degree air at the same pressure. Additionally, a heated air-charge raises the temperature in the combustion chamber, increasing the risk of detonation as the air-charge temperature increases.

Cooling the air-charge before it enters the engine reverses these negative side effects. A cooler, denser air-charge improves performance and thwarts detonation.

Forcing the air-charge through a heat exchanger is the most efficient way to extract heat. As the name implies, a heat exchanger transfers heat from one medium to another. The purpose, of course, is to improve performance by producing a denser air-charge by removing heat.

Intercoolers and Aftercoolers

Intercoolers and aftercoolers are heat exchangers. An air-to-air heat exchanger transfers heat from high-temperature air to low-temperature air. In a similar manner, radiators use water to transfer heat energy to air. Typically, the high-temperature medium is listed first, as in the case of a radiator, which is a liquid-to-air heat exchanger. A transmission oil cooler integrated into the radiator is an example of a liquid-to-liquid heat exchanger. The coolant absorbs heat given off by the hot transmission oil.

According to Spearco Performance Products, which engineers, manufactures, and markets heat exchangers, intercooled air can increase horsepower output by as much as 18 percent. Fundamentally, although a number of variables influence engine performance, a minimum 1 percent power increase for each 10 degree reduction in air-

Intercooler Efficiency

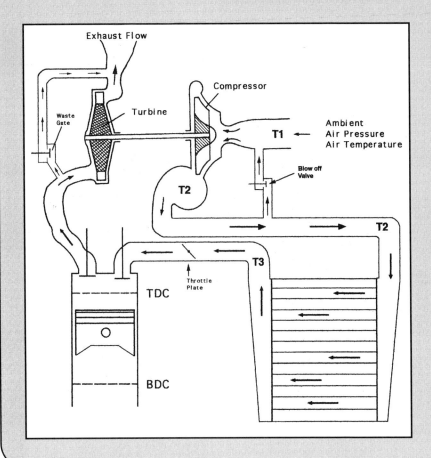

Efficiency is defined as the ratio of the temperature drop of charge air across the intercooler to the maximum temperature potential available for cooling, that is, $E = T2 - T3$ divided by $T2 - T1$ where T3 is the intake manifold temperature or temperature out of the intercooler; T2 is the compressor discharge temperature or the temperature into the intercooler; and T1 is the ambient temperature, which is assumed to be the same as the compressor inlet temperature. Consider a 300-degree Fahrenheit charge air temperature (T2), 150 degrees Fahrenheit out of the intercooler (T3) and a 90-degree ambient temperature (T1).

Efficiency =
$$\frac{300 \text{ degrees} - 150 \text{ degrees}}{300 \text{ degrees} - 90 \text{ degrees}} = 71\%$$

This intercooler is removing 71 percent of the air-charge temperature. Obviously, the higher the efficiency, the cooler the charge air. The cooler the air-charge, the higher the performance potential. *Spearco*

charge temperature can be anticipated. That is to say, reducing the air-charge temperature 10 degrees will promote a 1 percent power gain. Power can be increased by approximately 8 percent for every 10 percent increase in air density. Obviously, either intercooling or aftercooling is a good investment.

Increasing the detonation threshold by cooling the air-charge has additional advantages. It is possible, for example, to run 3 or 4 additional pounds of boost without increasing the octane rating of the fuel or reducing the timing lead.

Further, the cooling effect carries through to the exhaust temperature. Reducing the air-charge temperature by 200 degrees decreases the exhaust gas temperature 200 degrees, which makes for a cooler exhaust manifold.

Lowering the temperature throughout the process also reduces the load on the cooling system. Although the temperature reduction is small by comparison, the effect can be dramatic considering that most factory cooling systems are marginal at best.

Air and water coolers each have advantages and disadvantages, but with the exception of cost and a minimal weight penalty, efficient intercoolers provide an excellent return on investment.

Air-to-air intercoolers are simple, have no moving parts, and consequently are very popular. Yet they are quite large, typically requiring an abundant amount of open space. Also, an air-to-air cooler and the plumbing needed to connect it is almost always located forward of the front wheels, which adds weight to the nose of a vehicle.

Air-to-water intercoolers are more compact and are not limited as to location because a forced air source is not required. They are, however, more complicated, require maintenance, and in some applications, come with a higher weight penalty. Still, unlike a non-force-fed air-to-air cooler, bolting the water reservoir portion of a water cooler system in the trunk can shift weigh to a more desirable location.

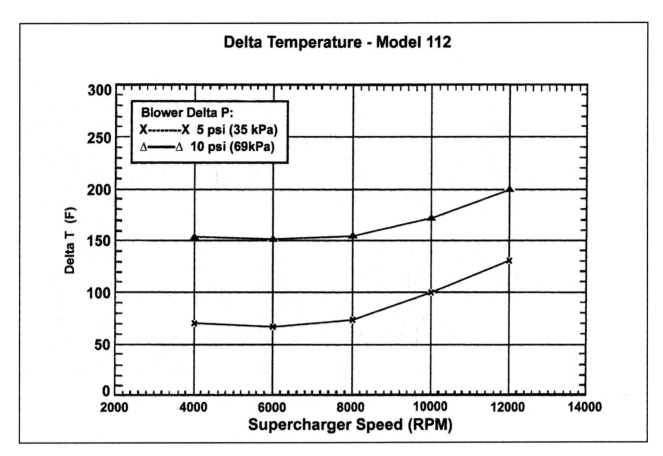

Roots superchargers typically generate high air-charge temperatures, because a small amount of compressed air leaks past the rotors. Eaton successfully controls the inherent trait by incorporating advanced machining procedures that hold tolerances to a minimum. Improving containment improves overall efficiency, which limits the amount of heat transferred to the air. *Eaton Corporation, Supercharger Division*

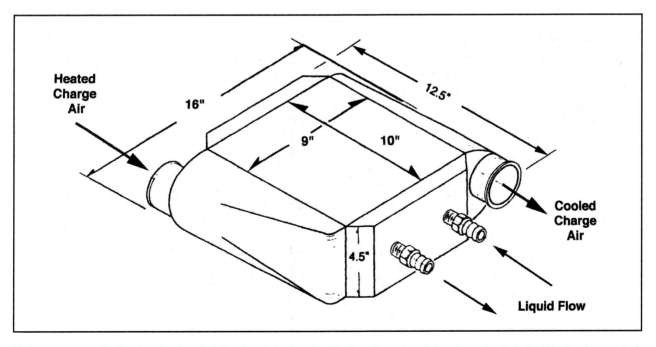

It's important to note that heat transfer characteristics of an air-to-air cooler differ from those of an air-to-water cooler. Air-to-liquid heat exchangers (typically called aftercoolers) use low-temperature liquid to cool the air-charge. Heat is transferred from the discharge air (heated charge air) to the liquid as it passes through the core. *Spearco*

Loop Air-to-Liquid Systems

Typical closed-loop air-to-liquid systems use a liquid-to-air heat exchanger (radiator) to cool the water. Conventional air-to-water/water-to-air systems (shown in solid lines) are not as efficient as a properly sized air-to-air intercooler because the liquid returning from the front heat exchanger (radiator) is warmer than the ambient air. This is true because a radiator can never achieve 100 percent efficiency, but rather is closer to 70 percent. Given these parameters, the water entering the intercooler will be between 110 and 130 degrees (or warmer) on a 90-degree day.

Circulating ice water from a reservoir dramatically improves the efficiency of a water-cooled system (shown here in broken lines), but the effects are relatively short lived. Cooling the charge air with water that is 40 or 50 degrees colder than the ambient air offers tremendous advantages in the short term. The system can be downsized to minimize weight.

Drag racing and other competitive sports requiring short bursts of high power can make use of these advantages. For others, the additional cost, the installation complexities, and the weight penalty may deplete the overall benefits. Equal-capacity air-to-air intercoolers are lighter, simpler, and less costly.

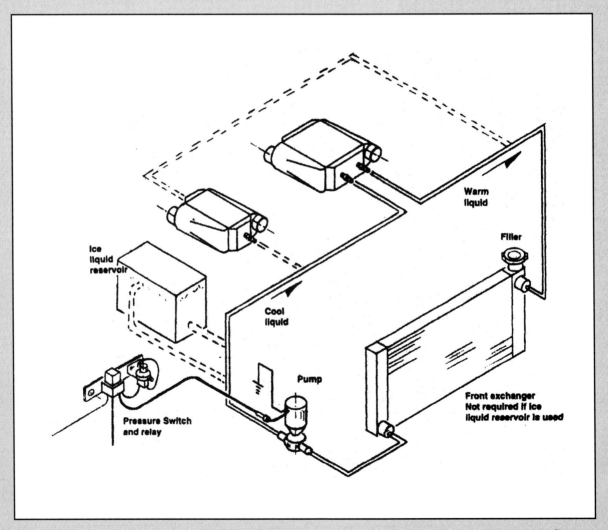

Spearco

2.3-Liter Turbo, 173.9 Horsepower per Liter

It's hard to visualize a stock-bodied, 4-cylinder 1987 Merkur XR4ti traveling 186.090 miles per hour. It's equally hard to imagine a 156ci engine capable of generating 400-plus horsepower. Rick Byrnes, Ford Motor Company engineer and land-speed record holder, explains how to prepare a turbocharged, intercooled 2.3-liter engine for such a feat.

Obviously, durability is a major concern; more specifically, the engine must be strong enough to

An Esslinger Engineering .600-inch-lift, steel-billet roller cam combined with stock roller followers reduces valve stem and lash adjuster loads. The Esslinger patented valve stem caps provide a large, radiused contact point and keep the arms properly aligned with the valve tips.

complete back-to-back 5-mile top-speed runs at Bonneville. Beginning at the top, Esslinger Engineering assembled the cylinder head, starting with a Motorsport M-600049-A231 "D" port big-valve iron casting. Machine work was kept to a minimum in an effort to preserve structural rigidity. The perimeter of the combustion chambers was moved outward to provide a more centrally located spark plug and each was enlarged to 68-cc.

Intake valve pockets and exhaust runners were slightly massaged, matched, and polished. Standard 1.890-inch SVO stainless-steel intake valves were paired with Inconnel 1.590-inch exhaust valves. Inconnel will withstand extremely high exhaust temperatures. Knowing 27.5 pounds of boost would have a tendency to force the intake valves open, springs were upgraded to provide 110 pounds of seat pressure and 350 pounds of open pressure. Production Viton valve stem seals were shortened to provide additional room for Esslinger's own Chrome Moly spring retainers and 10-degree keepers.

The Motorsport block features siamesed bores for added strength. Joining the cylinders also limits bore distortion under extreme loads. Cooling is a major factor during long-distance high-speed runs. To ensure adequate coolant flow between the head and block, additional holes were drilled in the gasket

(continued on page 94)

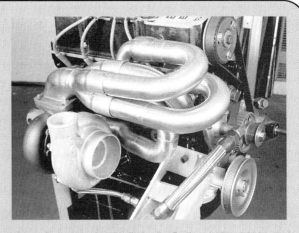

Watson Engineering hand-built the Jim Fueling–designed 304 stainless-steel exhaust header. An antireversion chamber, or AR ball, is located at a strategic point in each tube to deter reversion. The Garrett T04 turbocharger can deliver 50 pounds of air per minute. The estimated horsepower figure came from calculating the distance, time, vehicle weight, and speed at both the dragstrip and Bonneville.

Devising a way to keep the air-charge temperature under control posed additional problems, so a sprayer system was fabricated to mist water directly in front of the intercooler when boost reached a preset limit. Water was plumbed to the handmade jets from a pressurized reservoir located at the rear of the passenger compartment.

(continued from page 93)

surfaces. The Fel-Pro solid-core "wire-ring" head gasket was also modified. Progressively larger holes were added between each cylinder: 1/8-inch holes between number 1 and number 2 cylinders, 3/16-inch holes between 2 and 3, and 1/4-inch holes between cylinders 3 and 4.

To ensure even coolant flow, the diameter of the water transfer holes at the rear of the gasket was reduced. A thermostat was retained for a quick warmup, to help slow coolant flow around the cylinders, and to create back pressure in the engine block. To vent steam pockets that might form around the exhaust ports and to eliminate air pockets when the system is filled, passages added above the exhaust ports on the outside of the head were plumbed to a distribution block located on the firewall.

Stock cast-iron 2.3-liter auxiliary shafts have been known to break during high-rpm operation. To eliminate any possibility of failure, an Esslinger billet steel shaft with a removable distributor gear was installed.

An external Avaid single-stage high-capacity oil pump pulls lubricant from a fabricated 7-quart oil pan. The path of the oil flow through the engine was modified as well. The internal passageway that originally supplied oil to the cylinder head was plugged. An external port restricted with a .155-inch orifice was added at the rear of the cylinder head to supply oil to the cam and cam followers. A T-fitting was added to direct the remaining oil flow to the turbo.

High combustion temperatures transfer a lot of heat to the Metel Leve flat top pistons, the piston rings and the cylinders. Small oil jets were added to cool the piston domes and provide additional lubricant to the skirts and cylinder walls. The .040-inch jets, fashioned by drilling into the main bearing web, are fed by the main bearing oil feed passage. To help control any extra oil flying around the crankcase, a crankshaft scraper was fabricated and attached to the main bearing webs.

Steel-billet 5.625-inch Crower rods connect the PSC cross-drilled billet steel crank to the pistons. SPS socket-head cap screws secure the surface-ground 4140 steel-billet main bearing caps in place. A 3.400-inch stroke dropped the pistons .165 inch below the deck, which helped lower the compression ratio to 7.0:1. The .912-inch diameter wrist pins are secured with four Tru Arc snap rings, two on each end. Radial pin clearance is .001 inch.

Spearco's Intercooler Performance

Spearco's Intercooler Performance Chart illustrates the relationship between boost pressure and temperature compared to intercooler efficiency and pressure drop. The approximate increase in air density is shown as well.

First, locate the corresponding boost pressure on the left side of the chart. Project a horizontal line from that point right to the nonintercooled line, then extend a vertical line down to the Y axis to read air density.

For example, 10 pounds of nonintercooled boost at 244 degrees Fahrenheit will have a .095 lbs/cu./ft. air density. Extending the horizontal line to intersect an intercooler performance line will indicate the expected drop in temperature and pressure. The corresponding vertical line will show the resulting increase in air density. Extending the 10-psi boost line over to the sixth intercooler line indicates a potential 125-degree drop in air-charge temperature with a .5-psi drop in pressure with a .112-lbs/cu. ft. air density. This chart assumes a 90-degree Fahrenheit ambient temperature and .072-lbs/cu. ft. air density at sea level and a compressor with a minimal 70 percent adiabatic efficiency. As the chart illustrates, air density continues to increase with improved charge cooling and low pressure drop.

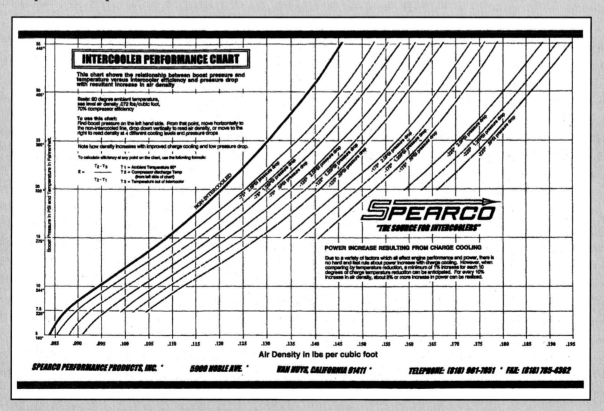

Engine Size	Diesel			Gas- Hi Performance Street Application			Gas - Racing		
1.2 - 2.3L	2-110	2-173		2-110	2-172	2-192	2-110	2-178	2-195
	2-113	2-195		2-113	2-173	2-195	2-116	2-180	2-198
	2-172	2-208		2-116	2-180		2-161	2-192	2-203
				2-161	2-181				2-205
2.4 - 4.0L	2-110	2-195		2-116	2-180	2-205	2-115	2-176	2-196
	2-113	2-208		2-161	2-181	2-207	2-167	2-179	2-205
	2-172			2-175	2-194		2-174	2-182	
	2-173			2-178			2-175	2-194	
4.1 - 7.5L	2-175	2-205		2-115	2-179	2-205	2-176	2-205	
	2-178	2-207		2-167	2-196	2-207	2-182		
	2-180			2-174	2-199		2-197		
	2-181			2-176			2-199		
7.6 - 8.5L	2-115	2-179	2-205	2-176	2-205		Consult		
	2-167	2-182	2-207	2-182			Spearco for		
	2-174	2-194		2-197			Recommendations		
	2-176	2-199		2-199					

An intercooler must be sized and configured properly for the application. Spearco offers a general selection chart indicating production cores that can be used for a number of popular engine sizes and applications. To obtain more detailed information, consult the individual performance chart for a production core. *Spearco*

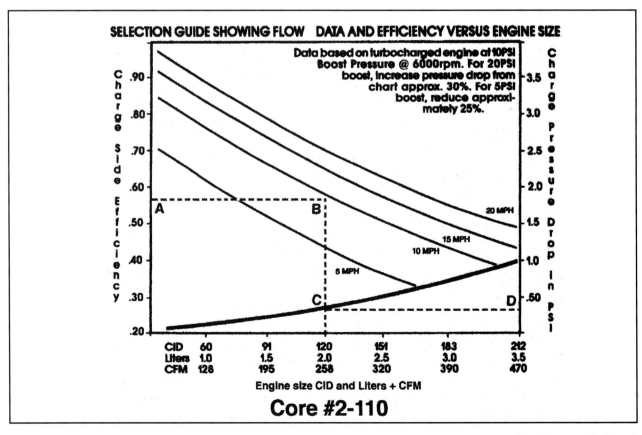

Using this example for a number 2-110 Spearco core, at a 10-mile-per-hour (B) ambient side face velocity, the efficiency will be 57 percent (A) with a .4-psi pressure drop across the core (D) for a 2-liter engine consuming a maximum of 258 cfm (C). Ideally, the efficiency of the core should be 75 percent or greater with a pressure drop of no more than 1 psi. *Spearco*

Accessible Technologies has been promoting the benefits of intercooling since 1994. ATI's ProCharger kits include a matched air-to-air intercooler that further enhances the advantages of forced induction. This table illustrates the potential effect of an efficient intercooler. *Accessible Technologies, Inc.*

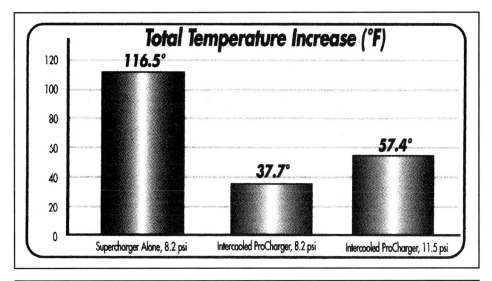

More power can be can be extracted from a denser aircharge, provided the air/fuel mixture ratio is calibrated properly. Cooling the air-charge increases its density. This graph, circulated by Accessible Technologies Incorporated (ATI), illustrates the potential performance increase based on air density alone. *Accessible Technologies, Inc.*

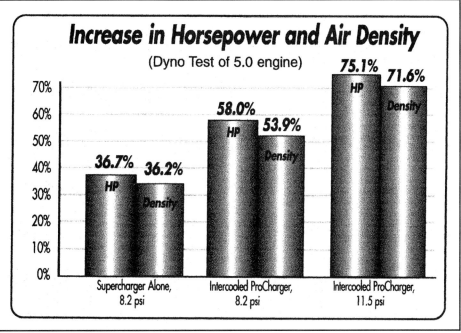

An air-to-water/water-to-air system such as this Vortech 8N301-010 kit can circulate tap water or iced water. Note that the radiator will act like a heater when the temperature of the cooling medium is lower than the ambient air temperature. Fabricating a bypass valve to eliminate the water-to-air heat exchanger (radiator) will optimize the system when circulating ice water. *Vortech*

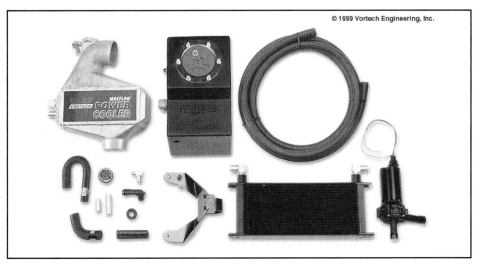

Chapter Six
Nitrous Oxide Injection

British chemist Joseph Priestly is credited with discovering nitrous oxide gas in 1772. Interestingly, nitrous oxide does not occur naturally, which means to exist it must be man-made. The result of a purposeless experiment, the colorless, odorless gas would not make it into a piston engine until 1942.

During those 170 years between 1772 and 1942, Sir Humphry Davy of Bristol, England, tested the effects of nitrous oxide on the human respiratory system in 1799 and first coined the term "laughing gas." In 1844, Horace Wells then introduced nitrous oxide to dentistry as a painkiller. With little claim to fame beyond a dentist's office, nitrous oxide was popularized as a recreational drug by traveling performers in the early 1800s.

During World War II, the Germans injected nitrous oxide into high-altitude plane engines and ground vehicles in an attempt to increase power output. The introduction of jets near the end of the war all but eliminated the need for further testing, but the knowledge and performance improvements gleaned during those early tests found a home in automobile racing in the years following the war. Man's search for more powerful automotive engines was fueled in part by American soldiers who returned home with this experimental technology initiated by German engineers. These engineers discovered that an internal combustion

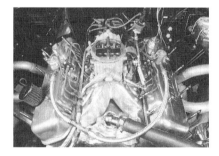

Nitrous oxide and fuel are transferred from their respective reservoirs to the solenoid valves through high-pressure braided steel hoses. These hoses are specific for nitrous oxide applications and contain a Teflon-coated inner tube. It is important these lines do not come into contact with any heat source, sharp edges, vibrating components, or parts that may squash them.

Introducing more air/fuel mixture into the cylinders produces more power. When properly calibrated, a 50-horsepower hit will add 50 horsepower to the bottom line. Likewise, ample amounts of fuel and nitrous oxide will add 500 horsepower to the naturally aspirated baseline. Durability is the single limiting factor.

Each nitrous oxide storage system or vessel contains a weight and a certification date and consists of a DOT-approved aluminum bottle, a siphon tube, and a bottle valve with a safety relief venting system.

For safety purposes, the bottle should never be installed within the interior of the vehicle. Nitrous oxide can cause suffocation, because the body cannot process the oxygen/nitrogen gas. Always place the bottle in a trunk, away from all light and heat sources. If the vehicle does not have a trunk, purchase a "blow down" kit designed to vent the gas to atmosphere, should the safety valve release.

engine injected with nitrous oxide and a proportionate volume of fuel will generate a seemingly endless amount of power.

In the 1960s, drag racers began utilizing the oxygen in nitrous oxide to enhance power output. By the 1970s, nitrous oxide had become a hot topic at the drag strip and a point of controversy among many spectators, car owners, and sanctioning bodies. The pronounced advantage that nitrous offered was seen as unfair. As a result, racers and officials eventually settled on a separate class for injected drag racers. Nitrous oxide's modest cost and controllability eventually became attractive features to even the casual speed freak.

Nitrous oxide is a covalent compound, meaning it is a combination of two gases. Its chemical composition consists of one oxygen atom attached to two nitrogen atoms, which gives the oxygen about 36 percent of the atom's

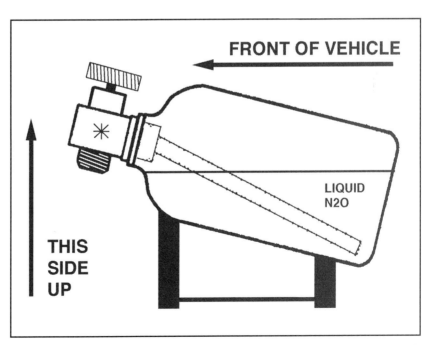

Valves range from a standard medical type up to the most current high-volume designs used for serious racing applications. High-flow valves reduce the chance of a pressure drop. Always use the most current, safest, and highest-flowing valve designed for the application. Likewise, ensure that the bottle is safely secured with high-strength DOT-approved precision brackets and mounting hardware.

total weight. Since nitrogen and oxygen don't naturally exist in this combination within our environment, nitrous oxide must be manufactured by using heat and a catalyst. All gases exist without a definite shape or volume due to their high amounts of thermal energy, and to store enough nitrous oxide for practical use, it must be condensed into a liquid.

Under normal atmospheric conditions (temperatures and pressures), nitrous oxide must be kept under pressure to remain in a liquid state. Condensing nitrous oxide into a liquid can be accomplished by either compressing it or lowering the temperature below its boiling point, which is -127 degrees Fahrenheit. Because it is impractical to keep nitrous at a steady 127 degrees below zero, applying pressure quickly became the norm. The variations of heat and pressure present a sliding scale. For example, it takes 10.857 pounds of pressure per Fahrenheit degree of temperature to condense nitrous oxide gas into liquid nitrous oxide. Thus, at 100 degrees Fahrenheit, approximately 1,087.5 psi is required; at 50 degrees, 534.5 psi is needed, and so on. At zero degrees Fahrenheit it only takes approximately 11 pounds of pressure to liquefy nitrous oxide. This is not an exact ratio because normal atmospheric air pressure is forever changing. Converting nitrous oxide back into a gas is simple: just release it into the atmosphere. Because the boiling point of liquid nitrous oxide is approximately -127 degrees Fahrenheit (at 14.7 psi atmospheric pressure), it will boil instantly when it rises above that point.

In current-day production for industrial and racing applications, sulfur dioxide is often added to nitrous oxide to inhibit its use as a recreational inhalant. It is also widely used as a propellant in aerosol products and as a tracer gas to locate leaks in vacuum and pressure lines.

Nitrous Oxide Injection Systems

The chemical properties of nitrous oxide make it an almost perfect catalyst for combustion. Nitrous oxide quickly expands from liquid to gas (boils) when released into the intake charge. As a secondary benefit, a large amount of heat energy is absorbed by the nitrous oxide during its rapid expansion through a process loosely termed as the "latent heat of vaporization," a process in which a boiling liquid will absorb heat energy as it changes (expands) from a liquid to a gas. The same cause and effect makes spray deodorant cold when it is applied directly to the skin and propane gas valves freeze over with ice when they are opened to the atmosphere.

Condensing a gas into liquid removes heat energy. Heat energy is then restored (absorbed) when the liquid changes (boils) back into a gas. The same process occurs when water is boiled on a stove, but at higher temperatures (+212 degrees Fahrenheit at 14.7 psi atmospheric).

The refrigeration process (the absorption of heat energy by the expanding gas) cools the intake charge, thereby increasing its overall density (cold air is more dense than warmer air because the atoms are closer together). To reiterate, nitrous injects a high concentration of oxygen atoms into the engine while cooling the air-charge at the same time. It is a

Nitrous Temperature	Corresponding Pressure
-30	67
-20	203
-10	240
0	283
10	335
20	387
30	460
40	520
50	590
60	675
70	760
80	865
90	985
95	1050

The solenoid handles the nitrous oxide flow via an electro magnetically controlled plunger. The maximum capacity assigned to the solenoid should be at least 20 percent greater than the pressure in the bottle and a flow rate larger than the total flow area of the metering jets. If the solenoid is not large enough to handle the pressure behind it, the coil may fail.

Through the years, switches used to activate nitrous oxide systems have evolved and become increasingly safer and more predictable. There are manual switches designed to fit shifters or steering wheels for those who require total control. Others are designed to only activate the nitrous system at certain preset parameters.

Throttle-mounted switches can be easily activated when the engine is not running or when it is running at an rpm too low for safe operation. For these reasons, electronic switches activated by rpm offer an improved range of safety. Master controllers can be set to apply the nitrous oxide all at once or in stages.

win-win situation with virtually no compromise.

In addition, once converted from liquid to gas, nitrous oxide remains suspended, which allows it to efficiently mix with the fuel. This even distribution increases the likelihood that the nitrous oxide molecules will mix efficiently with the fuel molecules, which reduces the possibility of puddling (fuel falling out of gaseous suspension into a liquid form). The dense, highly concentrated air/fuel charge increases combustion pressures as it burns, which in turn transfers a large amount of energy to the crankshaft.

Nitrous oxide injection is a fairly easily understood application. The system requires hoses to transfer liquid nitrous oxide and gasoline from their respective storage containers to the engine and a valve attached to each hose to activate the flow. An orifice or jet controls the amount of flow, and a nozzle or nozzles disperse the liquid in a predictable spray pattern designed to both mix the two elements and spread them evenly over a large area. Calibration is a product of jet size (orifice) and rate of delivery (pressure and volume).

Computing and maintaining the optimum ratio of nitrous oxide to gasoline is further simplified by the kit manufacturers themselves. With no actual mechanical parts to contend with, a user need only obtain knowledge of application, installation, use, and troubleshooting to achieve satisfactory results. Many companies assure that drivers with average mechanical ability can correctly assess the application, install the system, and use nitrous oxide injection to their best advantage.

When installed and used properly, nitrous oxide injection is very safe and predictable. Engine failure occurs only if the system is installed incorrectly, used improperly, or if an unforeseen malfunction occurs, such as inadequate fuel delivery caused by a faulty solenoid valve. Nitrous oxide injection systems are only used on demand and generally above 2,500 rpm at full

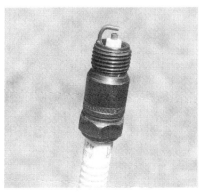

Spark plugs are often another point of interest. Select a plug with the proper heat range for the cylinder head. Aluminum heads dissipate heat more quickly than iron heads.

Install a spark plug with a shortened negative electrode and a .030- to .035-inch gap. A standard (long) negative electrode shrouds the spark and can become a glow plug if it absorbs enough heat. The superheated electrode can ignite the fuel early, causing detonation.

throttle. The cost-per-horsepower ratio makes nitrous oxide injection one of the most affordable and popular performance enhancements on the market. As with any engine modification, a little homework will go a long way to ensure success.

Nitrous oxide must be purchased from an authorized distributor. Because it is not as readily available as gasoline, some advanced planning is required. Depending on your particular location, a distributor may be as close as your nearest parts store or 100 miles away. When dealing with an industrial supplier, nitrous oxide is somewhat application specific, meaning there are

If the fuel pump supplies both the engine and the nitrous system, the volume of fuel must support the total horsepower output of the engine (mass flow per unit time). In this example, a mechanical fuel pump supplies fuel to the carburetor. A separate fuel line and electric pump feed the nitrous oxide system.

The stand-alone nitrous system has its own pressure regulator. The electric fuel pump servicing the nitrous system is activated only on demand. Always set the regulator to the flowing fuel pressure rate, not the static rate. In this application, the fuel supply system for the engine does not require a regulator.

single-stage system is the simplest, utilizing only one injection of nitrous oxide into the engine upon activation of the system. With a dual-stage system, there are two different applications of nitrous oxide, one following the other.

The methods used to open the solenoid(s) vary widely from the simplest push-button switch to a computer-operated controller that all but eliminates the possibility of human error. Electronic devices can trigger the nitrous when, and only when, the engine reaches a predetermined speed. Many dual-stage systems use a throttle switch to activate the first-stage and manual switch (driver controlled) to bring on the second stage. The manner in which the nitrous oxide is supplied to the engine varies from manufacturer to manufacturer.

Dry Versus Wet Airflow

An intake manifold is simply a collection of individual tubes or runners that feed each cylinder from a common plenum. The diameter (cross-sectional area) as well as the shape and the length of the runners determine its efficiency. Carbureted and throttle body fuel injection manifolds are designed to accommodate wet airflow—the mixture of air and fuel. Ford's Sequential Electronic Fuel Injection (SEFI), GM's Tuned Port Injection, and all other port-injected systems utilize a dry airflow manifold, so named because they do not flow air and fuel in combination, only dry air.

Because dry air is less dense compared to a mixture of air and fuel, the differences between each respective manifold design are very important, particularly when their roles are reversed. For example, a dry flow manifold is converted into a wet flow system when nitrous oxide and fuel are injected behind or in front of the throttle body. Because the manifold was not designed for wet flow, the modification can set a series of events in motion that can lead to a violent

medical grades and industrial or automotive grades. Also, distribution centers will only fill authorized containers that have been safety certified.

Nitrous oxide systems are available for both carbureted and fuel-injected engines. Relating to the way the nitrous and fuel is introduced into the engine, there are three basic designs: a Wet System, a Dry System, and a Direct Port Wet System. The Dry System and the Direct Port Wet System are best suited to fuel injection. They are specifically designed to accommodate high rates of fuel and nitrous oxide, and, most importantly, the fuel is injected very close to the intake valve.

Typical nitrous systems are available in either single or dual stage, meaning the initial single shot can be supplemented with a second shot as engine speed increases. Although there is technically no limit to the number of stages, even the most sophisticated racing systems usually stop at three. A

explosion. In extreme cases, the force of the explosion can literally destroy the manifold, the engine, and in some cases, the hood of the car. Nitrous oxide explosions are legendary and can be very destructive.

The problem is caused by a condition called "puddling." To be effective, atomized fuel must remain mixed or suspended in the air, or in this case, the nitrous oxide and air. Because fuel is considerably heavier than air, the fuel molecules have a tendency to fall out of suspension—the fuel molecules simply separate from the air molecules. Wherever fallout occurs, liquid fuel condenses and forms a puddle. Once pockets of raw fuel form in the intake, the explosive potential is multiplied exponentially. A normal backfire can ignite the raw fuel, because there is an abundance of oxygen present.

Slow air movement or turbulence promotes fuel separation, thus fallout occurs when the airflow slows as it passes through tight bends, odd shapes, or large open areas. A particularly bad air "speed bump" or pocket is called a dead spot. A small amount of air simply becomes trapped in a dead area at some point in the rpm range. These areas could be considered an engineering flaw except the size and shape of a production manifold is usually compromised by cost, packaging, and production methods. But as long as the manifold flows only dry air, the discrepancies are a nonissue. A dry manifold simply must supply the cylinders with an abundance of clean air.

Some dual-plane manifolds can be equally troublesome when fed a very large amount of nitrous and fuel. Although they are wet flow systems, most production dual-plane manifolds are engineered to promote low-speed performance. As a result, their uneven-length runners typically navigate a number of twists and bends.

To minimize the possibility of puddling, never activate a nitrous system at slow engine speeds, when air velocity in the intake manifold is low.

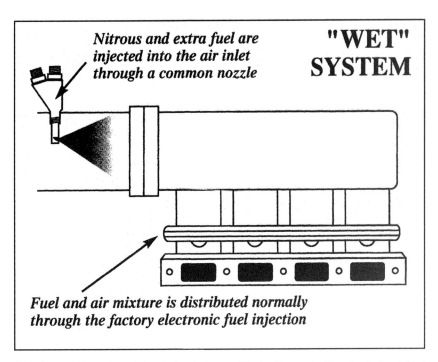

Wet nitrous oxide systems deliver fuel and nitrous oxide simultaneously either ahead of or behind the throttle body. The simplest method utilizes a single nozzle, which is also recommended for turbo- and supercharged vehicles. *Nitrous Oxide Systems*

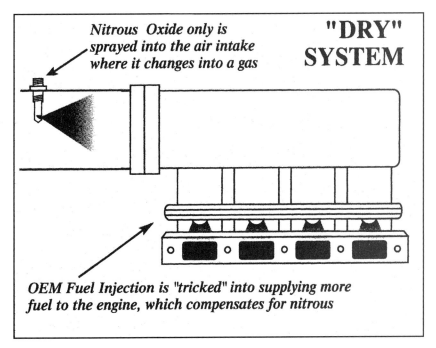

A dry system injects only nitrous oxide into the intake system. Additional fuel is delivered through the injectors by the vehicle's electronic computer controls. The dry system's chief advantage is that fuel is not present in the manifold. *Nitrous Oxide Systems*

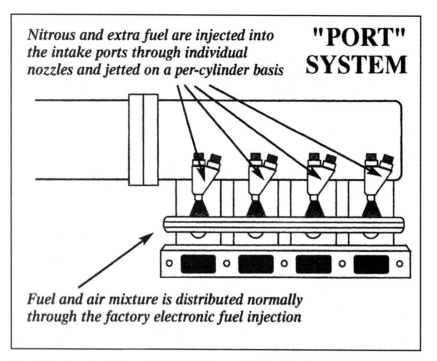

Nitrous and extra fuel are injected into the intake ports through individual nozzles and jetted on a per-cylinder basis

"PORT" SYSTEM

Fuel and air mixture is distributed normally through the factory electronic fuel injection

The direct port system is the most efficient, yet the most difficult to install. Nitrous oxide and fuel are injected directly into each intake runner through a single nozzle. Installation usually involves drilling and tapping a hole in each runner. *Nitrous Oxide Systems*

Single Nozzle N$_2$O Flow

Jet Size	Pounds per Hour	Estimated Horsepower
14	28.8	10
16	36	12.5
18	50.4	17.5
20	64.8	22.5
22	79.2	27.5
24	93.6	32.5
26	86.4	30
28	108	37.5
31	129.6	45
33	136.8	47.5
35	151.2	52.5
38	172.8	60
41	208.8	72.5
46	273.6	95
52	331.2	115
57	410.4	142.5
62	489.6	170
70	547.2	190
73	597.6	207.5
78	676.8	235
82	720	250
88	763.2	265

.093 solenoid w/ 24" D-3 jumper line
All tests performed at 1050 PSI.

Installing an electronic nitrous controller that prevents activation below a preset rpm can prevent the system from being activated accidentally. A controller can also add a number of other safety features such as fuel and/or nitrous pressure limits and a high-rpm cutoff.

Calibration

Few people know more about calibrating nitrous oxide injection than Mike Wood at Nitrous Express. His success is due in part to his ability to reduce abstract scientific principles to high-performance language that the world at large can understand. When described in easy-to-understand terms, horsepower by injecting the proper amount of nitrous and fuel is really very simple.

Calibrating nitrous oxide is simply a matter of applying the laws of fluid dynamics. The practical application is far simpler than the initial computation. Any fluid process, such as flow around an obstacle or through a pipe, can be described mathematically

by a specific equation that relates the acting forces—the dimensions of the system and its properties, such as temperature, pressure, and density. Newton's laws of motion and viscosity, the first and second laws of thermodynamics, and the laws of conservation of mass, energy, and momentum are appropriately applied.

Air/Fuel Ratio

The fundamentals lead back to an ideal air-to-fuel ratio, in this case oxygen contained in the nitrous oxide and gasoline (or alcohol). Nitrous oxide and gasoline mixed at a ratio of approximately 5:1 (5 parts of nitrous to 1 part fuel) will produce an air/fuel mixture ratio equal to 9.45:1 at a brake-specific fuel consumption (BSFC) of 0.5. There will be some variance because the "ideal" air/fuel mixture ratio is spread over a relatively large range. An 8:1 ratio is acceptable in some applications, but not advisable for the average user. A ratio between 4.5:1 and 6:1 is commonly accepted and considered "safe." A 6:1 nitrous/fuel mixture will equate to an 11.4:1 air/fuel ratio at a 0.5 BSFC. Higher-octane fuel will tolerate a leaner mixture without invoking the wrath of detonation.

Although the consequences of lean fuel detonation are hammered over and over, the experienced tuner also knows the risks resulting from an overrich fuel condition. It is widely accepted and commonly taught that a rich fuel mixture will not hurt an engine—the same has been said in various ways in this book. The concept has merit, but like every other variable, exceeding the limits of sound theory can cause perfectly good engine parts to break.

When dealing with naturally aspirated or low-boost forced induction, the risk associated with a moderately rich air/fuel ratio is slight, because typically the volume of fuel entering the engine is comparatively small. Further, the warning signs are

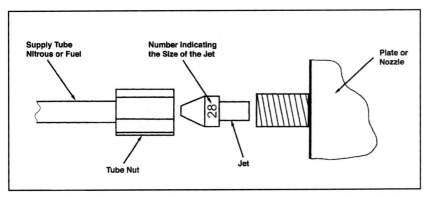

The jet is positioned "in-line" between the supply tube and the plate or nozzle. A high-quality filter on both the nitrous and fuel lines is highly recommended. A plugged nitrous jet will cause a full rich condition. A failed fuel supply will cause a severe lean condition.

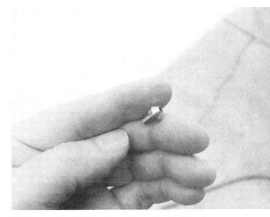

The tapered end of the jet seals against a flared tube. A scratch or nick in this area could cause a leak.

obvious. First, an overly rich fuel mixture will cause an engine to run poorly. Rich, black smoke bellowing from the exhaust, combined with a very slow throttle response provides additional clues. But nitrous oxide injection can pump a very large quantity of liquid fuel past the intake valves in a relatively short time. If the flow of nitrous trails off or the calibration is excessively rich, the fuel will not atomize properly. The cylinders literally fill with liquid fuel. When the quantity of liquid exceeds the minimum cylinder volume, the piston will not reach TDC on the compression stroke because liquid cannot be compressed. The momentum of the rotating assembly will then slam the piston into the solid barrier. The destruction that follows is similar to a chain reaction accident on a busy freeway.

Most catastrophic engine failures involving nitrous oxide injection are caused by an overrich fuel condition, while relatively few mishaps result from detonation. An experienced tuner will lean the fuel mixture to squeeze every BTU out of each drop of fuel while watching (and listening) for signs of detonation since optimum power will occur at or near the threshold. A novice or conservative operator will likely calibrate an overrich mixture to ensure the ratio is well within safe limits.

Fluid Dynamics

Fluid dynamics must be applied to arrive at a 5:1 ratio because we are dealing with two liquids. Fluid dynamics incorporate quite a large number of variables: the inside diameter of the hose or tube and its length, the pressure forcing the liquid through the hose, and the viscosity (weight) of the liquid are a few principal factors. Viscosity is further defined as the degree to which a fluid resists flow by an applied force. Viscosity is given a value or specific gravity (relative density), which is the ratio of the density of a substance to that of a reference material at a specified temperature. Water achieves maximum density at 4 degrees Celsius and is the scientifically accepted reference material. Simply put, specific gravity (sg) is the weight of a gallon of a given liquid compared to the weight of a gallon of water at a constant temperature. The difference is given as a ratio.

Whether or not the tube is bent, the number of bends and the angle of each bend is yet another issue. Twists and turns impede liquid flow. To simplify this explanation, we must exclude the resistance factor caused by the number and size of the bends in the tube, but we should add that the path of the nitrous hose should be as straight and direct as possible.

Fuel and nitrous flow are measured in pounds per hour (lbs/hr)—the

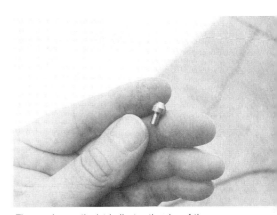

The number on the jet indicates the size of the orifice, as with carburetor jets.

In this example, the orifice is a .028-inch hole.

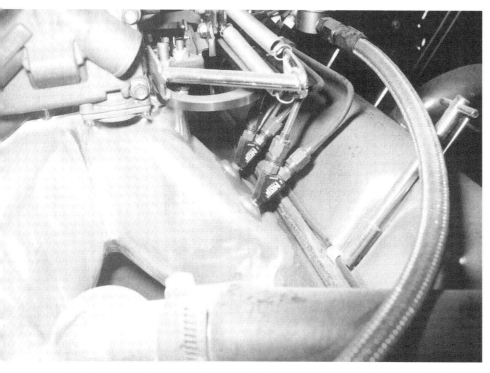

Nozzles are designed to both atomize the fuel and mix the two compounds as they are injected. This port system is calibrated using 8 fuel and 8 nitrous jets, one each per nozzle. This is a single-stage system that delivers one very large nitrous hit. A two-stage system might have a pair of fuel and nitrous lines feeding a single four-hole nozzle.

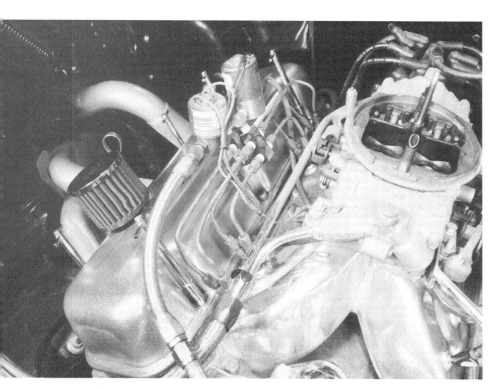

Plumbing the nitrous and fuel to each individual cylinder can pose a problem if you haven't taken Pipe Bending and Flaring 101. In this application, one fuel and one nitrous solenoid services four cylinders of a V-8 engine. The main fuel and nitrous lines feed a Y, which in turn feeds two solenoids.

explanation of Brake Specific Fuel Consumption (BSFC) in chapter 2 discusses this at length. Compared to gasoline, measuring nitrous flow is relatively simple, because liquid nitrous has a consistent weight, while the weight of a gallon of gasoline can vary depending on the brand and type. It is important that the pressure (and therefore the temperature) of the nitrous oxide be consistent. Nitrous Express keeps the nitrous pressure at a constant 1,050 psi for all laboratory testing. Using a Nitrous Express 100-horsepower plate system as an example, nitrous oxide is propelled through a .057-inch jet at 1,050 psi for 10 seconds. The weight differential of the bottle before and after the test indicates the amount of nitrous expelled. In this example, 1.1 pounds of nitrous escaped through the jet in 1/6th minute (ten seconds). Multiplying 1.1 by 6 equals the amount of nitrous flow per minute, or 6.6 lbs/min. Multiply 6.6 times 60 to convert pounds per minute to pounds per hour, which in this example equals 396. Divide 396 by 5.5 to determine the proportionate amount of gasoline needed to make 100 horsepower.

> 1.1 pounds of nitrous expelled through a .057 jet in 10 seconds.
> 1.1 lbs x 6 = 6.6 lbs/min
> 6.6 lbs/min x 60 = 396 lbs/hr
> 396 lbs/hr ÷ 5.5 = 72 lbs/hr

Therefore, to generate 100 horsepower using a 5.5:1 ratio the system must deliver 396 lbs/hr of nitrous and 72 lbs/hr of gasoline.

The same laws of fluid dynamics apply when computing fuel flow, but to be accurate you must first know the specific gravity of the gasoline used. Mike Wood at Nitrous Express uses .730 sg—a widely accepted average weight of a gallon of pump gasoline. If a gallon of water weighs 8.337 pounds (at 15 degrees Celsius), then a gallon of gasoline with a .730 sg weighs

6.086 pounds (8.337 x .730). Therefore, the system must deliver 11.7 gallons of fuel per hour (72 ÷ 6.1539). The flow bench indicates that a .046 jet will expel approximately 71 pounds of gasoline per hour when propelled by 4.4 pounds of pressure.

Applying these calculations, a Nitrous Express 100-horsepower plate system will deliver approximately 396 pounds of nitrous and 72 pounds of fuel per hour when equipped with a number 57 nitrous jet and a number 46 fuel jet, assuming the nitrous pressure is 1,050 psi, the fuel pressure is 4.4 psi, and the specific gravity of the fuel is .730. The system can be fine-tuned by varying the fuel pressure one or two tenths up or down. Fuel with a higher or lower specific gravity will also require a fuel pressure adjustment.

Tuning

Tuning a system having only two jets is relatively simple compared to a port system, which will incorporate at least two jets per cylinder. The flow rate through multiple jets is combined to produce a total flow rate of nitrous and fuel. In other words, a port system installed on a V-8 engine will meter through a minimum of 8 nitrous and 8 fuel jets. The combined flow through all 8 nitrous jets and the combined flow through all 8 fuel jets are factored to determine the nitrous/fuel ratio. Looking at it from another angle, one nitrous and one fuel jet is supplying a single cylinder engine times 8. If the nitrous/fuel ratio for each cylinder is 5.1, then the ratio for the engine will also be 5:1.

Nitrous Express street EFI systems are engineered for true plug-and-play performance. Simply install the system and drive. The engine management computer will keep the air/fuel mixture optimized throughout the full range of operation. No additional calibration is necessary.

Mike Wood further explains that Nitrous Express– advertised horsepower

Fuel Flow In Pounds Per Hour at .730 SG

Jet Size	1	2	3	4	5	10	15	20	25	30	35	40	45	50	55	60	65	70	75	80	85	90
14	2.02	2.80	3.47	3.95	4.24	6.66	8.20	9.07	9.75	10.52	11.10	11.77	12.45	13.03	13.51	14.00	14.48	14.96	15.35	15.93	16.12	16.60
16	2.51	3.47	4.14	4.73	5.11	7.43	8.49	9.26	9.94	10.81	11.29	11.97	12.55	13.13	13.61	14.09	14.57	15.05	15.44	16.01	16.41	16.70
18	3.66	5.79	6.85	7.82	9.07	13.13	15.54	16.99	18.34	19.50	20.66	21.62	22.78	23.55	24.62	25.49	26.35	27.13	27.90	28.58	29.35	30.22
20	4.82	6.95	8.40	9.84	10.81	15.44	18.34	20.46	22.01	23.46	24.81	26.06	27.22	28.43	29.54	30.70	31.47	32.73	33.40	34.47	35.24	36.30
22	5.60	8.11	9.55	11.34	12.55	17.57	21.24	23.94	25.49	27.13	28.48	30.12	31.38	32.82	33.98	35.24	36.49	37.55	38.71	39.87	40.93	42.00
24	7.53	10.71	12.84	14.29	16.22	22.88	26.84	29.44	31.66	33.79	35.91	37.55	39.29	41.03	42.67	44.12	45.47	47.11	48.37	49.43	50.98	52.23
26	8.78	12.45	14.77	17.86	19.69	26.45	30.80	33.60	36.20	38.62	40.64	42.87	44.80	46.63	48.47	50.11	51.94	53.58	55.32	56.77	57.93	59.86
28	10.42	14.77	17.95	20.46	22.30	32.63	37.65	41.31	44.41	47.31	50.11	52.33	54.84	57.25	59.38	61.60	63.53	65.56	67.58	69.32	71.16	73.09
31	13.42	19.69	23.65	27.03	30.60	43.44	44.02	48.27	52.52	56.19	58.99	62.27	65.27	68.07	70.58	72.89	75.40	77.63	80.00	82.07	84.19	86.41
33	14.48	20.46	24.62	28.00	31.38	44.41	50.20	55.03	58.41	62.85	66.23	69.51	72.51	75.69	78.69	81.29	84.19	86.60	89.31	91.43	94.23	96.45
35	15.44	24.52	27.03	31.76	35.43	48.08	52.91	57.93	62.37	66.52	70.00	73.47	76.76	79.85	83.03	85.83	88.83	91.53	93.94	96.45	99.06	102.00
38	20.95	28.09	33.21	36.98	39.68	55.80	62.56	68.65	73.96	78.78	82.94	87.09	91.24	94.91	98.29	102.00	105.00	108.00	111.00	115.00	117.00	120.00
41	22.98	31.66	37.36	41.80	45.57	63.43	70.48	78.40	84.48	89.69	94.14	98.96	104.00	108.00	112.00	116.00	119.00	124.00	128.00	132.00	135.00	138.00
46	27.51	37.75	44.80	49.72	53.97	74.82	87.38	95.78	103.00	109.00	115.00	122.00	127.00	132.00	139.00	144.00	149.00	153.00	157.00	162.00	167.00	171.00
52	30.70	41.32	49.24	54.74	59.76	103.00	121.00	130.00	140.00	150.00	158.00	165.00	174.00	180.00	188.00	195.00						
57	34.95	43.93	51.27	57.25	84.00	116.00	135.00	147.00	159.00	170.00	180.00	190.00	199.00	208.00								
62	49.14	69.51	81.29	91.34	99.35	140.00	171.00	200.00	215.00													

NOTES: All jet sizes are in thousandths
All numbers over 100 lbs/hr are rounded
revised 9-10-00

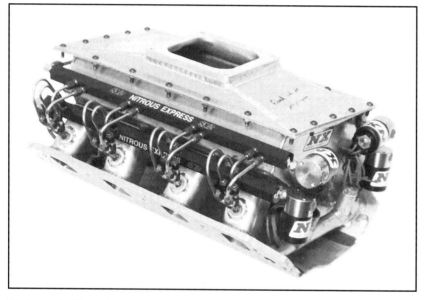

This impressive Nitrous Express assembly is a port injection system. Each fuel rail delivers fuel and nitrous to four Shark SX2 nozzles. Two pairs of solenoids control delivery to two rails. Depending on the application, both systems can be activated at the same time (single-stage operation) or triggered separately (two-stage operation). *Nitrous Express*

values are measured at the rear wheels and those gains are guaranteed.

As discussed many times thus far, achieving an ideal calibration is extremely important. One or two clicks either side of optimum can make or waste 10 horsepower.

Nitrous Oxide Manufacturers

There are many different nitrous oxide injecting systems to choose from. While several closely resemble each other, there are numerous specifications and particulars—some subtle, others major—that you should consider

before deciding which system is best for you. Remember that it is important to consider your performance, power, and practical needs while you evaluate the options available.

Nitrous Express

Nitrous Express uses the term "Next Generation" to describe its systems. The company works hard to incorporate new ideas to replace old, outdated nitrous systems, and it applies more than 50 years of combined experience to problem solving. Nitrous Express innovations are flow-

bench designed, dynamometer tested, and track proven. This, coupled with its technical support team, enables it to offer its safe and reliable Next Generation systems for both the novice and racer alike.

Nitrous Express Carbureted Systems

Gemini Twin This popular single-stage, direct-port plate system solves a variety of distribution problems common to single-plane manifolds. It is engineered to provide the exact amount of nitrous oxide and fuel mixture into each runner through a pair of tubes (two nitrous and two fuel). Gemini Twin is equipped with the only patented plate in the industry and is available in two series, Stage 6 (50 to 300 horsepower) and the potent Pro-Power (100 to 500 horsepower). Either system is available for gasoline or alcohol enrichment. The GT systems include the following:

- Billet aluminum construction
- Stainless-steel spray bars
- EMD-produced orifices
- Large body stainless-steel solenoids with a lifetime warranty
- Heavy-duty 60-amp antifly back relay
- Lightweight stainless-steel bottle brackets
- Unique 14-foot triple-insulated thermoplastic supply line

Gemini Quad This is a dual-stage plate system designed for competition or heavy-hitting street use. GQ kits range from 50 to 800 horsepower, depending upon application. This two-stage design is essentially a Stage Six and Pro-Power GT incorporated into one billet nitrous plate. Features include the following:
High-flow bottle valve (.312 orifice)
All D-6 hardware
D-6 triple-insulated thermoplastic supply line
15-pound nitrous bottle

Stage Six This is an entry-level plate system that offers advanced technology coupled with six power settings. Stage Six is a great option for the budget-minded racer because it is adjustable through six levels of performance from 50 to 300 horsepower. The tuner can increase the horsepower hit to take advantage of progressive engine modifications.

Hitman This is a low-cost, single-stage plate system designed for the novice performance enthusiast. It is available for Holley 4150, 4500, Spreadbore, and Quadra Jet carburetors and can be calibrated to deliver 100, 150, or 200 horsepower. Hitman is inexpensive, easy to install, and even easier to calibrate and use.

Fuel Injection Kits

Nitrous Express EFI kits are somewhat application specific in that the company lists no less than 59 separate part numbers covering 15 different car lines. Calibration provides nitrous hits as low as 35 horsepower for some 4-cylinder, front-wheel-drive imports, and up to a 300-horsepower blast for domestic V-8 engines. Next Generation are wet nitrous systems injecting nitrous and fuel into the intake manifold.

Shark and Piranha Nozzles

Nitrous Express is also very proud of its innovative nozzles including the Shark, Piranha and Shark SX2. Nitrous Express port-injected nozzle systems can be installed on virtually any engine, allowing fine-tuned calibration from 5 to 1,200 horsepower. Shark and Piranha nozzles accommodate single-stage injection. The Shark SX2 is designed to deliver a two-stage hit through a single nozzle. With fewer nozzles to install, there is less drilling and a single delivery device can be installed in an ideal location for optimum distribution. Shark SX2 nozzles

A number of protective options, such as this fuel pressure safety switch, can prevent a catastrophic failure. This switch will shut the system down in the event the fuel pressure drops below a safe level.

A solenoid-operated bottle valve can be wired for convenience, for safety, or both.

are capable of delivering up to 400 horsepower per nozzle in both single- and dual-stage configurations.

Solenoids

First, solenoids must be dependable. Second, the flow rate must exceed the capacity of the jet(s). High-flowing solenoids are essential to high-performance nitrous oxide applications. In this case, bigger can be better. Nitrous

Express solenoids are CNC machined and guaranteed for life. Reportedly, NE's Super Shark will flow 8.8 pounds of nitrous in 10 seconds. Others, such as the Iceman Pure-Flo, have an integrated purge port.

Nitrous Oxide Systems (NOS)

Nitrous Oxide Systems (NOS) is one of the leading, and perhaps the best-known, manufacturer of nitrous

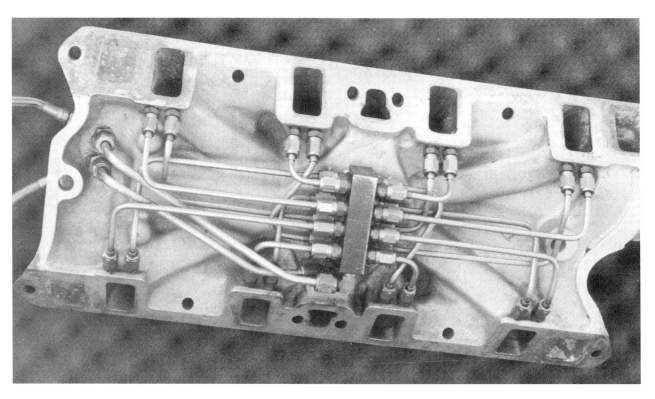

A stealth system requires imagination and talent. This sophisticated "hidden" port system uses a single nitrous and fuel nozzle to supply each cylinder.

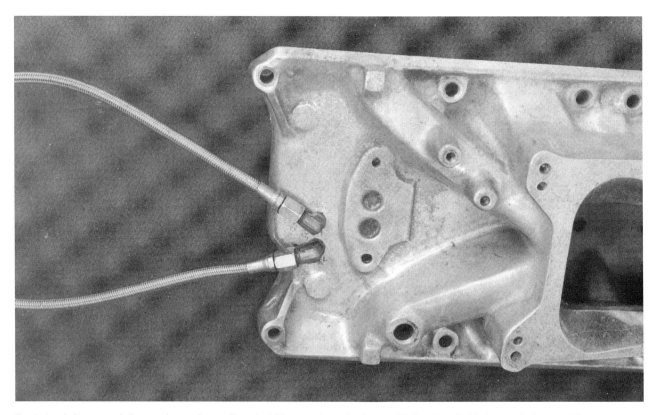

The fuel and nitrous supply lines are inconspicuous. Though visible, once the engine is assembled and installed in the car, the hoses will become camouflaged in the maze of wires, hoses, and cables behind the carburetor.

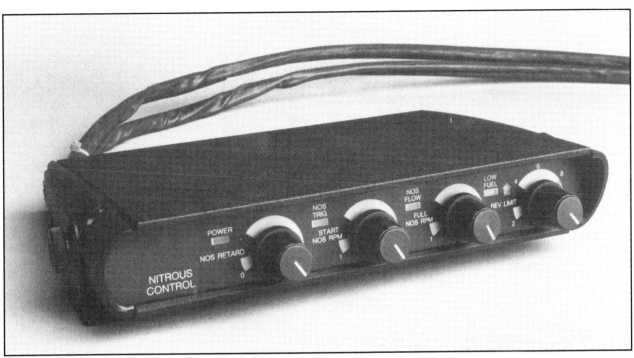

Jacobs Electronics' Nitrous Mastermind can activate the nitrous system at a preset engine rpm, shut off the nitrous flow in 1/100 of a second if the fuel pressure drops below a predetermined threshold, implement a programmed timing curve during nitrous activation, and provide rpm limit protection. *Jacobs*

oxide injection systems. NOS single-, dual-, and three-stage systems have powered some of the most successful race cars in the world. The company pioneered many innovative components, features, and controls that have become commonplace. Few manufacturers have contributed more to the success of nitrous oxide injection.

Powershot and Super Powershot These kits are entry-level economy systems designed for carbureted V-6 and V-8 engines. Both are equipped with highly accurate spray bars. Unlike the Powershot, the Super Powershot has changeable jets. The anticipated power gain will be between 90 and 150 horsepower. Both systems are manually activated by the driver.

Cheater and Dual Shot Cheater These plate systems were designed for engines with a displacement of 350 ci or larger. The Cheater is available in both a single- and dual-stage configuration, giving the driver the ability to

control the application as necessary. The first stage of the Dual Shot Cheater is activated by a throttle switch on the carburetor, and the driver manually controls the second stage. Both systems are adjustable by simply changing the nitrous and the fuel jets. Estimated performance gains are 150 to 250 horsepower with the Cheater, and 100 to 250 horsepower with the Dual Shot Cheater.

Big Shot and Dual Stage These systems will each deliver 200 to 400 additional horsepower and should be installed on extensively modified race engines. Both take advantage of new technology using a "fogging" plate that greatly enhances atomization and distribution of the mixture. With the Dual Stage Big Shot, the driver maintains control by manually activating the second stage. These systems add power gradually through two sets of solenoids.

Sophisticated Plate and Hidden Systems Annular Discharge plates take advantage of a staked circular pat-

tern to optimize delivery and atomization. They will fit beneath a 1050 or 1150 Holley Dominator carburetor with either an open or four-hole mounting flange. These systems will deliver up to 500 horsepower.

The Double Cross plate is equivalent to two Big Shot plates stacked on top of each other. The placement of the spray bars creates the best distribution of nitrous oxide and fuel.

Top Shot A Top Shot nitrous system is installed in the air cleaner assembly and can support a 75- to 150-horsepower hit. Top Shot is equipped with adjustable nitrous and fuel jets.

Sneaky Pete Another unique system NOS offers is called Sneeky Pete for obvious reasons. Sneeky Pete is a pocket-sized nitrous bottle that is designed to be inconspicuous. Fuel comes from jetting the carburetor a little overrich. No other fuel source is required. The bottle is small enough to fit in a tote bag or briefcase.

111

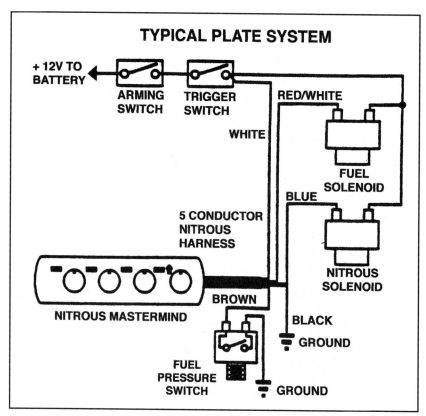

TYPICAL PLATE SYSTEM

+ 12V TO BATTERY

ARMING SWITCH

TRIGGER SWITCH

RED/WHITE

WHITE

FUEL SOLENOID

BLUE

5 CONDUCTOR NITROUS HARNESS

NITROUS SOLENOID

NITROUS MASTERMIND

BROWN

BLACK

GROUND

FUEL PRESSURE SWITCH

GROUND

A fuel pressure switch installed in the fuel line, just upstream from the solenoid, monitors fuel pressure. Should the fuel pressure fall, Mastermind will close the nitrous solenoid by interrupting the electrical path to ground. A simple plate system will typically have one nitrous and one fuel solenoid. *Jacobs*

Under the Manifold Cheater These kits can generate up to 150 extra horsepower. Obvious detection is limited because the lines and nozzles are installed on the bottom of the intake manifold. These direct port injection systems deliver a shot of nitrous oxide without the visual telltale signs.

Electronic Fuel-Injected Kits

NOS designed its electronic fuel-injection kits to work in conjunction with original-equipment manufacturer hardware. NOS manufacturers specific kits for tuned port Camaros and Firebirds, as well as dry systems for the LS-1 and a special 50-state emissions- legal LT-1 system. All of these kits deliver from 100 up to 150 horsepower.

NOS also manufactures a unique dry 75- to 150-horsepower kit for 5-liter Mustangs that is 50-state emissions legal. Systems for the 4.6-liter SOHC and DOHC engines are also available from NOS. Chrysler gets attention with 75- to 135-horsepower systems specially packaged for the Viper, the Dakota, and the Neon. And NOS offers a number of kits for import cars, ranging from 40- to 60-horsepower wet and dry kits to specific direct port systems that can effectively add between 80 and 225 horsepower. Although most of the above systems are technically emissions legal, they may not be legal for sale or use on certain pollution-controlled vehicles in some states.

Direct Port Systems

Direct port is the most efficient way to deliver the correct amount of fuel and nitrous. Because each cylinder is equipped with its own separate nozzle, each can be tuned independently for maximum performance. To help overcome the differences in flow characteristics, camshaft profiles, and other variables, NOS has a wide range of nozzles and systems to choose from.

Sportsman Fogger This port injection system can deliver 50 to 250 additional horsepower and is suited for most domestic, foreign, carbureted, or fuel-injected engines. Adjustable nitrous and fuel jets regulate the power levels.

Pro Shot Fogger and Pro Shot Fogger 2 The Pro Shot Fogger was designed to be installed on highly modified V-8 engines equipped with race-quality components. Horsepower gains range from 150 to 500-plus in certain applications. The Pro Shot Fogger 2 boasts the same benefits, but differs in that it is a two-stage system consisting of Fogger nozzles and a special spray bar plate installed under the carburetor.

Pro Shot Twin Fogger Engineered for the serious performance enthusiast, Pro Shot Twin Fogger is capable of generating from 150 to 1,000-plus horsepower. This extreme-horsepower kit combines two complete Pro Shot Fogger systems. Needless to say, racing fuel is required.

Pro Race Fogger This is another system designed for probuilt race engines. Pro Race Fogger's single-stage system is capable of 150- to 600-horsepower gains and comes with a choice of fogger nozzles and low-restrictive solenoids.

Supercharger and Turbocharger Kits NOS has designed a number of systems specifically for factory and aftermarket turbocharged or supercharged engines. These systems are designed to eliminate turbo lag and increase torque. Additionally, because the temperature of injected nitrous oxide is approximately 127 degrees below zero, forced induction systems duplicate the effectiveness of an intercooler by reducing the air-change temperature by as much as 75 degrees. Extremely high cylinder pressures are normal, so forged pistons, rods, and cranks are highly recommended. A high-performance ignition system is also suggested. Horsepower gains between 30 and 40 percent are typical.

Nozzles

Original Fogger and Fogger 2 Nozzles NOS original, patented Fogger nozzles provide individual calibration for each cylinder and are available in either 90-degree left or right angles or a 180-degree spray pattern.

Fogger Annular Discharge Racing Nozzles These nozzles mix the nitrous and the fuel outside the nozzle tip in a unique pattern for better control. Properly installed, the nozzle tip will not protrude into the intake air stream. A flush nozzle will not disturb the airflow.

Soft Plume 90-Degree Fogger Nozzles Soft Plume nozzles were specifically designed for smaller-displacement engines.

Fan Spray/Jet Spray Nozzles These nozzles are perfect for applications where regular nozzles may not fit, such as under-the-manifold direct port systems. They spray at either a 90-degree angle or straight.

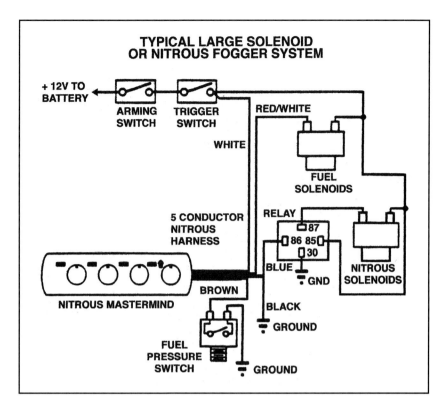

A nitrous control designed to manage a staged system will accommodate multiple pairs of fuel and nitrous solenoids. Large solenoids or multiple solenoids require a relay. Although installation and operation vary from one manufacturer to another, the fundamental principles of all electronic nitrous controls are similar. *Jacobs*

Chapter Seven
Fuel

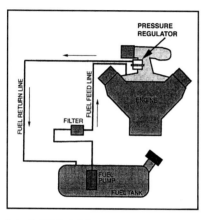

A basic EFI fuel delivery system consists of a fuel pump, filter, and pressure regulator. The arrows indicate the direction of fuel flow. The pressure regulator restricts the return path to the tank. Forcing fuel through the metered restriction creates pressure in the line between the pump and the pressure regulator. *Vortech Engineering*

The most common problems associated with forced induction are preignition and detonation. Either will produce a pinging or rattling sound, particularly when the engine is under load or operating at part-throttle. All vehicles can experience detonation or preignition regardless of whether they are equipped with forced induction.

Preignition, as the name implies, is ignition that occurs too early in the cycle. If, for example, the negative electrode on the spark plug can not get hot enough to glow red, the heat from the wire will ignite the fuel charge long before the electrical spark arrives.

Detonation is a sudden and uncontrolled explosion. It's difficult to think in milliseconds, but the air/fuel mixture *must* burn at a controlled rate no matter how fast the engine runs. The air/fuel mixture should never explode, but rather it should burn very quickly. In a compression ignition (diesel) engine, the heat from compression alone is sufficient to ignite the air/fuel charge. The same thing can occur in a spark ignition engine if conditions are right. Either condition can be caused by a number of problems , including the following:

- A lean air/fuel mixture
- Too much timing lead
- Excessive operating temperature (ineffective coolant)
- Excessive air-charge temperature (forced induction)
- Poor-quality fuel (low octane)
- Lugging (engine rpm too low for load conditions)
- Too much compression (compression ratio too high)

To maintain an ideal air/fuel mixture ratio, the volume of fuel must increase in direct proportion to the volume of air. If the fuel enrichment system cannot keep up with the demand, the air/fuel mixture will lean out. That's why an onboard fuel pressure gauge is more important than a boost gauge. A faltering fuel pressure reading is a sure sign of trouble.

The air/fuel mixture ratio should be between 13.6 and 14.7:1 during naturally aspirated operation (no boost) and 10.5 to 12.5:1 under boost. A 10.5 to 1 air/fuel ratio might be considered too conservative by

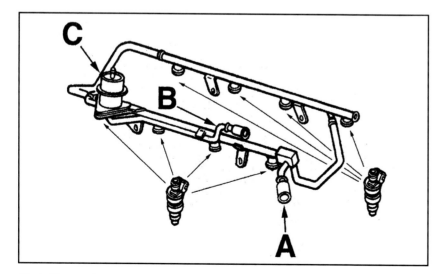

The fuel loop services a smaller fuel loop that feeds the injectors for typical V-6 or V-8 applications. High-pressure fuel enters at A and low-pressure fuel exits at B after passing through the pressure regulator C. Feeding the injectors from a pressurized loop ensures an adequate supply of fuel to each injector.

some, but it is a safe estimate considering the precision, or lack thereof, of the fuel enhancement systems included with most forced induction kits.

Maintaining an "ideal" air/fuel mixture is difficult. Overdriving the injectors (port injection system) with a high-pressure fuel pump and an FMU is a widely accepted practice. Typical fuel rail pressure in a loop system (which returns unused fuel to the tank) should be approximately 35 to 45 psi naturally aspirated, and between 60 and 100 psi under boost. Any number of problems can cause inadequate fuel pressure. For example, a fuel filter might become clogged or not allow sufficient flow. A clogged fuel injector (port injection) can cause an individual cylinder to lean out. A failing electric fuel pump can bench-test OK, but fail consistently when the engine and the fuel delivery system are under full load.

Ignition timing is equally critical. The spark plugs must fire progressively earlier in the cycle as engine speed increases, otherwise performance will suffer dramatically. Too much timing lead will cause detonation, and too little will hurt performance. Skirting the threshold of detonation will generate optimum performance without damaging the engine.

It all sounds simple enough, but the load on the engine; airflow dynamics through the engine; the density, temperature, and the amount of humidity in the air; and the atmospheric air pressure change continuously, and at times very quickly. Fuel delivery and timing lead must also change to ensure optimum performance.

Diagnosing a troubled engine is not terribly difficult. Consider the engine assembly as a number of integrated systems consisting of fuel, electrical, ignition, mechanical, and so on. Eliminating trouble-free systems will eventually isolate the problem within a single system. Then test only the components that make up that particular system.

Gasoline Tip

The octane number is a measure of how fast or slow a fuel burns. The higher the octane rating, the slower the fuel will burn. The octane number is found by computing (R+M)/2 or AKI where R is the research octane number, and M is the motor octane number. Research octane is needed for low-rpm/part-throttle operation, and motor octane is needed for high rpm/WOT/full power operation. (R+M)/2 is a good overall guide to octane.

Other facts and tips concerning gasoline include the following:

- Some gasolines contain oxygen compounds such as MTBE or alcohols. These additives promote horsepower output.
- Aromatics, such as toluene and/or xylene, should be limited in racing gasoline.
- Aviation-grade gasoline is good for low-rpm, high-altitude operation, but is not formulated for automotive use.
- Leaded racing gasoline is only legal for off-highway-sanctioned racing events.
- Burning leaded fuels in a pollution-controlled vehicle will damage the emissions hardware.

The octane rating should be as high as possible. Too much octane is safe; too little can be disastrous. The higher the octane rating, the more timing lead the engine will tolerate. To a point, the greater the timing lead the more power the engine will generate. Low octane and/or too much timing lead will cause detonation or preignition. Detonation is abnormal combustion that occurs after the spark plug fires. Some or all of the fuel mixture will explode or burn uncontrollably. Preignition is abnormal combustion that occurs before the spark plug fires. The excessive cylinder pressures created by these explosions can break ring lands or unseat a head gasket. Controlled combustion defines a smooth, consistent burn with no abnormal combustion.

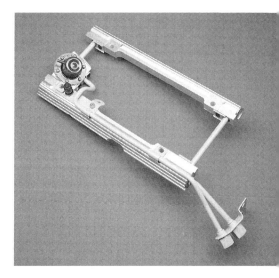

Retain the loop when upgrading the fuel delivery system. If the injectors are placed in a series, like Christmas tree lights, the last injector in line might be deprived when full power is ordered. Install an Accel high-volume fuel rail assembly or one similar to it. *Mr. Gasket*

Most factory fuel pressure regulators are non-adjustable. Opt for an adjustable regulator to facilitate fine-tuning, like this Kenne Bell billet adjustable regulator, designed for Ford cars and trucks equipped with a fuel return. Adjust the fuel pressure to obtain an optimum air/fuel mixture ratio during nonboost conditions.

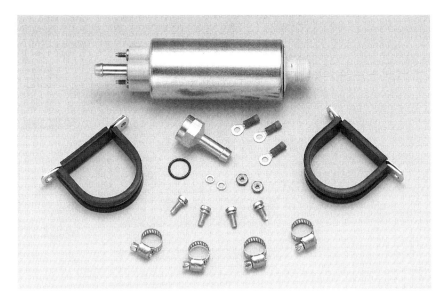

High-volume, low-pressure mechanical or electric fuel pumps designed to be used with carburetors will not deliver enough pressure for a fuel injection system. Additionally, in-line electric pumps designed for a loop system will not work on dead-end or returnless systems, because they do not incorporate an internal bypass valve.

Because dense air/fuel mixtures burn faster, high-boost pressures demand higher octane fuels and/or less timing lead. Likewise, high air-charge temperatures require higher octane.

Diagnostics 101

Diagnosing a detonation or preignition problem isn't terribly difficult. First, the forced induction system must be either eliminated or implicated as the source of the problem. Use the diagnostic procedure listed below to help pinpoint the cause. Please note: These diagnostic procedures represent an overview and as such are not intended to circumvent procedures recommended by a qualified service technician. An experienced diagnostician will file this list under "Hints, Tips, and Suggestions."

Supercharger Diagnostics

Remove the supercharger drive belt or disconnect the discharge manifold to isolate the supercharger system. The engine will now operate in a naturally aspirated mode. If the detonation subsides, a problem with the supercharger's fuel enhancement system is likely. Check the auxiliary injectors,

the fuel pump, and/or the FMU. If the engine continues to detonate, the ignition timing is suspect. A heavily modified engine is more difficult to diagnose, because a number of systems have been changed or upgraded. Also keep in mind that problems can overlap. An air/fuel ratio meter will indicate a lean fuel condition with or without the blower connected.

Turbocharger Diagnostics

Removing the discharge manifold eliminates the load on the impeller, but the turbocharger can reach excessive speeds when the pressures on either side of the engine (intake and exhaust) are uncontrolled. Therefore it is not safe to run a turbocharger at any appreciable speed with the discharge manifold disconnected. Instead, adjust the wastegate and/or the bypass valve to systematically reduce the amount of boost the turbocharger generates. Richen the fuel in progressive steps until the detonation subsides. Increase boost and fuel until the desired values are achieved. Add timing in small increments until the engine detonates, then back out timing until the detonation subsides.

Below are other procedures and conditions to consider.

Air/Fuel Ratio

It is difficult to dial in the air/fuel mixture ratio without a device to measure the outcome; therefore, an air/fuel ratio meter is highly recommended. In the absence of a meter, adding fuel (richening the mixture) is relatively safe. An excessively rich air/fuel ratio will make the engine run poorly, but will usually not cause damage. Remove fuel until the engine pings under load, then richen the mixture until the noise subsides. In reverse order, add timing until the engine pings, then remove just enough timing to eliminate the noise. Also, keep in mind that blower motors are heat sensitive, meaning calibrations for 60-degree weather will be too aggressive when the temperature rises to 90 degrees.

Modifications—Electronic Fuel Injection Only

Modifications that improve airflow through the engine, such as headers, heads, and intake manifolds, will lean out the air/fuel mixture. A typical electronic fuel injection system will attempt to compensate for the additional airflow providing it is a feedback system (a feedback system is covered in greater detail in chapter 8.)

Most standard (base) forced induction kits are engineered for stock, unmodified engines, which means the fuel enrichment system is calibrated for stock airflow values. Engine modifications designed to further improve performance can tax the fuel delivery system. In the event airflow exceeds the maximum threshold, the fuel enrichment system must be upgraded. In other words, if the fuel enrichment system cannot keep up with the demand, the engine will run lean. Once the fuel enrichment system has been upgraded, the air/fuel ratio must be recalibrated to achieve optimum performance. Increasing the out-

put of the supercharger by installing a smaller blower pulley (providing there is sufficient latitude to do so) will also lean the air/fuel mixture.

Computer Enhancements

Most computer enhancements, such as piggyback chips or reprogramming modules, are designed to enhance the performance of a naturally aspirated engine. However, few have the ability to "understand" forced induction, unless they are specifically programmed or engineered for that purpose. Most chips engineered for naturally aspirated engines make power by leaning the air/fuel ratio, increasing the timing lead, or both. Chips programmed for forced induction will *add* fuel (richen the air/fuel mixture) and *subtract* timing, which means a blower chip's programming is the

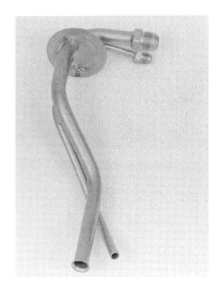

Some in-tank pumps may actually cause a restriction if demand exceeds its capacity. Upgrade to one or perhaps two high-capacity, external in-line pumps in place of the in-tank pump. This large-diameter pickup and return tube assembly can be installed in place of a 1979–1993 Mustang in-tank pump assembly.

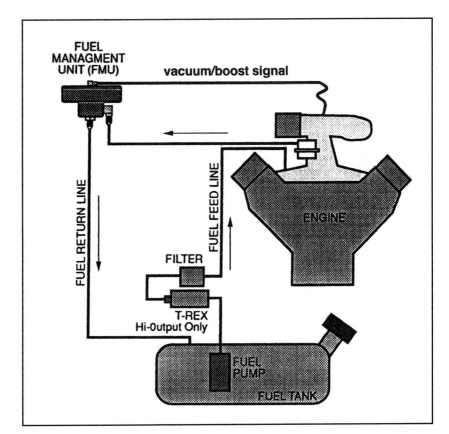

Boost causes the FMU to gradually close off the fuel return path, thus raising fuel rail pressure. Fuel pressure will increase in direct proportion to boost pressure. If the fuel pump(s), the FMU, and the fuel injectors are calibrated properly, fuel pressure will overdrive the injectors to provide an ideal air/fuel mixture ratio at each rpm point. *Vortech*

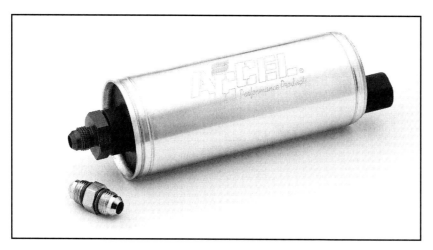

The typical advertised full capacity of a fuel pump is measured with no restriction. Fuel pump ratings that provide only the amount of horsepower the pump will support do not provide enough information. Fuel flow at a given pressure is essential data. Accel's 74702 pump is rated at 70 gallons per hour at 45-psi pressure. *Accel*

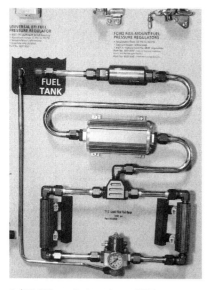

A $50,000 car that produces 450 horsepower with help from a $5,000 forced induction kit requires an adequate fuel delivery system. Paxton's premium system features billet fuel rails, filter, and pump, as well as an adjustable pressure regulator and a liquid-filled gauge.

exact opposite of a naturally aspirated chip. Therefore, installing an off-the-shelf computer chip on a blower motor is a recipe for detonation.

Fuel

The performance potential of the fuel is equally important. Low-octane, fast-burning fuels can predetonate due to the increased cylinder pressures associated with forced induction. Never burn fuel with a rating lower than 91 octane. Store a can of octane-enhancing fuel additive in the car in the event premium fuel is not available or if the ambient temperature climbs to triple digits. Use octane booster anytime detonation persists.

Spark Plugs

Paxton recommends copper-core spark plugs gapped to .035 inch and opposes platinum plugs or a larger gap setting. Wide plug gaps produce a hotter, albeit weaker, spark.

Ignition System

It's hard to keep a campfire lit during a tornado. Increased airflow dynamics and cylinder pressures with a blower will tax a stock ignition system. If the fuel doesn't light, the engine will bog or miss. Upgrade, or at the very least renew, the secondary ignition system if the engine misses under boost. Substandard or weak plug wires, coils, distributor caps, and so on, will likely fail when subjected to increased load.

Aftermarket Airflow Meter

An aftermarket mass airflow meter can also cause a lean fuel condition. A value sent from the mass air-flow meter tells the processor how much air the engine is ingesting at any given second. The processor adds the right amount of fuel based on that reading. To ensure that the chemistry is accurate, the meter must be calibrated for a particular engine size (airflow rate) and injector size (pounds per hour). The calibration must be modified if you change the parameters, as if by installing larger injectors or increasing the flow rate of the injectors by increasing the fuel rail pressure.

Recalibrating the electronics in a mass air meter is difficult. Some aftermarket manufacturers recalibrate the meter by varying the size of the sampling tube. The diameter of the sampling tube is proportional to the diameter of the main bore (ratio). Changing the ratio forces the meter to send an erroneous value to the processor. Computing the amount of error constitutes a change in calibration; hence the operation "recalibrates" the meter. If the computation is accurate, the meter will function within accepted parameters. If the calibration change misses the mark, an erroneous value could cause the processor to lean or richen the air/fuel mixture. An air leak between the meter and the throttle body will also produce an erroneous signal.

Fuel Management Unit

If detonation does not occur during naturally aspirated operation, but reappears when the blower is connected and making boost, the fuel enrichment system is the likely cause. The blower will lean the air/fuel mixture very quickly if the FMU is not working or is malfunctioning. Make sure the vacuum/pressure port is connected to the intake manifold. If the FMU doesn't "see" boost, it will not function.

Use a compressed air source and a pressure regulator to test the FMU. Simulate boost by pressurizing the vacuum/pressure port. With the pump(s) running, fuel pressure should increase at a corresponding rate with boost pressure. For example, a 12:1 FMU will increase the fuel pressure 12 pounds for each 1 pound of boost.

Fuel Hoses

Check to ensure that the fuel hoses are connected to the proper "in" and "out" port on the FMU. If these hoses are crossed, fuel pressure will hold the valve open.

Pressure Switch

Some systems incorporate a pressure switch, sometimes called a Hobbs switch, to activate the auxiliary fuel pump. Test the normally open switch to make sure it is supplying power to the pump shortly after the pressure in the intake manifold switches from negative to positive (vacuum to boost). The switch should close after sensing approximately 1 pound of boost. If more boost is required to close the switch, the fuel pump is coming online too late. Replace the switch and retest the system. Monitor fuel pressure with a full-time onboard gauge to ensure that the pressure enrichment system is functioning properly.

Vacuum and Pressure Leaks

A standard supercharger kit installed on a stock engine should produce from 5 to 8 pounds of boost, depending on the application. If a newly installed system produces low boost pressure and the engine detonates, the air/fuel mixture is lean, and/or there is too much timing, and/or the octane rating of the fuel is low. If these values are correct, check for vacuum leaks and pressure leaks around the discharge manifold. Make sure the hose leading to the gauge is not kinked or leaking. Check the FMU pressure port hose. Check the mass air meter wiring connection. Make sure the inline pump is not installed backward—the "in" line should come from the fuel tank and the "out" line should go to the engine—and ensure the negative and positive power leads are connected properly. Reversing

the leads could cause the fuel pump to run backward.

Altitude

Because air at higher altitudes is less dense, boost pressures will also be less. For example, operating a blower system in Denver (approximately 5,200 feet above sea level) will produce less boost pressure than the same system in Death Valley, which is several hundred feet below sea level. Increasing the blower speed to compensate for high altitude is a viable modification, but keep in mind the change will create an excessive boost condition as altitude decreases.

Excessive Boost

Excessive boost is a rare condition, but it can happen. As stated earlier, unmodified or "standard" supercharger kits should generate between 5 and 8 pounds of boost when installed on a stock engine. Boost values much over 8 pounds can cause premature engine failure. Excessive boost creates excessive cylinder pressures, which can overpower the head gaskets. Once the gasket seal has been breached, compression can leak into the cooling system. Following the return path, coolant can then leak into the cylinder(s) and/or the crankcase when cylinder pressures are low or after the engine has been turned off.

Either condition can cause a catastrophic failure. If boost levels are excessive, measure the diameter of the crankshaft and blower pulleys. Compare those measurements to the manufacturer's specifications for the application. If the crank pulley is larger or the blower pulley is smaller, the supercharger will run faster than the recommended limit set by the factory. A faulty or misadjusted wastegate can overspeed a turbocharger, which will create excessively high boost pressures. Install a pop-off valve in the discharge tube as a safety device. Should the wastegate malfunction, the pop-off valve will safely discharge the pressure.

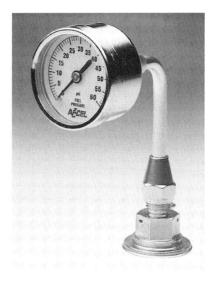

An accurate fuel gauge is an extremely important instrument. Low or no fuel pressure causes a lean fuel condition. Electric fuel pumps have been known to fade away slowly or telegraph an intermittent warning of impending doom. Closely monitor fuel pressure, investigate inconsistencies, and don't assume the gauge is bad. *Mr. Gasket*

Several Paxton Automotive Novi supercharger systems incorporate a "venturi" device that mounts in the air intake tube or manifold. The venturi is designed to increase air velocity, and in doing so, it reduces the supercharger's maximum boost capability. If the venturi has been removed or was not installed, the system will likely generate excessive boost. Increasing or eliminating the factory-set rev limit or changing the transmission shift points can also cause a supercharger or turbocharger to overboost the engine. Spinning the engine faster also spins the supercharger or turbocharger faster. Speed beyond engineered limits can cause damage to the point of total destruction.

Fuel Delivery

Most base or entry-level supercharger or turbocharger systems are not designed for sustained full-power operation—a 5-mile, wide-open throttle, full-power pass at Bonneville, for example, or one full-speed lap on a 1-mile oval. This is not because of durability concerns. The blower or

Adding fuel though auxiliary injectors is an excellent way to supplement the fuel delivery system, provided they are sized properly and can be calibrated to a high degree of accuracy.

Controlling auxiliary injectors with an electronic feedback system is ideal. A feedback system will automatically adjust fuel delivery to a near ideal air/fuel mixture ratio at all times. A programmable system can be adjusted or set to deliver a given amount of fuel at various rpm points and/or boost levels.

turbocharger will likely withstand the punishment. In most cases, the fuel delivery system will be unable to keep up with the engine's fuel requirements over an extended period of time.

At an ideal BSFC of .48, an engine generating 400 horsepower will consume 192 pounds of fuel per hour, a figure that jumps to 240 pounds of fuel for a 500-horsepower engine. At that rate, the fuel delivery system must transfer a minimum of 4 pounds of fuel from the fuel tank to the engine every 60 seconds. No need to wonder why race cars are equipped with fuel lines the size of a garden hose.

Most entry-level forced induction kits include either an auxiliary or a replacement fuel pump to increase fuel pressure and volume, but typically the stock fuel lines remain unchanged. Typical factory fuel lines are 5/16-inch ID or less. Applying the same .48 BSFC, a stock engine generating 225 horsepower requires 108 pounds of fuel per hour, or 1.8 pounds of fuel per minute. Expecting the same 5/16-inch fuel lines to deliver between 3 and 4 pounds of fuel per minute is risky at best. The factory fuel lines are simply too small.

Forced induction kits work because street-driven performance vehicles usually generate peak power for no more than a few seconds at any one time. As a point of reference, the average factory production musclecar will cover the quarter-mile in 15 seconds, give or take a second. There is rarely the need, or the opportunity, to stand on the throttle any longer than 30 seconds. A 5-second power squirt from stoplight to stoplight or a full throttle burst on a freeway on-ramp is more the norm.

Should a daring motorist tackle the Pikes Peak Hill Climb in a 5.0-liter Mustang equipped with a base supercharger or turbocharger system, it is likely the supply of fuel to the engine will fall short long before the car reaches the top. When the fuel delivery system fails to keep up with the demand, the air/fuel mixture becomes lean. When the air/fuel becomes too lean, combustion temperatures can surpass the melting point of aluminum. At that point, the pistons will start to deteriorate. This scenario usually results in a costly lesson.

To reiterate the point, the key factor here is time. Sustained power requires an ample supply of fuel for as long as the demand exists. Short bursts of power (20 seconds or less) consume comparatively small amounts of fuel. A stock fuel delivery system *cannot* support a 500-horsepower engine at full power for an extended period of time, and overdriving the pump or installing a larger pump is not an ideal fix. If the fuel system cannot keep up with the demand, every second of sustained full power operation will take the engine that much closer to destruction. Full-throttle operation for one second beyond the point of fuel starvation can kill the engine. Pushing the envelope is similar to playing Russian roulette. Eventually the gun will fire.

Interpreting Dynamometer Data

Dynamometer data is test data and the validity of the results depends

Dynamometer Data

A lot can be learned from a typical engine dynamometer data sheet besides peak torque and horsepower. Notes in the middle of this page describe the hardware and any special settings or adjustments. Note that the data shown is the average of two previous dyno runs.

Reading from left to right, the first vertical column illustrates the rpm range of the test. Column 2 lists the corrected torque numbers generated at each data point. When the measured variables are factored in, the data is said to be "corrected." Some or all of the measured variables are left out of uncorrected data. The third column lists the horsepower generated at each data point, and the fourth is the computed break specific fuel consumption figures listed in pounds per hour.

The air/fuel (A/F) ratio is also computed. Typical for a supercharged engine running an FMU, the example shown ran a rich mixture. The next column indicates manifold pressure. Because the numbers are positive, not negative, the values represent the amount of boost generated by the supercharger at each data point. The eighth column logs the fuel pressure at the injectors, and the ninth column shows the time it took the engine to sweep past each particular data point. The total length of the dyno pull—38.7 seconds—is listed at the bottom of column nine. The heading of column 9 indicates the data underneath is the exhaust gas temperature (EGT) of number four cylinder listed in degrees Fahrenheit, when in fact, the hardware was modified to measure the inlet air-charge temperature. The inlet air-charge temperature shows just how much the supercharger heats the incoming air-charge compared to ambient.

The amount of temperature added to the air-charge is a product of compressor efficiency—or inefficiency, to be more accurate. The less efficient the compressor, the more the air is heated. Note at the end of the pull that the inlet air-charge temperature is 300 degrees Fahrenheit.

```
PRINT # 139  C9        VORTEC.CFG   No Fric. Fact  Apr 19 '95   3:27 PM   Pg 1
  DUTTWEILER PERF
Engine:_                      Customer:_
Special conditions:_
                      ** up to 4 lines as shown **_____

C9   Wed Mar 1 '95   12:38 PM   3000 TO 5800 RPM         AVG of: A7745 A7746
  BARO:29.95   Disp:302    Bore:4    ATmp:75    VORTC:1          INJ:0

          HP:       RPM:        BOOST:       TORQUE:      RPM:
Custmer:  :  VORTEC 302    ENGINE:   302 FORD          IGN Timing: 10
Comment : TESTING PRODUCTS  SUPER FORD MAGAZINE
```

Average of 7745 and 7746. World Products aluminum heads, A-Trim blower with 2.75-inch pulley, Vortech manifold and adjustable FMU, 80mm MAF, 65mm TB, 30 lb injectors, 6 degrees initial timing. Injectors are static at 5000 rpm. Last test using 30 lb per hour injectors.

RPM BAND	C TORQ Ft-Lbs	C PWR CHP	BSFC #/HrHP	Fuel F #/Hr	A/F RATIO	MAN P PSI	FUEL P PSI	EGT 4 Deg F	TIME SEC
3006	312.6	178.9	0.601	104	10.010	3.84	55.5	165	3.2
3100	316.8	187.0	0.648	117	10.017	4.09	56.0	151	1.2
3200	324.4	197.7	0.622	119	10.002	4.38	56.0	136	1.7
3300	331.3	208.1	0.479	97	10.005	4.66	56.3	141	0.9
3400	341.8	221.3	0.491	106	10.002	4.96	56.6	161	1.1
3500	349.2	232.7	0.584	132	10.005	5.26	56.9	162	1.0
3600	356.0	244.0	0.613	145	10.007	5.57	57.5	167	1.0
3700	362.6	255.4	0.610	151	10.002	5.90	58.0	144	1.4
3800	367.7	266.0	0.621	160	10.005	6.23	58.4	156	1.1
3900	378.9	281.4	0.629	172	10.005	6.57	58.9	181	2.3
4000	386.4	294.3	0.633	181	10.002	6.90	59.4	171	1.9
4100	394.0	307.5	0.647	193	10.005	7.26	59.6	153	1.0
4200	405.4	324.2	0.635	200	10.002	7.60	60.1	157	1.9
4300	412.5	337.7	0.640	210	10.005	7.95	59.6	189	1.2
4400	417.5	349.7	0.650	221	10.005	8.27	59.6	210	1.2
4500	423.5	362.9	0.654	230	10.005	8.62	59.9	170	1.4
4600	427.9	374.8	0.656	239	10.002	8.95	60.0	167	1.2
4700	434.3	388.7	0.655	247	10.000	9.29	60.3	172	1.4
4800	441.7	403.7	0.640	251	10.000	9.60	60.8	236	1.3
4900	446.9	416.9	0.627	254	10.146	9.91	61.1	222	1.4
5000	449.2	427.6	0.622	258	10.422	10.19	61.4	193	1.2
5100	451.3	438.2	0.609	259	10.706	10.44	62.1	202	0.9
5200	445.3	440.8	0.608	260	10.979	10.62	62.0	206	1.0
5300	429.5	433.2	0.620	261	10.928	11.23	62.7	250	1.2
5400	396.2	407.3	0.660	261	10.884	11.88	63.3	234	1.1
5500	388.1	406.4	0.665	262	11.064	12.16	63.5	214	1.5
5600	380.8	406.1	0.662	261	11.284	12.38	63.6	233	0.9
5700	369.6	401.1	0.673	262	11.729	12.30	63.8	278	2.1
5777	358.4	394.2	0.689	264	12.024	12.05	63.6	300	0.8
AVRG	390.8	328.3	0.623	200	10.294	8.11	59.7	186	38.7

AVERAGE RESULTS From <3006> RPM to 5700 RPM   DEPAC # 17

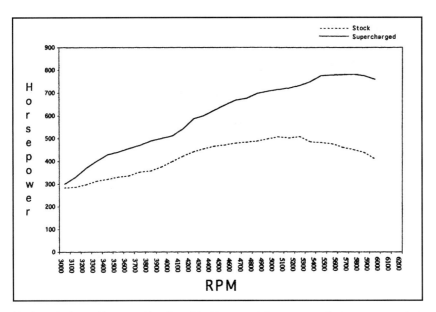

Much can be learned from graphing dyno data. These graph lines compare the horsepower output, naturally aspirated versus supercharged. In this example, not only is the power output up throughout the entire rpm range, but the peak data point was shifted to a faster engine speed. Naturally aspirated peak power occurred near 5,300 rpm.

Horsepower Contained In Gasoline

Horsepower	Lbs/Hr	Gal/Hr
1,000	500.00	82.115
975	487.50	80.101
950	475.00	78.047
925	462.50	75.994
900	450.00	73.940
875	437.50	71.886
850	425.00	69.832
825	412.50	67.778
800	400.00	65.724
775	385.50	63.342
750	375.00	61.616
725	362.50	59.562
700	350.00	57.509
675	337.50	55.455
650	325.00	53.401
625	312.50	51.347
600	300.00	49.293
575	287.50	47.239
550	275.00	45.185
525	262.50	43.131
500	250.00	41.077
475	237.50	39.023
450	225.00	36.970
425	212.50	34.916
400	200.00	32.862
375	187.50	30.808
350	175.00	28.754
325	162.50	26.700
300	150.00	24.646
275	137.50	22.592
250	125.00	20.538
225	112.50	18.485
200	100.00	16.431
175	87.50	14.377
150	75.00	12.323
125	62.50	10.269
100	50.00	8.215

This fuel "flow chart" assumes a .50 BASF using fuel that weighs 6.068 pounds per gallon (.730 specific gravity). For example, an engine generating 500 horsepower will consume 250 pounds, or 41.077 gallons, of fuel per hour whether it is naturally aspirated, turbocharged, supercharged, or injected with nitrous oxide.

on the level of accuracy and precision of both the equipment and the method of data acquisition. Quality dyno data requires a lot of time and expense. There are no shortcuts. Any and all variables that could influence the test results must be either controlled or measured. Control variables would include oil and water temperature, the quality and quantity of the fuel, and the consistency of each test session. Variables that cannot be controlled, such as atmospheric air pressure, humidity, and temperature, must be measured and noted. The measurements then become variable factors that are used to quantify the test results. Disregarding any variable reduces the test data to a nonrepeatable one-time sample. Controlling, and adjusting for uncontrollable variables, provides reliable test data that could be repeated at any time in the future or at a remote location. Unfortunately, most publicized dynamometer results are nonrepeatable samples because one or more of the aforementioned variables are not controlled or measured. Further, variables can be used to influence dynamometer results in a favorable direction. In

fact, it is far easier to manipulate dyno data using predictable variables than it is to generate accurate, repeatable data. For example, in most applications, dropping the coolant temperature from 200 to 100 degrees will generate higher power numbers with no other changes.

Most automotive enthusiasts are familiar with dyno data but, oddly, few question its validity.

As a general rule, high-end engine dynamometers generate the most repeatable data, providing all of the variables are addressed consistently and according to accepted guidelines. It can then be assumed that all repeatable data is also the most accurate data.

On the other end of the spectrum, the majority of the nonrepeatable samples are generated using chassis dynamometers. The accuracy of a nonrepeatable sample is not in question here. A nonrepeatable sample can produce accurate data. It simply must be categorized as a sampling based on the variables that were in force at the time the test was administered. Back-to-back runs logged on the same day can detect instant

mechanical enhancements or tuning adjustments. But the data is only valid at that particular time on that particular day if all of the variables were not addressed.

For example, drive a car around town for two hours then, without turning the engine off, strap it to a chassis dynamometer and perform

Chassis Dynamometer

Drive-on or chassis dynamometers have become very popular in recent years because, like drive-through fast food, they are convenient, easy to use, and produce near instant results with very little set-up time. In addition, the data extracted from a chassis dynamometer is usually basic and uncomplicated. Because a number of controlled and uncontrolled variables are ignored during most drive-on dyno sessions, more often than not, the data must be categorized as nonrepeatable samples.

That's not to say chassis dynamometers are incapable of producing repeatable data. On the contrary, if each controllable and noncontrollable variable is addressed, chassis dyno data can be every bit as accurate *and* repeatable as any data generated by an engine dynamometer. Unfortunately, few operators comply with these minimum requirements. Further, including the transmission, drive axle, and tires as part of the data acquisition hardware adds more variables to the mix.

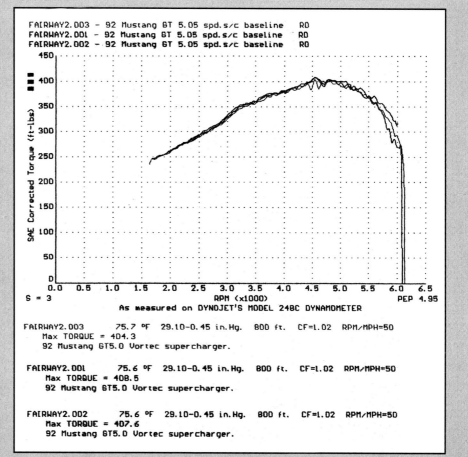

FAIRWAY2.003 - 92 Mustang GT 5.05 spd.s/c baseline   RO
FAIRWAY2.001 - 92 Mustang GT 5.05 spd.s/c baseline   RO
FAIRWAY2.002 - 92 Mustang GT 5.05 spd.s/c baseline   RO

As measured on DYNOJET'S MODEL 248C DYNAMOMETER

FAIRWAY2.003   75.7 °F   29.10-0.45 in.Hg.   800 ft.   CF=1.02   RPM/MPH=50
    Max TORQUE = 404.3
    92 Mustang GT5.0 Vortec supercharger.

FAIRWAY2.001   75.6 °F   29.10-0.45 in.Hg.   800 ft.   CF=1.02   RPM/MPH=50
    Max TORQUE = 408.5
    92 Mustang GT5.0 Vortec supercharger.

FAIRWAY2.002   75.6 °F   29.10-0.45 in.Hg.   800 ft.   CF=1.02   RPM/MPH=50
    Max TORQUE = 407.6
    92 Mustang GT5.0 Vortec supercharger.

Slippage in the torque converter (if it is an automatic transmission), the gear selected for the run, the rear axle ratio, the tire diameter, and any traction loss between the tires and the rollers will usually degrade the accuracy of the data. Estimating the unknown frictional loss imposed by the drivetrain further taints the data, because this figure can vary widely.

three full-power tests back to back. Shut it down and wait for one hour, then start it, let it idle for two minutes and perform another full-power test. More often than not, the fourth pass will show the highest horsepower number. Depending on the vehicle, it could be as much as 15 horsepower more. In most cases, allowing the car to cool for as little as 20 minutes will have similar effect to a lesser degree. Oil and coolant temperatures are major variables.

To put it into context, the torque and horsepower numbers recorded by a nonrepeatable sampling are only valid at that very instant. They are not representative of the engine's true and accurate output because the dyno data can only be repeated if and when all the variables coincide at another point in time. Variables can change from morning to afternoon, making it difficult to repeat a test on the same day.

A final word on dyno data: automotive enthusiasts are trained to focus on the peak power number, the highest torque and/or horsepower number logged during the dyno run. Under these circumstances, a 5-horsepower gain at the peak is said to be a successful change. In reality, a gain or loss at each and every data point should be taken into account before the modifications should be considered a success or failure. Case in point: if a modification produces a 5-horsepower gain at its peak, say at the 5,000-rpm data point, but sacrifices 10 horsepower at the 3,000-rpm data point, there is a net loss, not an overall gain.

Fuel Management and Injector Sizing

The remainder of this chapter is reprinted with permission from MSD Ignition's *Fuel Management Catalog.* The complete catalog can be downloaded in PDF format from their Web site at www.msdignition.com.

Determining the correct fuel flow through a group of electronic fuel injectors is similar to jetting a carburetor. In either case, the fuel flow must complement the airflow requirements of the engine over a broad rpm range. A carburetor may employ three or more separate control circuits—such as idle, transfer, and power—to meter the fuel curve over the full operating range. An injector must also supply a small amount of fuel to support idle, a large amount of fuel during wide-open, full-power conditions to prevent high-rpm lean-out, and be infinitely adjustable in all points in between. Consequently, an injector must have a wide "dynamic range" of operation.

The length of time an electronic injector is held open by the Engine Control Unit (ECU) dictates the amount of fuel delivered. It is "pulsed or energized" for short periods of time (milliseconds) at idle. The length of each pulse becomes longer as rpm and airflow increase. Electronic fuel injectors can open and close hundreds of times per second. Each opening and closing event is called a cycle. The length of the cycle is called the pulse width. Injectors too large or too small for the applica-tion can cause drivability problems, such as rough idle, surging, poor throttle response, or high-rpm lean-out. The same conditions occur when the jets in a carburetor are oversized or undersized.

Sizing injectors is based on the projected power output of the engine (horsepower) at a given BSFC. To ensure accurate calibration, consider the following:

- The projected horsepower output of the engine must be realistic. Don't shoot for a number that would satisfy an unobtainable goal.
- BSFC will typically range from .40 to .60 for SI (spark ignition) engines. An 0.5 BSFC is a reasonable initial estimate for most applications.
- The total flow rate needed to supply the engine with an adequate amount of fuel is the combined flow rate of each injector. Therefore, a multiplier (0.8 in the following examples) is needed to compute a practical, maximum flow rate for each injector, based on an effective real-world operating pulse time and fuel flow. A 100 percent operating pulse time, or width, meaning the injector is open all the time, is unrealistic. The following formula uses an 80 percent operating or "duty" cycle, which is more ideal. Some competition engine management systems may impose an 85 or 95 percent duty cycle, but overdriving the injectors for long periods of time can overheat the coil, which can cause irregular fuel delivery rates or decrease low-rpm performance.

When implementing these guide-lines, use the following formula to compute the individual injector flow rate in pounds per hour:

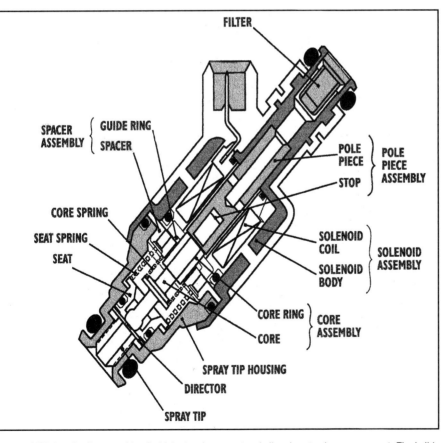

MSD "top feed" competition fuel injectors incorporate a ball-and-seat valve arrangement. The ball is lifted off the seat when the injector coil is energized. Fuel then passes through six metering holes in the injector tip. The holes project a tight 10- to 15-degree cone-shaped spray pattern. *MSD*

Injector Flow Rate (lbs/hr) =

horsepower x BSFC
# of injectors x 0.8

For example, to calculate the individual injector flow rate in pounds per hour for a 650-horsepower V-8 engine using 8 injectors, assuming a BSFC of 0.5, factor:

lbs/hr = $\dfrac{650 \times 0.5}{8 \times 0.8}$ **= 50.78**

Therefore, 8 50-lbs./hr injectors (MSD part number 2013) operating at 80 percent duty cycle will comfortably support approximately 650 horsepower when supplied with 43.5 psi fuel pressure.

To compute the performance of an injector with a known flow rate, use the following formula.

HP = $\dfrac{\text{Injector flow rate # of injectors x 0.8}}{\text{BSFC}}$

For example:

HP = $\dfrac{50 \times 8 \times 0.8}{0.5}$ **= 640**

Note: High-performance applications, forced induction, nitrous oxide injection, and extremely high-rpm operation (rotary engines for example) may require larger injectors.

ECU Compatibility

Determining the correct fuel flow is only part of the process. The injector must also match the operating parameters dictated by the ECU. Injector driver circuits are available in one of two styles: saturated or peak-and-hold. It is important to note that the two styles are not interchangeable, so it is very important that the driver circuit of the injector match the driver circuit used by the ECU.

Saturated Circuit Driver and Injectors

The ECUs controlling most domestic EFI systems are equipped with a 12-volt saturated circuit driver, in part because it and the matching injectors are inexpensive, simple, and reliable. The ECU delivers 12 volts to the injector to energize the coil. A relatively high resistance value associated with the saturated circuit driver (12 to 16 ohms) keeps the current flow to the injector comparatively low, which promotes long life by limiting the amount of heat generated by the coil. Conversely, saturated circuit injectors are inherently slower to respond (opening and closing cycle) compared to the peak-and-hold style. A slow response time somewhat limits the useful operating range of the injector. By comparison, a typical saturated circuit injector will take 2 milliseconds to open and close while a peak-and-hold injector will react in 1.5 milliseconds. Half a millisecond may not sound like a long time, but it is an eternity when an engine is running at 5,000 rpm.

MSD offers two quick-response saturated circuit injectors: a 12-ohm 38 lbs/hr device (part number 2018) and a 12-ohm 50 lbs/hr shooter (part number 2013). The resistance can be measured by testing the injector plug leads with a digital volt-ohm meter (DVOM). Use Ohm's Law to calculate the current delivered by the injector circuit: I = E/R, where I is amps, E is battery voltage available to the injector, and R is the injector resistance in ohms. Therefore a 12-ohm injector supplied with 12 volts (I = 12 / 12) uses one amp of current.

Peak-and-Hold Driver and Injectors

Peak-and-hold systems are also referred to as current sensing or current limiting. They are more expensive and more complex than saturated circuit drivers. As a result, peak-and-hold systems are not commonly used on domestic original-equipment applications, but instead are typically incorporated in sophisticated high-performance aftermarket management controls.

Most peak-and-hold drivers feature low 2- to 5-ohm resistance. The peak current is the amount required to quickly jolt the injector open, and the hold current rating is used to keep it open as long as the ECU commands. The kick from the higher voltage is needed to keep the fuel delivery stable when a comparatively high flow rate is called for. These drivers still deliver 12 volts, but due to the low resistance, the current flow is very high. Computing the amperage of a 2-ohm injector using Ohm's Law (I = E/R) or 12 / 2 = 6. Therefore a 2-ohm injector will draw 6 amps.

To emphasize the obvious, a saturated circuit injector cannot tolerate 6 amps of current flow. Peak-and-hold drivers also use one of two values: 4-amp peak/1-amp hold and 2-amp peak/0.5-amp hold. Even though 6 amps may be available to operate the injector, the maximum current allowed is either 2 or 4 amps, depending on the particular driver's limit. For example, MSD 2014 (72 lbs/hr, 2-ohm) and 2015 (96 lbs/hr, 2-ohm) injectors require a 4/1-amp driver.

Injector Points

A performance EFI system is only as reliable and powerful as its injectors. Elaborate electronic management systems are useless, if the injectors cannot meter the fuel delivery to a high degree of efficiency on command. MSD competition fuel injectors are engineered to meet or exceed the demands of even the most sophisticated control system. Flow rates are available to support from 250 to 1,300 horsepower.

MSD Competition Fuel Injectors

- MSD C Competition Fuel Injectors feature the following:
- Stainless-steel ball and seat metering for maximum internal sealing
- MULTEC metering design, producing superior fuel charge flow for consistent fuel delivery at any rpm
- Six-hole injector metering,

producing totally atomized and 10- to 15-degree spray pattern

- Fuel flow rates set and calibrated during manufacture to ensure precise flow rates
- Recessed deliver holes to resist clogging

Alternative Fuels

MSD competition fuel injectors are compatible with alcohol-based racing fuels. When using 100 percent methanol, the entire fuel system should be flushed with mineral spirits or gasoline after every race. Methanol residue may retain water, which will corrode any part that isn't stainless-steel. The working components inside MSD injectors will withstand long-term use, but over time alcohol fuel will cause the external O-rings to swell. It is advisable to keep an extra set of O-rings (part number 2100) on hand. Also, the comparable fuel requirement of methanol to gasoline is approximately 2 to 1, so double the injector size when determining fuel flow.

Bigger Isn't Always Better

A stock, street-driven EFI engine incorporating an O2 feedback, closed-loop control system will rarely show a performance gain simply by installing higher flowing injectors. During closed-loop operation, the ECU will try to compensate for the additional fuel in an attempt to maintain a near perfect air/fuel mixture ratio. If the injectors are not too large (approximately 10 to 20 percent larger) the stock ECU may be able to compensate.

If the airflow capabilities of the engine have not been altered (intake and exhaust systems remain stock) it is unlikely the stock ECU can pull out enough fuel to prevent an overly rich condition. At that point, unburned fuel will enter the exhaust system. Eventually the "Check Engine" light will alert the driver to the error. If the problem is left unchecked, the catalytic converter

could be damaged and/or other problems could occur.

It may be easier and more cost-effective to raise the fuel pressure to obtain a 10 to 20 percent increase in fuel flow at the injectors. The benefits of higher-flowing injectors can only be realized by increasing the airflow through the engine (i.e., upgrading the intake, cylinder head, and exhaust systems). Also, it will be necessary to install a chip or to reprogram the stock ECU to accommodate larger injectors.

Injector Balancing

Balancing or matching the flow rates of each injector in a stock application has some performance merit, but the benefits are far reaching for a high-performance engine. For these reasons, the static flow rate (wide open) for MSD competition injectors is held to a 1.5 to 3 percent tolerance variable.

Direct Replacement Injectors

Some MSD competition fuel injectors can be installed as direct-replacement injection in some factory applications. The following are a few recommendations:

PN 2010—Replaces the secondary injector on ZR-1 Corvettes

PN 2011—This is a replacement

for the GM Quad IV, 2.3-liter DOHC engine

PN 2016—A direct replacement injector for the GM 5.0-liter engine

PN 2016—Ford 5.0-liter engines, matches the stock flow rate

PN 2017—A replacement for Chevrolet 5.7-liter engines

PN 2019—Direct replacement to for earlier LT-1 engines

Increasing Fuel Pressure

MSD competition fuel injectors are flow rated with 43.5 psi of fuel pressure, but like any electronic fuel injector, they will flow more fuel at a higher system pressure. Increasing fuel pressure also creates a finer fuel spray for improved atomization and uniformity.

To obtain optimum performance, make sure that the correct injector is combined with the appropriate driver and do not increase fuel pressure above 72.5 psi (5 bar). The following chart illustrates the point. This is a pulsed test of two high-flow injectors, part number 2014 (72 lbs/hr) and part number 2015 (96 lbs/hr). Both injectors were pulsed using the correct electronic driver at an 85 percent duty cycle, which equals 10.4 milliseconds on-time.

Measurements were taken using fuel with a 0.788 specific gravity. Static flow would be higher if the injec-

---

Static Flow Driver Type Resistance

The approximate static flow rate listed in the chart assumes a 43.5 psi (3-bar) fuel pressure and a specific gravity of 0.788.

Part Number	Static Flow	Driver Type	Resistance
PN 2010	.21 lbs/hr	12V Saturated Circuit	12 Ohms
PN 2011	.26 lbs/hr	2/0.5A Peak & Hold	2 Ohms
PN 2012	.34 lbs/hr	2/0.5A Peak & Hold	2 Ohms
PN 2013	.50 lbs/hr	12V Saturated Circuit	12 Ohms
PN 2014	.72 lbs/hr	4/1A Peak & Hold	2 Ohms
PN 2015	.96 lbs/hr	4/1A Peak & Hold	2 Ohms
PN 2016	.19 lbs/hr	12V Saturated Circuit	16 Ohms
PN 2017	.22 lbs/hr	12V Saturated Circuit	16 Ohms
PN 2018	.38 lbs/hr	12V Saturated Circuit	12 Ohms
PN 2019	.24 lbs/hr	12V Saturated Circuit	12 Ohms

Static Flow Driver Type Resistance		
Fuel Pressure	PN 2014 (72 lb/hr) Pulsed Flow (lb/hr)*	PN 2015 (96 lb/hr) Pulsed Flow (lb/hr)*
30	.60	.78
40	.69	.91
50	.77	.100
60	.82	.109

* @ 10.4 milliseconds

tors are held wide open (100 percent duty cycle), meaning this data is more accurate for a real-world application using an electronic engine management control system that implements an 85 percent duty cycle.

If the static (nonpulsed) fuel flow at a given fuel pressure is known, use the formula below to compute the flow at a different pressure.

F2 = [(P2 P1)] x F1

F2 is the calculated injector static flow in pounds per hour (lbs/hr) at the adjusted fuel pressure.

P2 is the adjusted fuel pressure.

P1 is the known (rated) fuel pressure.

F1 is the static flow in lbs/hr at its rated fuel pressure (P1) in psi.

For example, an MSD 2018 injector is flow rated (static) at 38 lbs/hr at 43.5 psi. To compute the sta-tic flow at 60 psi, plug the numbers into the formula:

F2 = [(60 ÷ 43.5)] x 38

F2 = 1.1747 x 38 = 44.6 lbs/hr

Therefore, a #2018 injector will deliver 44.6 lbs/hr at 60 psi. Divide by 6 to convert pounds per hour to gallons per hour.

Additional Fuel and Boost System Components

The following products were designed for improved fuel flow performance and boost regulation on forced induction applications.

Mustang Turbo Fuel Systems by CarTech

Bell Engineering offers three high-volume fuel systems. The CarTech Stage 1 fuel system consists of a single inline fuel pump and filter, 1/2-inch ID supply line, and 3/8-inch ID return line. The Stage 2 system adds two 1/2-inch ID extruded aluminum fuel rails and a CarTech adjustable fuel regulator in place of the factory fuel rails. All other components are the same. The CarTech Stage 3 Renegade Fuel System is designed to support 1,000-plus horsepower, and includes a CarTech pickup tube and synthetic filter, two 250-liter-per- hour Renegade fuel pumps, number 8 supply line, number 6 return line, two 1/2-inch ID fuel rails, a CarTech EFI fuel regulator, a relay kit, and all the hose clamps and ends needed to install the system.

Chapter Eight
Electronic Controls

Air is easy; fuel and timing are hard. Adapting a blower to force air into an engine isn't too terribly difficult. Pipes, gear ratios, cfm, pressure variables, are all manageable. Maintaining a perfect air/fuel mixture ratio once the cylinders are filled with high-density air remains the most difficult problem for both factory and aftermarket engineers. Although self-compensating electronic controls have eliminated the need for bulky mechanical devices, keeping the air/fuel mixture perfectly calibrated to accommodate a performance modification is not easy.

Consider ignition timing, air/fuel ratio, air density, and volume on one side of a chemical equation that equals optimum power. Only the right amount of each component will promote complete combustion (extracting all of the energy stored in the air/fuel charge). The engine will still make power even if each component varies slightly, but it will be less than maximum. Timing that is advanced beyond an ever-shifting threshold causes detonation, but not enough timing constricts power. Too much fuel slows the combustion process and wastes energy; too little causes the combustion chambers to overheat. Either of these conditions will inhibit the engine's ability to generate optimum power.

Just knowing the formula isn't enough. The amount or value of each ingredient changes as the speed of the engine and atmospheric conditions change.

Dialing in just the right amount of timing and fuel for a given volume of air with a known density isn't extremely difficult if the rpm of the engine remains fixed. A steady-state dynamometer test is a perfect example where the load and rpm of the engine remain constant. While in this steady state, timing and fuel can be adjusted for optimum power because the airflow dynamics remain constant. Complications arise when the fixed values become variable. Automotive engines are dynamic in that the value of each necessary component is constantly changing. The temperature, density, and volume of the air ingested by, or forced into, the engine is also in a constant state of change. Fuel requirements vary dramatically with engine speed and load as well. In response to these changes, ignition timing and fuel delivery must vary in correct proportion, otherwise the performance potential of the engine will fall short of optimum.

Carburetors are mechanical metering devises. They react to atmospheric changes and airflow requirements to maintain an ideal air/fuel mixture ratio. Unfortunately, a carburetor's optimum performance range is somewhat limited, because the mechanical parameters remain fixed. Assuming the standard operating range of a passenger car engine is 1,000 to 6,000 rpm, a typical carburetor will deviate from an ideal air/fuel

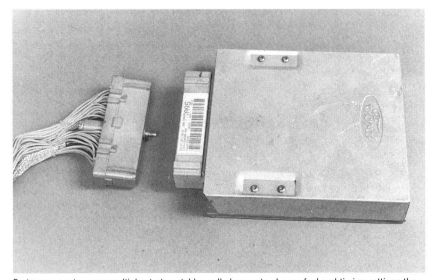

Factory computers use multiple strategy tables called maps to change fuel and timing settings thousands of times per second, but electronics designed to control a naturally aspirated engine cannot understand positive intake pressure (boost). Many OE processors can compensate for three or four pounds of boost, but, unfortunately, the factory parameters are limited.

mixture ratio at some point in that range. Usually carburetors are set up to deliver a near perfect air/fuel ratio early in the operating range, say from 1,000 to 3,000 rpm. An ideal air/fuel ratio here will produce adequate performance and maximum fuel economy because an engine typically operates in this range 80 to 90 percent of the time. A carburetor will normally overcompensate with excess fuel when a call for full power is ordered, which creates a rich fuel mixture. Allowing the mixture to go overly rich is safer than leaning the air/fuel mixture beyond acceptable limits. Mechanical limitations prevent a carburetor from "reacting" to all of the variables until or unless a person physically changes the hardware.

Computer Controls

The greatest advancement in automotive engine management in the last 20 years is the computer. Engineers use computers to engineer computerized engine controls. Original-equipment manufacturers tag their individual computer control electronics with different names such as electronic engine control (EEC) or engine management system (EMS). Industry jargon aside, it's a computer, a super- fast-thinking microprocessor that "reads" information from a group of sensors, evaluates the data in a millisecond, and then issues a series of commands to a group of actuators. The actuators perform work such as regulating the throttle bypass valve to keep the engine idling within a predetermined rpm range, or opening and closing a switch or valve. An electronic fuel injector is one example of an actuator.

The network of sensors, controls, wiring, and the microprocessor make up the electronic control system. Controlling fuel delivery and the ignition timing lead are high on the computer's priority list. The computer dictates the opening and closing cycle (pulse) of the fuel injectors, effectively regulating the air/fuel mix-

ture ratio while making minute timing adjustments thousands of times per second.

A typical Ford EEC-IV or EEC-V onboard computer will take "readings" from the following sensors and switches:

Air Conditioning Cyclic Switch
  (ACCS)
Brake On/Off (BOO)
Crankshaft Position Sensor (CKP)
Delta Pressure Feedback EGR
  Sensor (DPFE)
EGR Valve Position Sensor (EVP)
Engine Coolant Temperature
  Sensor (ECT)
Fuel Pump Monitor (FPM)
Heated Oxygen Sensor (HO2S)
Ignition Control Module (ICM)
Intake Air Temperature Sensor
  (IAT)
Knock Sensor (KS)
Barometric Pressure Sensor
  (BARO)
Mass Airflow Sensor (MAF)
Manual Lever Position Sensor
  (MLP)
Octane Adjust (OCT ADJ)
Park Neutral Position Switch
  (PPS)
Self-Test Input (STI)
Throttle Position Sensor (TPS)
Transmission Control Switch
  (TCS)
Transmission Speed Sensor (TSS)
Transmission Oil Temperature
  Sensor (TOT)
Tripminder (EVCM)
Vehicle Speed Sensor (VSS)

Electronic controls vary greatly from one manufacture to another, which means every system may not utilize all of these inputs. Most are essential, such as the heated oxygen sensor(s), the ignition control module, and the barometric pressure sensor. Some are optional or specific to a particular engine or vehicle, such as a knock sensor. Others are part of the emission control system.

Armed with the information supplied by the sensors, a Ford microprocessor makes adjustments,

then sends commands to the following actuators:

Canister Purge Solenoid (CANP)
Data Output Line (DOL)
Data Link Connector (DLC)
EGR Vacuum Regulator (EVR)
Electronic Pressure Control
  Solenoid (EPC)
Nonsequential Fuel Bank 1
  (Bank 1)
Nonsequential Fuel Bank 2
  (Bank 2)
Sequential Fuel Injector 1-8
  (INJ 1-8)
Fuel Pump (FP)
High Fan Control (HFC)
Idle Air Control Solenoid (IAC)
Low Speed Fan (LFC)
Malfunction Indicator Light
  (MIL)
Secondary Air Bypass Solenoid
  (AIRB)
Secondary Air Diverter Solenoid
  (AIRD)
Spark Output (SPOUT)
Torque Converter Clutch
  Solenoid (TCIL)
Transmission Shift Solenoid 1-4
  (SS1-4)
Wide Open Throttle A/C Cutout
  Relay (WAC)

The input data describes the current operating conditions, and the output commands make physical changes to the control system(s) or actuators. For example, the mass airflow meter tells the processor how much air the engine is consuming. The processor compares this reading to the data reported by the throttle position sensor, which measures throttle angle. All the while, the oxygen sensors are "reporting" how much oxygen (ratio) is in the exhaust. Too much oxygen in the exhaust indicates a lean air/fuel ratio; too little means the ratio is too rich. The processor does the math, then regulates fuel and timing using preprogrammed logic called a strategy. Emissions controls are also activated or deactivated as required.

The latest computers control the following engine and drivetrain functions:

Ignition timing
Fuel delivery (injector pulse width)
Secondary air injection
Automatic transmission shift points
Speed control system (integrated)
Torque converter lock-up
Transmission line pressure
Air conditioning compressor
EGR valve
Engine cooling system electric fan
Fuel pump operation
Fuel vapor recovery system
Idle rpm
Check engine light/check
    transmission light

Strategy is a preprogrammed list of choices the microprocessor uses to "make decisions." Humans determine a course of action based on logic, common sense, and experience. A computer uses programming (i.e., all of the logical choices must be programmed into memory in advance). The computer then follows a predetermined course of action based on the values provided by the sensors. If the reading from sensor A is 1 and the reading from sensor B is 2, then the command to actuator C must be 3.

The "basic engine strategy" is based on normal inputs and outputs, including extreme operating conditions, such as extreme ambient temperatures. Adaptive strategies allow the processor to learn certain variable conditions, commit them to memory, and then use them to become more proficient. To over-simplify an example, if readings from sensors A, B, and C are within a predictable range, the processor will "read" maps A1, B1, and C1. If, however, readings from sensor A remain consistently high, the processor may substitute map A2 in place of A1.

Programming can also include strategies that can prevent unnecessary damage if something goes wrong. A failure, or what the processor per-

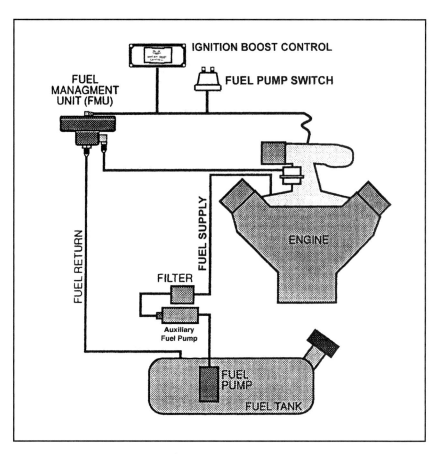

An ignition boost control retards the timing lead in small increments while the fuel pump switch, sometimes called a Hobbs switch, activates the auxiliary fuel pump(s) as boost pressure increases. Calibrating and synchronizing all of the components that make up a forced induction system is essential–and sometimes difficult. *Vortech*

ceives as a failure, prompts the best example of a strategy beyond the basic engine strategy.

When everything is operating normally, all the input and output data falls within set parameters. If something goes wrong—for example, a sensor might die or a connection might be broken—the processor diverts to an "operator notification of failure" strategy, which turns on the malfunction indicator light (MIL), better known as the "check engine" light. A trouble code indicating the cause of the problem is then stored in the keep-alive memory (KAM). A technician can extract and erase the trouble code using a scan tool. When the problem has been repaired and the computer is happy, the check engine light remains off.

If the failure has the potential to cause engine damage, the processor is programmed to engage the "failure mode effects management " or FMEM strategy. Let's say the coolant temperature sensor dies. The check engine light comes on, alerting the driver to a problem. FMEM then substitutes a value for the coolant temperature based on intake air temperature and how long the engine has been running. Functions that depend on an accurate coolant temperature reading will run in a default mode. In our example, the computer will run the electric cooling fan on high to ensure that the engine doesn't overheat. In short, FMEM allows the engine to operate satisfactorily in spite of a minor failure and it will take steps to prevent damage to the engine. The glowing check engine light tells the operator things aren't quite right but because the engine continues to run satisfactorily, the problem is not serious.

In the case of a serious electronic failure, which is something known to cause damage, the "hardware-limited operating strategy," or HLOS, kicks in. In an effort to prevent or limit damage, HLOS severely restricts operation by imposing default values. Ignition timing is fixed at 10 degrees advanced, and fuel delivery is restricted to a safe value. At that point the engine will run badly and peak rpm will be limited as long as HLOS is in control, but it will continue to run. In other words, better start looking for a service center, because your fun is done until the problem has been repaired. HLOS is commonly called, for obvious reasons, limp-home mode.

The severity of the failure and its potential to cause engine damage is compared to hundreds of programmed scenarios. From there, the processor will implement a failure strategy to protect the engine. Before OBD-II, emissions system components were included in these strategies only if their failure could cause engine damage. OBD-II now takes failure strategies to the next level of control by including all emissions equipment, its operation, and its efficiency.

As monitoring systems go, OBD-II has a lot of power. As long as emissions levels are within specifications, OBD-II is happy and the vehicle runs fine. OBD-II will turn on the MIL and store a code in the KAM on the second drive cycle if any malfunction causes emissions to exceed one-and-a-half times the allowable standard. OBD-II can also trigger FMEM and HLOS strategies if necessary. "Any malfunction" means if a key sensor fails or is disconnected, the air/fuel ratio runs too lean or too rich or any emissions component, or the system fails to operate up to a predetermined minimum standard.

Hypertech's power modules implement reprogrammed air/fuel ratio and spark advance values, in addition to a number of electronic driveline enhancements. A dual tuning module can switch between two optimized strategies: The Street Runner power chip for naturally aspirated conditions and the nitrous chip when nitrous oxide is injected.

The efficient operation of these computer-controlled functions defines "drivability." Incorporating all of these components and systems makes computer-controlled cars far superior compared to the carbureted cars of yesterday. Implementing computers was paramount. Today an EEC will run an engine efficiently whether the car is driving across the Rocky Mountains in December or through the Mojave Desert in August.

Computer-Perceived Modifications

Before OBD-II, aftermarket programmers and chip manufacturers expanded the versatility and adaptability of electronic engine controls to near omnipotence. Today, programmers must learn how to work within the parameters of OBD-II. Because OBD-II monitors the operation *and* efficiency of all the emission systems, the quality of the exhaust will soon become a primary consideration when planning any performance modification.

Adding forced induction further complicates the issue, because unless the vehicle was so equipped by the factory, the onboard computer only understands natural aspiration. Information contained in the strategy maps can relate only to negative pressure (vacuum) in the intake manifold. The ability to understand positive pressure in the intake manifold is not included in the programming. Further, fuel delivery, that is, the computer's ability to regulate the air/fuel ratio, is designed to accommodate stock airflow values. The computer doesn't understand mass air (density) values above stock operating conditions. In short, factory processors do not have the ability to learn, or adapt to, radical performance modifications.

Some computers tolerate forced induction better than others. Generally, speed density systems are more tolerant than mass air systems. Speed density does not use a mass airflow meter to measure the amount of air entering the engine. Fuel management is a function of throttle angle, ambient conditions, normal operating temperatures, rpm, and feedback from the oxygen sensor(s). If the air/fuel mixture ratio remains within acceptable tolerances, the oxygen sensor will respond with a normal signal. In other words, the volume of air/fuel mixture flowing through the engine is a nonissue.

Comparatively, mass air meters have a somewhat limited range of operation and forced induction constitutes a radical change. Some mass air systems can accept forced induction better than others. It depends on the range of flexibility built into the stock computer. Further, converting a mass air setup to speed density is possible, but not recommended because it violates federal emissions laws.

Instrumentation for
Air/Fuel Mixture Measurement

Immersed in the depths of irony, a typical owner of a high-performance engine shop will likely choose to purchase a $5,000 tool chest over a high-quality air/fuel ratio meter. However, justification for such an expense contradicts sound economic theory because, although a two-story tool chest looks impressive, it cannot be used to make money. It can only provide housing for the productive tools.

Needless to say, a potential customer should not be impressed by the size of a mechanic's toolbox. An optimum level of performance is far more important. For that reason alone, an accomplished tuner will own a precision air/fuel ratio meter and perhaps a smaller, older toolbox.

An air/fuel ratio meter can deliver invaluable information that might otherwise remain elusive. One- or two-tenths of an air/fuel mixture ratio point can mean the difference between using or wasting energy. The definition of "complete combustion" includes extracting 100 percent of the energy contained in every molecule of fuel. Obtaining and maintaining complete combustion can only be accomplished when a near-perfect amount of air and fuel are present in the cylinders at the

same time. Anything less will not generate optimum performance.

Reading spark plugs to assess the air fuel mixture is both antiquated and imprecise. Giving a lifelong reader his due, it's better than no reading at all, and one experienced at detecting subtle changes will likely win more races than a nonreader. Viewed from a realistic level of perspective, reading spark plugs can narrow the search to the correct city and perhaps the right ballpark, but beyond that, optimum changes in calibration rely more on an educated guess than applied science.

ETAS

ETAS, Inc., an electronics manufacturer in Ann Arbor, Michigan, markets a line of affordable, precision air/fuel ratio instruments. Close examination of ETAS instruments will better explain why an efficient air/fuel meter is not only convenient, but necessary.

ETAS Inc., originally developed an affordable AWS signal-conditioning unit that uses a BOSCH LSU wide-band lambda sensor to accurately measure air/fuel ratios in SI engines. It is compact, simple to operate, and can be used as a full-time onboard monitor or a dynamometer test instrument. The 1.5x3x6 inch instrument weighs 1.3 pounds. An optimized analog PID temperature control ensures that the LSU sensor reaches operational temperature rapidly and also helps deter damage during extreme variations in exhaust temperatures. The AWS 0-5V real-time analog output can be connected to an external data acquisition unit for recording purposes. The gasoline air/fuel ratio measurement range is 11.0 to air with a +/- 2% tolerance factor. Maximum continuous exhaust operating temperature is 1,560 degrees Fahrenheit.

The ETAS LA 3 is an independent measuring unit used to determine lambda, air/fuel-ratio, or oxygen, when combined with a Bosch

LSU broadband lambda sensor. LSU is a planar two-cell marginal current sensor that will accommodate multiple functions through a modular structure. The LSU sensor combines a Nernst-concentration cell (sensor cell) with a pump cell that transfers oxygen ions. It not only measures the exact stoichiometric ratio point ($\lambda = 1$), but also provides leaner and richer mixture ranges. Every LA 3 meter is adjusted separately for the LSU sensor. Special operation electronics are implemented in the lambda meter for this purpose. Internal electronics convert signals from the pump and sensor cell and control the electronics used to regulate the temperature of the sensor. Data can be transferred to an IBM-compatible PC on demand via a 24V serial measurement bus (SMB). LA 3 will also accommodate multiple applications through the same SMB interface.

Display and adjustments are managed with the VS100 measurement program VSI or INCA software (updates can be downloaded from the ETAS Web site). A single interface can be set to monitor up to 16 units at one time. Because measurement data is permanently displayed, an SMB unit can also be used as a standalone device. A fixed keypad allows the user to set all default parameters, including switching the display from λ to O2, manipulating the character lines, or adjusting the low-pass filter. The deviation of $\lambda = 1$ is stabilized by a compensating measurement process.

Pump current is a product of absolute value and magnitude. A digital PID controller guarantees a constant sensor temperature. The measured values (λ, O2 or A/F) are permanently displayed and can be accessed by a scaleable analog output. The values are transmitted via the integrated serial interface (SMB) to an IBM-compatible PC on demand. Additional A/D-channels or thermoscans can be cascaded and run through one interface using settable device numbers. Key features include the following:

- Wide range of measurement for lambda, oxygen, and air/fuel-ratio
- Short measurement system settling time
- Self-calibrating on power up
- Digital low-pass filter of the first order can be adjusted separately for SMB interface
- LC display or analog output
- Three lambda characteristic maps (in front of/after catalytic converter, user-defined)
- Two heating characteristic maps for sensor (default or user-defined)
- Characteristic lines can be switched (in front of/after catalytic converter)
- Analog output of physical value (scaleable)
- Optimized sensor heating control
- High temperature range of exhaust gas
- Online display via integrated LC display
- Configuration via keypad
- Formware and characteristic line update using a PC
- VS100 software VSI integrated measurement is supported
- VSG graphical evaluation of measurement data
- INCA software measurement and adjustment program.

LA 2 is a standalone device engineered to measure lambda using an LSM11 Bosch lambda sensor. LA 2 can be connected to a PC via a 24V serial bus as well. Once the temperature of the sensor ceramics is factored in, the lambda value is calculated from the sensor voltage. Real-time lambda values are continuously shown on the backlit display and can be transmitted to an analog output. Data can be displayed and stored using the VS100 measurement program or INCA measurement and calibration software. The LA 2's range of functionality includes the following:

ETAS LA 3 Technical Data	
Designation:	**Characteristics:**
Dimension:	120-mm W x 55-mm D x 60 mmH
Voltage supply	
Input voltage	6 to 36 V DC polesafe
Input current max.	600 mA for 12 V
CPU board	
CPU	68332 Motorola
RAM	256 Kbyte
Flash-EPROM	256 Kbyte
Sensor heating	
Input voltage	6 to 36 V DC polesafe
Input current max.	5 A
Heating	Integrated heating control via digital PID controller
Inputs	Lambda Sensor LSU
Measuring tolerance ± 1.5 % (depending on sensor)	
Measuring range Lambda	
Air/fuel-ratio	0.7 to 32.0
	0 to 22%
	10.2 to air
Settling time	2 ms cycle time
Outputs	
Analog output	0 to 8.2V (scaleable). Short-circuit safe and external voltage safe up to 40 V.
Internal resistance	2 Kohm
Serial interface	Cascadable with other units via a V24 (RS232), 38400 baud serial bus (max. 16 units)
User interface	
Display	8-digit backlit LCD with contrast adjustment, external display available as an option
Keypad	For configuration of basic adjustments
Environment	
Temperature range -40 to +80°C (display -25 to + 75°C)	

- Measurement range from 0.75 < (<1.65 with a Bosch LSM11 Sensor
- Analog output of the physical value
- Sensor heating control via AC internal resistance of the (-sensor
- High exhaust fume temperature range
- Measurement tolerance of from ±2.5% to ±4.5%, depending on area
- Online display on integrated LCD display
- Up to 16 cascadable SMB units
- 12V power supply can be passed-through via SMB cable
- SMB interface (V24)
- INCA measurement and configuration program
- VS100 Software
- VSI for integrated measurement

- VSG graphical evaluation of measured data

HKS

Japanese automotive engineers Hasegawa, Kitagawa, and Sigma launched an aftermarket company (appropriately called HKS) that manufacturers and distributes electronic controls and pressure valves designed specifically to add control to an otherwise unruly turbocharger system. Import turbocar enthusiasts the world over turn to HKS in search of power, stability, and durability. Many devices are application-specific, while others could be adapted to any turbocharged vehicle.

Vein Pressure Converter

Factory mass airflow meters are difficult to reprogram and can restrict airflow to the turbocharger. A number of aftermarket supercharger and turbocharger kit manufacturers recommend eliminating the device entirely. HKS markets a popular unit called a vein pressure converter or VPC, which converts both airflow meter and air mass sensor systems to a speed density system. The VPC's 16-bit central processing unit reads its own intake air temperature sensor and absolute pressure transducer (B-MAP sensor) signals and subsequently supplies the engine management computer with adaptive values. In addition to replacing the factory airflow metering device, in some cases it can also override the factory maximum boost fuel cutoff feature. HKS's VPC also has the ability to create programs to take advantage of larger fuel injectors and high-output turbochargers.

The pressure sensor should be mounted slightly higher than the throttle body with the fitting facing down. Mount the sensor and the air filter away from water and high temperatures. The 4-millimeter hose should be kept as short as possible and the inline air filter should be placed no more than 2 inches from the pressure sensor. If there is only one pressure source on the intake manifold after the throttle body, use a 4-millimeter tee to splice into the line, making sure the other side does not relieve the pressure. If there are two sources in the intake manifold, use one for the pressure sensor and tee the line you remove into the other source.

If possible, mount the air temperature sensor fitting into the intake manifold after the throttle body. If this is not possible, drill a hole and use a 1/8-inch NP tap to create a port just

ETAS LA 2 Technical Data

Designation:	Characteristics:
LA 2 Dimensions	115 mm W x 155 mm D x 60 mm H
Power supply	
Input voltage	9 to 20 V DC pole-safe
Input current max.	400 mA
λ-sensor heating	
Input voltage	9 to 15 V pole-safe
Input current max.	8 A
Heating	Integrated heating control via AC internal resistance of the λ-sensor
Input	
Measurement tolerance ranges $\lambda < 1$	
U = 14.5 V and exhaust fume temperature 300 to 700 °C	
$\Delta\lambda = \pm 2.5$ % (sensor-dependent)	
$\lambda = 1$	$\Delta\lambda = -2$ % to + 1 % (sensor-dependent)
$1 < \lambda < 1.3$	$\Delta\lambda = -4$ % to + 2.5 % (sensor-dependent)
$1.3 < \lambda < 1.65$	$\Delta\lambda = \pm 4.5$ % (sensor-dependent)
Output	
Analog output	0-75-1.65 V = value 0.75-1.65. Short circuit proof and external voltage-safe up to 30 V. Internal resistance 2 KOhm
Serial interface	V24 (RS232), 38400, Cascadable with additional units (max. 16 units)
Display	3-digit backlit LCD display with adjustable contrast
Environmental conditions	
Temperature range	−25 to +80 °C (Display 0 to +75 °C)

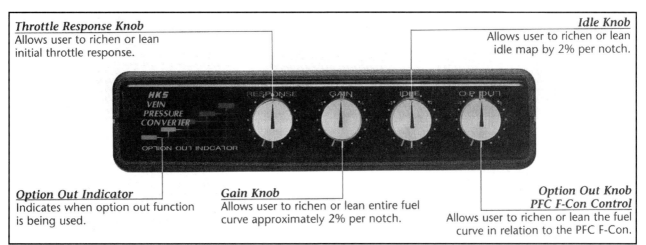

Throttle Response Knob
Allows user to richen or lean initial throttle response.

Idle Knob
Allows user to richen or lean idle map by 2% per notch.

Option Out Indicator
Indicates when option out function is being used.

Gain Knob
Allows user to richen or lean entire fuel curve approximately 2% per notch.

Option Out Knob
PFC F-Con Control
Allows user to richen or lean the fuel curve in relation to the PFC F-Con.

Vain pressure converter (VPC) built by HKS.

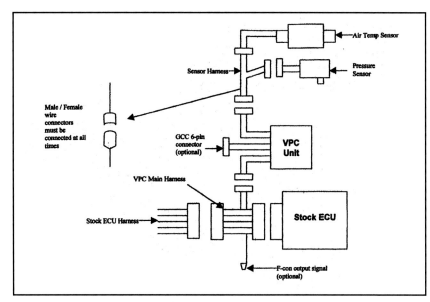

Wiring schematic illustrates how a VPC interacts with the stock system. *HKS*

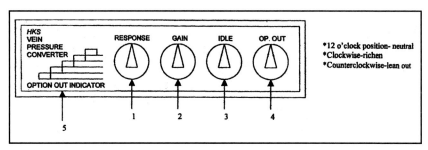

Calibration instructions for a VPC begin here. *HKS*

before the throttle body. Do not mount the air temp sensor after the cold start injector or an A/C controlled injector. Connect the air temperature sensor harness to the air temperature sensor and run the harness through the firewall to the F-con harness mounting location.

Locate the stock ECU using the factory repair manual, then install the main VPC harness between the ECU and the ECU harness. Mount the VPC control unit in the desired location, utilizing the mounting bracket supplied with the kit. Connect the main VPC and sensor harness to the VPC control unit. Make sure the wire with the male/female connector on the sensor harness is connected at all times.

Set all knobs set at the 12 o'clock position to center baseline values.

Rotating the Response knob clockwise will increase fuel delivery; counterclockwise rotation will decrease fuel delivery. Overcompensation toward increased fuel delivery will cause the VPC to be more sensitive to on-and-off throttle situations, which can cause the engine to hesitate. Rotating the gain knob will change the VPC output voltage (lean or rich) through the rpm band. Each notch is a 2 percent adjustment lean or rich. Overcompensating toward rich (clockwise) may cause fuel cutoff and/or hesitation. Adjusting the idle control knob will change the air fuel mixture below 1,300 rpm.

The option out knob is used to control an F-Con unit, assuming one is available for the application. Each notch represents a 2 percent adjust-

ment, lean or rich. The option out wire on the VPC harness goes to the number 17 position on the F-Con harness (see diagram). If a VPC is used in conjunction with a GCC (graph control computer) and an F-Con, disconnect the GCC from the F-Con and connect it directly to the VPC control unit using the 8-pin connector.

The GCC can control the VPC output voltage by each rpm value displayed. If the GCC is turned too far clockwise (rich), fuel cutoff may occur. The first LED on the Option Out Indicator will light up red to show the VPC unit is operating. Each LED will light up red to indicate a 10 percent increase in fuel added to the F-Con. The VPC reads boost pressure through the factory ECU and decides how much fuel the F-Con should add. The LED indicator light will be on whether or not an F-Con is connected.

Vein pressure converters are available for a number of import and domestic vehicles. A 49-state notation means the kit has been certified for use on emission control vehicles in all states except California for that particular application. A California kit is legal in all 50 states.

Programmed Fuel Computer Management System

A programmed fuel computer management system (PFC F-CON) includes a plug-in fuel management device designed to refine the air/fuel mixture ratio of a turbocharged engine. F-Con optimizes the factory injector pulse width signal by intercepting, and then recalibrating, the original settings dictated by the original-equipment manufacturer's engine control unit (ECU). The modified signal provides a longer pulse width for factory injectors or a shorter pulse width for larger aftermarket injectors. The system ensures an ideal air/fuel ratio during high-boost conditions. Certain PFC F-Con kits include a fuel cut defenser (FCD) to override the

HKS Vain Pressure Converter Application Chart

		ROM
DODGE / EAGLE		
4601-M07US	Stealth R/T w/Stk Inj & InTank F'Pump 90-93 Calif	Z11AT18B
4601-M08US	Stealth R/T w/Stk Inj & InTank F'Pump 90-93 49 St	Z114918C
4601-M09US	Stealth R/T w/550 Inj & InTank F'Pump 90-93 Calif	Z11AT18D
4601-M10US	Stealth R/T w/550 Inj & InTank F'Pump 90-93 49 St	Z114918D
4601-M11US	Talon 5-Speed w/Stock Injectors 95-98	D33WINA
4601-M12US	Talon 5-Spd w/Stk Inj, Sport Trbo & Bosch F'Pump 95-98	D33AT18B
4601-M01US	Talon w/Stock Injectors 89-94 Calif	D136T
4601-M02US	Talon w/Stock Injectors 89-94 49 State	D138
4601-M03US	Talon w/Stk Injectors & Bosch F'Pump 89-94 Calif	D27AT18A
4601-M04US	Talon w/Stk Inj & In-Tank F'Pump 89-94 Calif	D27AT18B
4601-M05US	Talon w/550 Inj & Bosch Fuel Pump 89-94 Calif	D135BT1
4601-M06US	Talon w/550 Inj & Bosch F'Pump 89-94 49 State	D137B3
MAZDA		
4601-Z01US	Miata w/ Stock Cams 90-93 (Requires F-Con)	NA35N18A
4601-Z02US	Miata w/ HKS Cams 90-93 (Requires F-Con)	NA35N18B
MITSUBISHI		
4601-M11US	Eclipse 5-Spd w/Stock Injectors 95-98	D33WINA
4601-M12US	Eclipse 5-Spd w/Stk Inj, Sport Trbo & Bosch Fuel Pump 95-98	D33AT18B
4601-M01US	Eclipse w/Stock Injectors 89-94 Calif	D136T
4601-M02US	Eclipse w/Stock Injectors 89-94 49 State	D138
4601-M03US	Eclipse w/Stk Inj & Bosch F'Pump 89-94 Calif	D27AT18A
4601-M04US	Eclipse w/Stk Inj & In-Tank F'Pump 89-94 Calif	D27AT18B
4601-M05US	Eclipse w/550 Inj & Bosch Fuel Pump 89-94 Calif	D135BT1
4601-M06US	Eclipse w/550 Inj & Bosch F'Pump 89-94 49 State	D137B3
4601-M07US	3000GT w/Stk Inj & In-Tank F'Pump 90-93 Calif	Z11AT18B
4601-M08US	3000GT w/Stk Inj & In-Tank F'Pump 90-93 49 State	Z114918C
4601-M09US	3000GT w/550 Inj & In-Tank F'Pump 90-93 Calif	Z11AT18D
4601-M10US	3000GT w/550 Inj & In-Tank F'Pump 90-93 49 State	Z114918D
NISSAN		
4601-N01US	300ZXTT w/Stock Injectors 90-96	Z32T217
4601-N02US	300ZXTT w/485 Injectors 90-96	Z32T27B
4601-N03US	300ZX Non-Turbo w/Stock Injectors 90-96	Z32NA18A
DODGE / EAGLE / PLYMOUTH		
4201-M001US	Conquest 84-86 Non-Intercooled	ES40
4201-M005US	Laser 89-94 w/Stock Injectors	E177
4201-M005US	Talon 89-94 w/Stock Injectors	E177
MAZDA		
4201-Z010US	Miata 90-93 W/Stock Injectors	ES94
4201-Z009US	Miata 90-93 w/VPC	E104V
4201-Z003US	RX7 Twin Turbo 93-95 w/HKS Exhst, SMF & EVC	FD3VN1
4201-Z013US	RX7 TT 93-95 w/In-Tank F/P, Full Turbo & I/C	FD3VS2
4201-Z002US	RX7 Turbo II 89-91	E149
4201-Z012US	RX7 Turbo II 89-91 w/Sport Turbo	E1102
4201-Z001US	RX7 Turbo II 86-88	E149
4201-Z011US	RX7 Turbo II 86-88 w/Sport Turbo	E190
4201-Z005US	323GT & 323GTX 88-89	E569
4201-Z004US	626GT 86-87	E548
MITSUBISHI		
4201-M005US	Eclipse 89-94 w/Stock Injectors	E177
4201-M004US	Mirage 85-86	E348
4201-M009US	Starion 88-89	E540
4201-M008US	Starion ES / ESIR 85-86 w/Intercooler	E540
4201-M001US	Starion ES / LE 84-86	E540
NISSAN		
4201-N001US	300ZX Turbo 84-89	E405
TOYOTA		
4201-T006US	Supra Turbo 86.5-88 w./Stock Injectors	E155
4201-T007US	Supra Turbo 86.5-88 w/550 Injectors	E164
4201-T013US	Supra Turbo 86.5-88 w/550 Injectors & VPC	E105V
4201-T008US	Supra Turbo 89-92 w/Stock Injectors	E155
4201-T009US	Supra Turbo 89-92 w/550 Injectors	E164
4201-T014US	Supra Turbo 89-92 w/550 Injectors & VPC	E105V
4201-T010US	Celica All-Trac 88-89	E148

factory high-boost fuel cut-off threshold. Fuel delivery may be adversely affected if a FCD is used without an F-Con or similar type of supplemental fuel system.

Install the PFC F-Con by simply sandwiching the intercept harness in between the factory wiring harness and the ECU, and then connect the pressure sensor. Reconnect the factory harness to the ECU to return to the stock configuration. An interchangeable ROM chip allows the F-Con to be programmed for a number of specific applications. Adding a mixture controller or graphic control computer (GCC) will provide additional tuning.

Turbo Timer

A turbo timer extends turbocharger life by allowing the engine to idle for a preset amount of time after the ignition key has been turned "off." Keeping the engine idling for a short time allows engine oil and coolant to cool the turbine, shaft, bearing, and impeller. If the turbo is not allowed to cool down, burnt oil will adhere to the bearing and shaft. The process is called "coking." Coking is the number-one cause of bearing failure. HKS engineered the first commercially available turbo timer in the early 1980s.

Turbo timers can be hard wired (cut and splice) or connected with an application-specific, plug-in wiring harness. The unit uses and/or interrupts the battery, accessory, ignition, start, and parking brake light circuits. When activated, the unit will keep the engine running for up to 9.99 minutes after the ignition has been turned off and the key removed. It will be necessary to modify some factory-installed alarm systems to accommodate the timer. The unit is also equipped with a safety circuit that is activated with the parking brake. A turbo timer can be installed and/or adapted to fit on any gasoline or diesel application without legal limitations.

A quick-installation harness provides plug-in-play simplicity. The triple-plug installation harness plugs into the factory harness and the turbo timer pigtail. Only the safety wire requires a splice.

Currently, HKS quick-installation harnesses are available for 28 import and domestic applications. Clean air laws do not govern turbo timers because they do not change the emission output of a vehicle. They simply keep the engine running for a short period of time to allow the water and turbocharger temperatures to stabilize before total shutdown.

Electronic Valve Controller IV

It is necessary to control boost levels in order to achieve optimum performance from a turbocharger. An electronic valve controller IV (EVC IV) Part #4503-RA006, adds electronic precision to an otherwise mechanical wastegate system. EVC IV is a microprocessor that provides immediate push-button selection of preset boost levels. To return to factory boost settings, simply switch the EVC unit off. All adjustments are accessible from the passenger compartment of the vehicle and can be changed on the fly. Fuzzy logic gives the EVC the ability to learn the vehicle's boost pressure curve. This learning feature reduces turbo lag without overboosting. Essentially, an HKS EVC allows the driver to "dial up" the vehicle's maximum performance potential.

The EVC IV is the fourth-generation of the first electronic boost controller sold for passenger vehicles, and can be used on both internal and external wastegates. EVC IV is not capable of reaching boost levels lower than stock and will maintain its programming even if the vehicle's battery is disconnected or the unit is unplugged. Most factory-turbocharged vehicles are equipped with a secondary boost limiting system (fuel cut-off system or pop-off valve) to safeguard against wastegate failure.

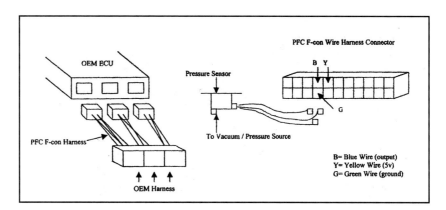

PFC F-Con wiring diagram. *HKS*

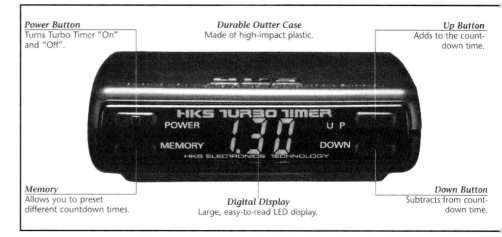

HKS turbo timer. *HKS*

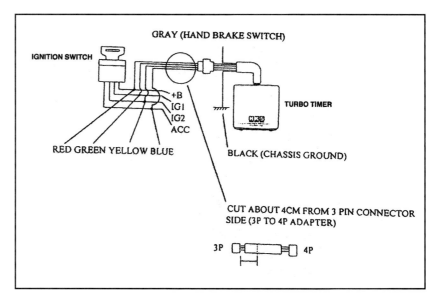

Turbo timer wiring diagram. *HKS*

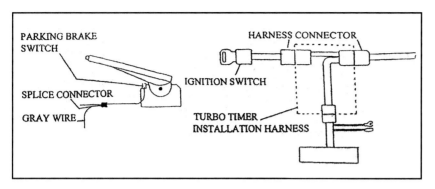

Turbo timer installation harness. *HKS*

DODGE / EAGLE / PLYMOUTH	
4103-RM001	Colt 85-88
4103-RM001	Conquest 83-89
4103-RM001	Laser 89-93
4103-RM001	Stealth R/T 90-96
4103-RM001A	Talon 95-98
4103-RM001	Talon 89-94
FORD	
4103-RZ001	Probe GT 88-92
MAZDA	
4103-RZ001	MX6 GT 88-92
4103-RZ002	RX7 Twin Turbo 93-96
4103-RZ001	RX7 87-91
4103-RZ001	323 GT & 323 GTX 88-89
MITSUBISHI	
4103-RM001A	Eclipse 95-98
4103-RM001	Eclipse 95-98
4103-RM001	Galant VR4 91-92
4103-RM001	Mirage 85-88
4103-RM001	Starion 83-89
4103-RM001	3000GT VR4 90-98
NISSAN	
4103-RN001	200SX 84-88
4103-RN001	280ZX 81-83 (Adapter Required)
4104-RA001	Adapter for 280ZX 81-83
74109-025100	300ZX TT 90-96
TOYOTA	
4103-RT003	Celica All-Trac 90-93
4103-RT001	Celica All-Trac 88-89
4103-RT003	MR2 91-95
4103-RT007	Supra TT 97-98
4103-RT004	Supra TT 93-96
4103-RT003	Supra 91-92
4103-RT001	Turbo Truck 86-88
MISCELLANEOUS	
4104-RA004	3-pin to 4-pin connector

Turbo timer installation harness application chart. *HKS*

EVC IV will not raise boost pressures beyond the factory limit. If the vehicle is equipped with a fuel cut defense system, excessive boost pressures may cause engine and/or turbocharger damage. Additionally, no electronic device can control boost pressures above the maximum efficiency point of the turbocharger; therefore, boost pressure drop at high rpm may not be totally eliminated. In addition, a boost pressure device will not compensate for pressure loss due to improper turbocharger sizing, nor will it prevent boost creep or boost spikes due to inadequate wastegate flow capacity, lean air/fuel ratio, or poor compressor design. Excessive back pressure may not be eliminated. The EVC IV monitors pressure on the discharge side of the compressor and the intake manifold. Electronic Valve Controller EZ (EVC EZ) Part #4503-RA008 is an economical version of EVC IV.

Fuel Cut Defencer

An HKS fuel cut defencer (FCD) is an electronic device that overrides the high-boost fuel cut-off function imposed by the factory. The FCD will widen the area of high boost, allowing a turbocharged engine to attain much higher boost settings. Installation requires a simple hard wire splice into either the VPC/F-Con or factory ECU harness. Be advised, this product bypasses the factory safeguards that would otherwise prevent excessive boost levels. Under these conditions, it is possible to damage the turbocharger, the engine, and the drivetrain.

HKS strongly recommends installing a supplemental fuel enrichment system to prevent a lean fuel condition. Current applications include the following: Mazda RX7 Twin Turbo manufactured November 1991 and up; Mazda RX7 Turbo manufactured from March 1989 to October 1991; Mazda RX7 Turbo manufactured from September 1985 to February 1989; Mitsubishi Eclipse/Eagle Talon/Chrysler Laser manufactured from October 1989 through 1994; Mitsubishi Starion ES/Plymouth Conquest 1983-1986; Mitsubishi Mirage 1985–1986; Mitsubishi Starion ESI/ESIR/Plymouth Conquest TSI 1985–1986; Nissan 300ZX Twin Turbo 1990–1996; Nissan 300ZX Turbo 1984–1988; Toyota MR2 Turbo manufactured December 1991 and up; Toyota Celica Turbo manufactured from September 1989 to August 1991; Toyota MR2 Turbo manufactured from October 1989 to 1991; Toyota Celica Turbo manufactured from September 1989 to July 1991; Toyota Celica Turbo manufactured from October 1986 to September 1989; Toyota Supra Twin Turbo 1993 and up; Toyota Supra Turbo manufactured from January 1988 through 1992; and Toyota Supra Turbo manufactured from January 1986 to December 1987.

Air Fuel Ratio Regulator

As the name implies, an air/fuel ratio regulator (AFR) regulates the air/fuel mixture ratio. It alters calibration by changing the airflow voltage output to the vehicle's factory computer. This particular device was designed for lightly modified vehicles requiring only slight fuel adjustments. The 12-setting dial indicator allows the user to make the air/fuel mixture richer or leaner by approximately one ratio point (total) in either direction. Each notch on the dial will adjust the A/R by approximately 0.2 of a ratio point. This enables the user to dial in the best possible mixture.

HKS offers two AFR units, each identified by the type of factory air metering system. The D-Type AFR is designed to work with vehicles utilizing a pressure sensor (D-Jetro) that is measured by speed density. The L-Type AFR is designed for vehicles with an airflow meter with voltage readings measuring from low to high (hot wire type). These systems control

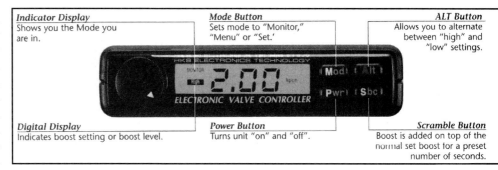

Electronic valve controller IV (EVC-IV) engineered by HKS, Inc. *HKS*

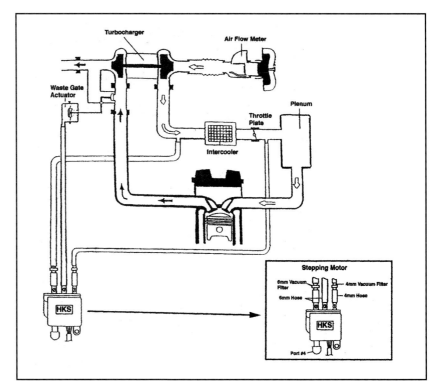

EVC-IV block diagram. *HKS*

input signals to the vehicle's ECU to increase or decrease the air/fuel ratio. As with any device that adjusts the air/fuel mixture, overcompensation toward the lean (negative) side of the ratio can cause engine failure. Current applications include the following:
• Honda/Acura–NSX/Accord/ Vigor/Prelude/Integra/Civic/ Legend;
• Mazda—RX7; Mitsubishi/
• Dodge—3000GT VR4/ Stealth RT/Eclipse/Talon/ Galant VR4/Mirage/Starion;
• Nissan—300ZX TwinTurbo/

Sentra/NXCoupe/300ZX/ 300ZX Turbo;
• Toyota—Supra/MR2/Celica/ Camry/Corolla.

Graphic Control Computer

HKS' graphic control computer is designed to add flexibility to the VPC and PFC F-Con. GCC allows the tuner to alter the programmed fuel curve by adjusting the fuel pulse duration at a specific rpm. Five intervals of adjustment provide up to 16 percent fuel enrichment or 12 percent fuel deprivation in four different rpm

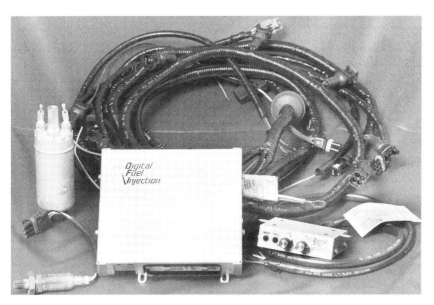
Fully programmable DFI computer, wiring harness, and sensors.

ranges. The GCC will interpolate or average between points of adjustment to ensure smooth fuel delivery. LEDs indicate whether the fuel mixture is in fact being altered by the GCC. The unit can also be used to adjust the fuel mixture under boost conditions when used in conjunction with an F-Con. GCC plugs into either the VPC or PFC F-Con harness.

Programmed for Performance

Factory production electronic engine management systems are extremely efficient, but from a performance point of view, they offer limited expandability. Most cannot be upgraded, reprogrammed, or modified internally. Programming codes are locked in nonremovable ROM chips. Sheets of data called maps can be overlaid many times, making reverse engineering, the art of decoding electronic code, extremely difficult and time consuming.

We know mechanical performance modifications increase the air and fuel flow through the engine. If the increase falls within the preset parameters that the factory computer can understand, then and chances are good it can handle the job. If the increases exceed the factory threshold,

the computer will interpret the change in air and fuel as a problem and retreat to a safe mode.

Correcting or amending these electronic miscommunications is a monumental problem. Companies that manufacturer high-performance electronic parts such as chips, piggyback processors, and programmable tuning devices make a living addressing these problems. Typically, these devices are designed to work in conjunction with the stock processor and are considered electronic patches for a self-imposed problem.

Replacing the stock computer with a fully programmable computer presents the only true ideal solution. Fully programmable engine control computers allow the tuner full latitude to calibrate fuel delivery and timing lead at any and all rpm points. Sophisticated systems will accept hundreds of program entries, ranging from cold-start fuel enrichment to off-idle timing retard under boost.

Stand-alone, fully programmable computers exist, but they also present legal problems for drivers who want more performance from their licensed, street-legal car, truck, or SUV. Factory engine management computers are certified by the government as part of

the drivetrain package—the engine, transmission, rear axle ratio, and tire size. The central processor is an intricate part of that system, because it controls the two main factors that dictate economy, performance, and emissions—the air/fuel mixture ratio and ignition timing lead. Even though aftermarket programmable computers can equal a factory computer in these two areas, none as yet have been certified, and it is doubtful any will ever be legalized for use on a pollution-controlled vehicle. The reason is simple. The government considers emission compliance top priority, while typical performance enthusiasts will likely place horsepower first on their list of needs. Quite simply, the government does not want to leave those choices up to the average consumer.

In other words, an aftermarket computer's main asset is also its downfall—full programmability. Unfortunately, because there are no preset limits, a turner can program an aftermarket computer to deliver optimum performance at the expense of economy and emissions output. So until or unless an aftermarket computer manufacturer can satisfy both the government and the performance enthusiast, fully programmable processors will remain "off-road only."

ACCEL's digital fuel injection (DFI) is a prime example of a non-street-legal, stand-alone, fully programmable engine control system. DFI's claim to fame is flexible performance programming covering all parameters and engine speeds. The system can be adapted to almost any multicylinder engine, providing a suitable throttle control is utilized. The base computer can be easily programmed to run any naturally aspirated engine. Using an engine or chassis dynamometer and a quality air/fuel ratio meter to measure the results, fuel and timing can be "dialed in" to near perfection.

DFI is also an ideal companion for forced induction application

Most supercharger kits designed for late-model returnless fuel systems trim both fuel and timing with a superchip. Depending on the output capacity of the blower, some kits may include larger injectors. Trimming large injectors is preferable to overdriving small injectors.

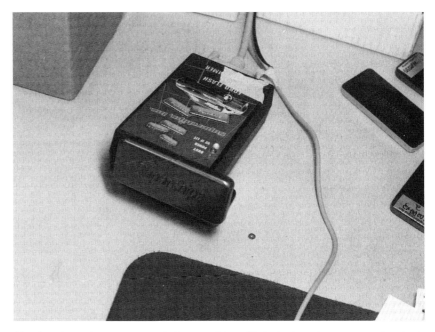

Very few aftermarket computer controls can match an OE electronic engine management system's ability to provide optimum drivability. Superchips are a cost-effective way to maintain ideal fuel and timing curves without sacrificing overall performance, because they work in conjunction with the factory computer.

because, unlike a stock computer, DFI understands positive intake pressure. Besides regulating the basic air/fuel and timing settings, DFI can switch to a programmable boost map when the computer senses pressure in the intake manifold. The CPU will add the proper amount of fuel, and regulate the ignition timing based on a customized "boost" map.

DFI can also control single-, dual-, or three-stage nitrous oxide systems. Once the nitrous system has been activated, the computer switches to a preprogrammed "nitrous" map, which contains rpm toggles to activate single- or multiple-stage systems as well as timing and fuel instructions.

A word of caution—a fully programmable computer is not for the fainthearted or the underfunded racer. Full latitude means a tuner can program an engine to destroy itself. Remember that pushing the envelope involves a certain amount of endurance testing—for both you and the engine. Engage the services of an experienced dynamometer operator and make sure he relies on a quality air/fuel ratio meter. Begin with a conservative programming that is rich with fuel. Lean fuel and add timing slowly until the desired results are achieved and be happy with a modest gain. Keep in mind those who go for broke typically go broke more often than they win.

The Laws of Clean Air

The government sentinel responsible for the air we breathe, the Environmental Protection Agency (EPA), accepts the latest regulations developed by the California Air Resources Board. These requirements call for a system that will monitor the performance of emission control components and functions. Further, the monitoring must be done onboard, and the results must be available to inspection personnel without the need for manufacturer-specific test equipment. The mandate was designated OBD, for on-board diagnostics. The primary difference between the last generation of computer controls and the current generation is the inclusion of OBD-II, the second-generation OBD system. The Federal Clean Air Act of 1990 requires that all 1996 and newer vehicles be equipped with OBD-II. Ford Motor Company began phasing in EEC-V and OBD-II in 1994. V-6 Mustangs and Thunderbirds/Cougars equipped with 4.6 SOHC engines were the first recipients.

OBD-II monitors the following components, systems, or functions:

- Exhaust gas recirculation (EGR)
- Heated oxygen gas sensor (HO_2S)
- Comprehensive components
- Catalyst efficiency
- Engine misfire
- Fuel system
- Evaporative system (1995 requirement)
- Secondary air system (1995 requirement)

Legalities pose an even greater challenge because federal and/or state laws cover automotive exhaust emissions. It is unlawful to remove, disable,

Extreme Performance Engine Control (EPEC)

Ford Motorsport markets a programmable mass air-control system called Extreme Performance Engine Control, or EPEC, that interfaces with a factory EEC-IV computer via piggyback processor and a laptop. Originally, EPEC was designed to work on 1988–1995 Mustangs and Cobras, but it will also work on other EEC-IV- equipped vehicles with EEC-IBV pinout. EPEC contains a default "safe" calibration file that can be recalled at any time, should the programmer stray beyond sensible boundaries.

Fully programmable options include the following:

Fuel Control – Idle, part-throttle, WOT, transition, air temperature correction, coolant temperature correction, injector offset correction, and absolute throttle position control

Spark Control–Idle, part-throttle, WOT, air temperature correction, engine temperature correction, barometric pressure correction, absolute throttle position correction, mass airflow spark correction, boost retard, and single- and two-stage nitrous oxide spark retard

Additional nitrous oxide programming includes minimum on-throttle angle, maximum off-throttle angle, maximum engine speed, "on" delay after maximum engine speed, stage one- and -two minimum engine speed, and spark retard. In addition, EPEC offers an overall fuel engine speed limiter, an overall spark engine speed limiter, a stage or launch limiter with dynamic rpm limiter and cut-in rpm control. To enhance EPEC's user-friendly capabilities, the software uses commonly accepted terms, such as air/fuel ratio and spark advance. The EPEC M-12650-M80 computer system requires one of two wiring harnesses—an M-12581-Z94 for 1994–1995 Mustangs or an M-12581-Z88 for 1988–1993 Mustangs.

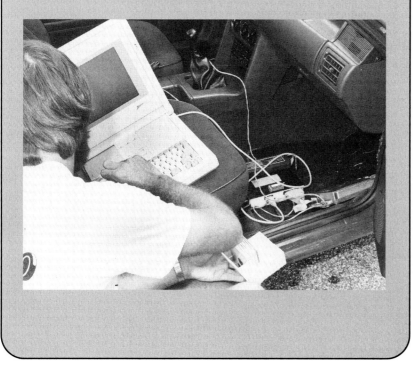

or tamper with an emissions system or component installed on a street-driven vehicle. Further, the emissions standards set forth at the time of manufacture must be maintained throughout the vehicle's useful life.

Each of the 50 states is responsible for regulating emissions and meeting federal air-quality standards. In California, which has some of the strictest emission requirements in the country, the CARB sets the criteria, which vary depending on which part of the state you are in. In many parts of the state, vehicles are required to pass an annual emissions test. CARB also regulates aftermarket components designed to enhance the power output of an engine because they have the ability to increase exhaust emissions. It is important that you be familiar with your area's emission laws and requirements.

Generally, any component that alters the airflow (air and fuel) through an engine cannot be installed on a vehicle licensed for street use in California unless it passes a CARB inspection. There are two basic test formats: certification and exemption. Certification testing is extensive. Complete engines must be certified unless they are exact replacement components. Stock or exact replacement parts must match the original factory specifications.

An exemption order refers to a numbered legal document that spells out legal parameters for a given part or assembly. Exemption means tests have shown that a nonstock part or assembly does not adversely affect emissions. If a component increases the amount of bad gases exiting the tailpipe, CARB will not legalize it for sale in California. Any power-enhancing component that has either not been tested, has failed a test, or is otherwise known to increase emissions must carry a "Not legal for sale or use in California on pollution-controlled vehicles" notice on the packaging and in advertisements. A

An EO number indicates that a forced induction system is "street-legal" in either 49 or all 50 states. The 50-state EO number for this particular Vortech kit is stamped into the identification plate under the model and serial numbers. The three numbers identify the system and the legal application(s).

"49-state street-legal" notice means the part is legal in all states except California and a "50-state street-legal" tag means the part is street-legal everywhere in the United States.

Certifications and exemption orders are application specific and restricted to a particular make, model, and year. Depending on the part, the exemption order may cover a span of years for a given engine family if the engine certification remains unchanged. For example, the 5.0-liter HO engine installed in Mustangs from 1987 to 1993 changed very little, if at all. Therefore, it is likely an exemption order for, say, an intake manifold, would cover all 1987–1993 Mustangs equipped with a 5.0-liter engine.

The Window of Opportunity

Emissions testing focuses on the low end of the rpm range because the engine in an everyday passenger car spends approximately 95 percent of its time below 2,500 rpm. If a performance part adds power above 3,000 rpm but does little or nothing to change the way the engine runs below 3,000, it will likely qualify for an exemption order. The window of opportunity for perfor-

mance engine components, including turbocharger, supercharger, and nitrous oxide injections kits, range from 3,000 to 6,500 rpm (or higher), which is rarely exercised by the average driver. For these reasons, aftermarket forced induction kit manufacturers seeking an exemption order typically design a system to come on line at 3,000 rpm or

above. This range of operation makes perfect sense, considering that the only practical purpose for a blower or nitrous oxide injection is to enhance wide-open throttle performance. Idling around town, the engine delivers good emissions-clean economy, because the power enhancement is a passive participant.

Multiple Headaches

Don't assume all aftermarket high-performance components offered by different manufacturers are compatible with each other, or that OBD-II will accept them once they are combined. Typically, components and/or packages are tested separately, not in combination with other manufacturers' products. For instance, OBD may trip the check engine light when a mass airflow meter, larger injectors, and a camshaft are combined, even though each has been issued an exemption order number. Additionally, most individual components are installed and tested on a totally stock engine. In other words, a large-bore throttle body will likely qualify for an exemption order if it is the only performance part installed on a stock engine.

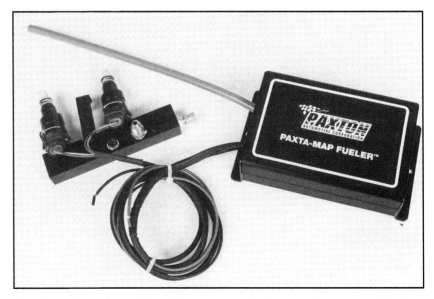

One of Paxton's supplemental fuel delivery systems is designed around a programmable microprocessor called Paxta-Map. Depending on the application, some Paxton supercharger kits include a PM, which provides a separate fuel map for up to three auxiliary injectors.

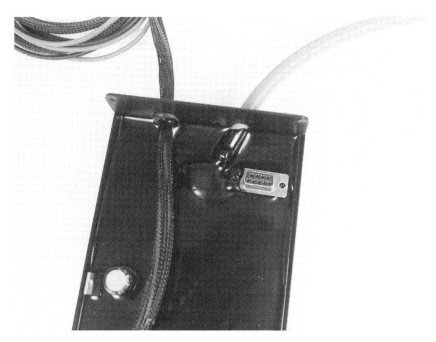

Paxta-Map must be programmed with a PC or laptop via this serial port. Paxta-Map is not a feedback system, meaning once the fuel curve is programmed, it is not self-compensating, and therefore the rate of fuel delivery remains fixed until it is reprogrammed.

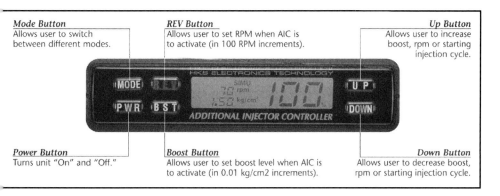

Mode Button
Allows user to switch between different modes.

REV Button
Allows user to set RPM when AIC is to activate (in 100 RPM increments).

Up Button
Allows user to increase boost, rpm or starting injection cycle.

Power Button
Turns unit "On" and "Off."

Boost Button
Allows user to set boost level when AIC is to activate (in 0.01 kg/cm2 increments).

Down Button
Allows user to decrease boost, rpm or starting injection cycle.

Turbo specialists HKS manufactures a stand-alone supplemental injector computer called AIC III (Additional Injector Controller). AIC can control up to eight high- or low-impedance injectors. Fuel delivery is based on two basic functions—boost pressure (0 to 36.259 psi) and rpm (1,000 to 12,000). AIC III will activate the injectors at the precise rpm (in 100-rpm increments) and boost pressure (in 0.01-kilogram-per-square-centimeter increments). *HKS*

A 50-state street-legal kit consisting of a camshaft, heads, and an intake manifold should work fine because the components were designed to complement each other. Further, for a kit to qualify for an exemption order, all components included in the kit were installed and tested at the same time.

Installing high-performance kits engineered for, and tested on, OBD-equipped vehicles is the safest way to avoid compatibility problems. A well-engineered, CARB-approved forced induction kit is a perfect example. Besides, given the potential for error, a well-engineered, street-legal forced induction kit will deliver a higher horsepower-per-dollar ratio with far less hassles in the end. The idea is to generate more horsepower without sacrificing drivability or compromising your legal position regarding emissions. As part of your research, ask questions about fuel management and how it will influence emissions. A copy of the CARB exemption order will define the parameters of the application but may not address all the legal issues in your city. In the end, compliance is your responsibility, not the kit manufacturer's.

Tuning for Forced Induction

Because necessity is the mother of invention, a large number of electronic devices designed to enhance control have hit the market in recent years. Unfortunately, a stand-alone, street-legal, programmable computer with the capacity to understand forced induction has yet to be offered. Until such a computer is available, a piggyback processor or programmable chip that capitalizes on the stock computer's self-adjusting capabilities remains the best option. Several individual electronic devices that address a number of single calibration issues are available. Incorporating one or combining several of these devices can greatly enhance your forced induction experience.

Since a large number of variables influence performance, it is important to set the major adjustments to achieve a workable baseline, then fine-tune each value to achieve optimum results.

First, make sure the engine is running correctly under natural aspiration. Adding forced induction to a troubled engine will only complicate existing problems and make them harder to calibrate and/or diagnose. A stock engine is easier to diagnose and tune because the factory calibration provides a stable baseline. Make one change at a time and test the validity of that change before making another change. Increasing the size of the injectors, throttle body, mass airflow meter, or anything else that increases airflow through the engine will have a negative effect on the factory baseline calibration. It is relatively easy to foil a well-running engine in an attempt to improve performance. Therefore, it is important to recalibrate the air/fuel mixture and timing once the improvements have been installed. Don't attempt to fix a problem by adding more hardware.

Add a high-powered ignition system and ensure that it is working properly before installing a forced induction kit. It is difficult to ignite large quantities of air/fuel, and most stock systems are not up to the task.

Factory computers have a range of tolerance—some greater, some less. Factory engine management systems are also self-adjusting, to a point. If the factory computer does not have an adequate range of adjustment to accommodate the modification(s), the tuner should add an adjustable piggy-back processor or replace the factory processor with a programmable aftermarket computer. In either case, the legal issue regarding emissions output should be considered.

Fully programmable computers are not street-legal, even if they are sophisticated enough to emulate the factory system. Likewise, not all piggy-back processors, chips, or tuning aids are street-legal. If the modification influences the factory calibration from idle to approximately 2,500 rpm, chances are good the vehicle will not pass an emissions test. Factory low-speed calibration provides optimum fuel economy with minimum exhaust emissions, and the settings are extremely sensitive.

Operating within the parameters of the stock processor will limit the opportunity for problems. The fuel management system is designed to adjust fuel and timing automatically, and most operate very efficiently within their individual range of tolerance.

The mass airflow meter should be trimmed for, or adjusted, to accommodate the flow capability of the injectors. The computer cannot correct a mismatch here. The computer reacts to the signals issued by the sensors. If the signal is out of range, the computer cannot compensate. Most

Jacobs Electronics' turbo timer is an adjustable timing control with rev-limit protection designed for GM HEI ignition systems. The unit provides two fully adjustable timing retard features: One can back out up to 15 degrees of timing anytime, and the other can retard timing an additional 15 degrees by rotating the boost retard knob. *Jacobs*

processors will read the mismatch as an error.

The injectors should be sized to complement, or support, the airflow through the engine. Undersized injectors will cause a lean fuel condition during high-rpm operation and oversized injectors can cause a rich fuel condition at low engine speeds. Likewise, excessive fuel pressure can cause a rich fuel condition. Conversely, low fuel pressure will normally not generate a lean fuel mixture, although all injectors require a minimum amount of fuel pressure.

Aside from delivering fuel to the cylinders, an injector must spray the fuel in a fine mist. Liquid fuel must vaporize and combine with oxygen before it will burn. A fine mist breaks the fuel into small particles. The smaller the particles, the quicker the fuel will vaporize. An injector delivering low-pressure fuel will spray a stream that will not vaporize easily.

Most computers do not monitor or adjust the fuel pressure. Once the ideal minimum fuel pressure is dialed in, adjust the fuel delivery by altering the pulse width of the injectors (the length of time the injectors remains open) electronically. If the parameters are outside the limits of the factory injectors, install larger injectors, then "trim" them electronically. Or add auxiliary injectors and a supplemental electronic device to control them.

Tuning for Supercharging and Turbocharging

Purchase and install an application-specific supercharger or turbocharger kit that bests suits your needs. Don't subscribe to the "bigger is better" theory. High-powered systems are difficult to calibrate and maintain. If the vehicle is licensed for street use, make sure the kit has an EO and is legal for use in your state.

Install the kit as-is out of the box to minimize complications. Tune the system to achieve optimum performance using the guidelines issued by the kit manufacturer. Purchase and install all recommended gauges, and install a fuel pressure gauge whether or not one is recommended. Fuel pressure is more important than boost pressure.

Test the vehicle on a chassis dynamometer to ensure that all systems are working properly. Use an SAE-approved diagnostic air/fuel ratio meter to ensure that the fuel enhancement system is calibrated properly. Fine-tune the system while running the vehicle on a dynamometer or a drag strip—not on the street.

Monitor the exhaust gas temperature with a quality pyrometer. EGTs approaching 1,500 degrees Fahrenheit indicate a lean fuel condition. Low EGTs indicate a rich fuel condition.

Follow the kit manufacturer's recommendations for spark plug type,

Computer Modeling

Calibrating engine performance with a calculator is difficult even for a math major. Thousands of variables must be measured, factored, and plotted. Engineers toil for months and sometimes years to develop a new engine design. Is it any wonder extracting the calculations for a major modification seems such a daunting task?

Things are invented because necessity is a mother. As proof, complex mathematical problems and the need for speed sparked the evolution of the computer. All computers are based on mathematical computation. It's debatable whether the math problems became too complex or the quest for enhanced productivity became too great. In either case, engine engineering is rooted in mathematics.

Engine modeling programs make good use of a computer's mathematical reasoning by transforming statistics into real-world values.

```
                                                           9- 7-1999
                                                            PAGE 3
ENGINE SPECIFICATIONS:        Displ: 349.85 cid 5.73 liters, 8 Cyls
                              Standard for Critical Loads:   4350.0 g's
Block Deck Ht:  9.025    Firing Angle:  90 deg   Bore:        4.000 in
cc/Cyl:        716.55    Compr Ratio:   12.80    Stroke:      3.480 in
Deck Ht/cc:   .0049 in   Compr Vol cc:  60.72    Rod Len:     5.700 in
Deck cc/Thou: .2059 cc   Rod/Stroke:    1.638    Recip Wt:    1029 gms
Total Piston Sq In: 100.53   Comp Dist = Pin to Deck Ht:  1.585 in
                             Bore/Stroke:                  1.149
Max piston speed occurs at:                             75 deg ATDC
Average Balance Factor:   Recip 50.99% of  2058 gms  = 1049.3 gms Recip
                          Plus Rotating     0 gms    = 1049.3 gms BobWt

*****************************************************************************
Engine speed at estimated Critical Tension for recip wt of 1029 gms:  8211 RPM
At  6149 RPM, Maximum recip Tension is  56.08% of estimated Critical
Max Piston Speed:          5859 FPM at 75 deg ATDC
Tension at TDC:            2440 g's ( -5534.5 pounds)
Compression at BDC:        1299 g's (  2945.9 pounds)
Total Ignition Advance:  37 deg's ( .335 msec ATDC combustion time)
```

Combined VE	Calculated Performance			Primary Exhaust Tubes	
103.5%	RPM	HP	Ft-#'s	O.D. in	Length in
Max TORQUE	4658	393.4	443.5	1.875	43.4
Max POWER	6149	482.9	412.5	2.000	28.6

```
To achieve this performance level you need:
 193 to  212 CFM Int Flow at 25 inches water by 78 deg ATDC
 A single Carburetor, rated at 1.5 inches Hg, of  715 to  768 CFM
 Intake Port Dimensions for Recommended (& Critical Velocity) Airflow
```

	Peak Vel.	Area	Circle		Square	
	Ft/Sec	Sq In	In	mm	In	mm
Recommended	365	2.55	1.801	45.74	1.635	41.54
Critical	690	1.78	1.505	38.22	1.367	34.71

Modeling programs are written by and for automotive engineers and serious end users. Engine Expert and DynoMation, both distributed by Allan Lockheed and Associates, are examples of two invaluable computer modeling tools. Both are extensive, affordable, and very easy to use and understand. The programs complement each other and allow the user to predict real world performance numbers. After inputing known measurements such as bore, stroke, rod length, compression ratio, timing advance, deck height, and so on, you can do the following:

• Compute the effect of alternate intake and exhaust systems on your engine's upper rpm power curve
• Investigate cam timing and valve lift best suited to your existing intake and/or exhaust system
• Evaluate a projected power band or maximize power at a particular rpm

DynoMation will compute:
• Intake and exhaust velocity (kinetic energy)
• Finite amplitude intake and exhaust waves
• Carburetor airflow capacity (naturally aspirated or forced induction)
• Intake and exhaust runner lengths, taper, and exhaust collector size
• Cylinder head airflow capacity
• Valve timing events

DynoMation requires a 486DX/66 (or larger) computer to run at optimum speed. The literature states it will run on a 386 with a math coprocessor, but a 486DX/66 computer is recommended.

Engine Expert will suggest optimum cam specifications, carburetor size, valve size, port size, and/or power bandwidth. These programs will predict the advantages of forced induction on the assumption the supercharger or turbocharger system is sized properly for the application. They will not tell you how to select the proper supercharger or turbocharger. They can, however, predict the power output of an engine enhanced with a forced induction system.

heat range, and gap. The heat range refers to the temperature of the ceramic material around the positive electrode. A plug with an incorrect heat range can foul if it is too cold or overheat if it is too hot. Learn to "read" spark plugs. A heavy black or dark gray residue on the plugs indicates a rich fuel condition. Tiny silver or black specks indicate a lean fuel condition. If the negative electrode shows signs of melting or is discolored, the combustion temperature is too high. Add fuel to richen the mixture.

If possible, eliminate the FMU completely. FMUs are not precision devices and most are nonadjustable. Install larger injectors in place of the FMU, then adjust fuel delivery with a programmable piggyback microprocessor or a custom chip. Computer controlled electronic fuel injectors provide a wide range of precision adjustments.

Although easier to install and use, a chip may not be the least expensive option. Off-the-shelf chips may not be programmed to accommodate all engine modifications, and most include an acceptable margin of error. Only an experienced programmer can calibrate a custom chip to suit a particular engine package.

Many blower kit manufacturers offer custom chips, but the service can only be performed at their facility. Experienced programmers who can "burn" a custom chip offsite, based on the engine specifications alone, are rare. Real-time programming on the vehicle is the only way to ensure that the calibration will be accurate and trouble free.

Install a larger radiator if the vehicle is equipped with a standard cooling system. Forced induction will generate additional heat, and most factory automotive cooling systems are marginal at best when new. Many trucks and SUVs designed to haul or pull heavy loads include upgraded cooling systems as standard equipment, but most cars and light trucks do not. An optional "towing package" usually includes a cooling system upgrade.

Tuning for Nitrous Oxide Injection

Calibrating a nitrous oxide system is difficult only because the tuner can adjust both the air and the fuel. A naturally aspirated engine consumes all the air it can. The fuel is then adjusted or calibrated to achieve a near ideal air/fuel mixture ratio. Increasing the volume of N_2O gas has the same effect as increasing the airflow into a naturally aspirated engine.

Nitrous oxide supplies the oxygen that supports combustion. The fuel produces power, not the nitrous; therefore, the ratio of N_2O to fuel must remain consistent to extract optimum power from the fuel. The amount of potential energy stored in a single unit of fuel is a known value (i.e., 300 horsepower will require 150 pounds of fuel per hour at a brake specific fuel consumption of .50). The same applies for a nitrous injection system. To generate X amount of horsepower, an engine must be fed with a proportional amount of fuel. To burn that fuel efficiently, a proportional amount of oxygen (nitrous oxide) must also be present.

Refer to the calibration procedure outlined in chapter 6 to set up a safe baseline, then fine-tune the system using an exhaust gas analyzer (air/fuel ratio meter) and a dynamometer. Learn to read spark plugs if you plan to optimize the system beyond the baseline. Jet changes present a large adjustment. Adjust the fuel pressure up or down in small increments to "dial in" the perfect calibration after a jet change.

If you are brave enough to inject a blower or turbocharger with nitrous oxide, the same rules apply. First calibrate to obtain an ideal air/fuel mixture ratio during naturally aspirated operation, then tune the fuel enhancement system to achieve optimum performance under boost. Compute the fuel needed to support the additional horsepower hit, then adjust the nitrous oxide to support the fuel. Fine-tune the nitrous as

needed to achieve a safe air/fuel mixture ratio under full load at wide-open throttle. Rely on a quality air/fuel ratio meter, a pyrometer, and a dynamometer.

Purchasing a nitrous oxide kit is a safe, logical beginning. Most nitrous kits come with factory calibrated guidelines—50-horsepower kit, 100-horsepower kit, 200-horsepower kit, and so on. If a well-designed, properly calibrated supercharger or turbocharger system will add 100 horsepower, a 100-horsepower nitrous kit will add 100 more. Naturally, all of this assumes the engine will tolerate the increase in power. Common sense must prevail, or the tuner shifts the focus from making power to durability testing.

Selecting a Forced Induction Camshaft

Selecting a camshaft requires some degree of work. It's actually easier to choose the right supercharger, turbocharger, or nitrous oxide injection kit for a particular application because there are few details to consider beyond make, model, year, and engine. By comparison, there can be half a dozen or more cam profiles available for an engine family in any given make, model, and year.

Researching cam profiles is similar to shopping for a personal computer—a lot of details must be sifted and shifted to arrive at the ideal match. Ideally, a cam should enhance power but not be too overwhelming. Extremes will compromise drivability.

Start with the physical requirements–make, model, year, and engine. That should narrow it down to, say, 50 or so production camshafts offered by at least a half-dozen manufacturers. Production, or off-the-shelf, cams are mass-produced copies of proven profiles. Listing the basic information will define the mechanical requirements, such as the size and shape of the bearing journals and the configuration of the bumps. Usually a cam profile will

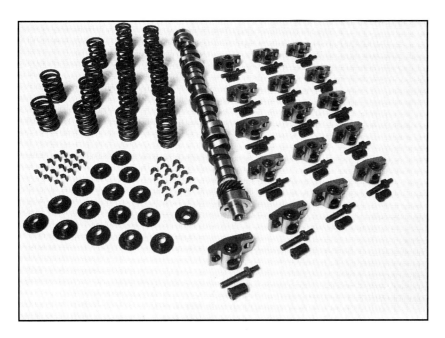

fit a given engine family over a spread of model years. In some cases it may fit only one engine in a small range of model years.

Production cams are available for a wide range of popular engines. The more popular the engine, the larger number of available camshafts. Conversely, there are fewer choices for less popular or limited- production engines. Most cam grinders offer customized service for unique applications or customer-specified grinds. Expect to pay a premium, should you require a one-of-a-kind profile.

The next choices are easy: naturally aspirated, forced induction, or nitrous oxide injection for street, street/strip, or race use? Street and street/strip use requires the buyer to select a CARB-approved cam grind. Custom-built street rods, cars built before 1974, and off-road vehicles can skirt the legal issue and breath easy, at least for now.

Details relating to camshaft profile—more specifically, how the cam will perform relating to power output, the power curve in relationship to engine rpm, and drivability should be considered next. Obviously, racers and those interested in serious competition will likely disregard drivabil-

ity as a minimum requirement. Conversely, street-driven cars must retain an acceptable amount of drivability to be enjoyable.

Sorting out camshaft profiles is best explained using examples such as those offered by Crane Cams. Crane is one of the few manufacturers that offer a large selection of varying profiles for nearly any application. Further, it is easier to describe cam profiles that are defined using standardized parameters. For example, one cam manufacturer may use .050-inch tappet lift while another may use .010-inch lift. It is simply easier to understand if all parameters are the same.

Using Ford's 5.0-liter HO engine built between 1985 and 1995 as the application, the choices are as follows:

Part Number 444211:

Naturally Aspirated—Good low- to midrange torque and horsepower, works with automatic or manual transmission and stock rear end gears.

Forced Induction—Good idle and daily usage with centrifugal or positive displacement centrifugal. Good low- to midrange torque and

horsepower, 2,200-2,600 cruise rpm, 8 pounds maximum boost with stock 9.2 compression ratio advised.

Nitrous Injected—Good idle, daily usage, with SEFI-type nitrous system. Good low- to midrange torque and horsepower, 2,200-2,600 cruise rpm, stock 9.2 compression ratio advised.

44211 is 50-state legal covering 1985–1993 (CARB EO # D-225-46), and the effective (basic) rpm range is between 1,500 and 5,000 rpm.

Part Number 444221:

Naturally Aspirated—Delivers good midrange torque and horsepower. Requires mass air low meter for best idle control. Works best with manual transmission. Auto may require higher stall converter. Use with 3.08 or numerically higher rear gears.

Forced Induction—Good idle, good midrange torque and horsepower. Daily usage with maximum 10 pounds of boost in a 2,400–2,800 cruise rpm range. Maximum 8.5 compression ratio advised; 1.7 ratio rocker arms are recommended.

Nitrous Injected—Good idle, good midrange torque and horsepower. Daily usage with SEFI-type nitrous system, 2,400–2,800 rpm off-nitrous cruise rpm. Stock 9.2 compression ratio advised.

444221 is 50-state legal covering 1985–1993 (CARB EO # D-225-46), and the effective (basic) rpm range is between 2,000 and 5,500 rpm.

Part number 444225:

Naturally Aspirated—Good midrange torque and horsepower. Designed to be used with 1.7 ratio rocker arms on mass air-equipped engine with aftermarket intake, heads, exhaust, and centrifugal supercharger.

Manual transmission okay or automatic with mild stall converter.

Forced Induction—Good idle and daily use with small supercharger generating maximum 10 pounds of boost. Good midrange torque and horsepower. Use 1.7 ratio rockers; 2,400–2,800 cruise rpm range. Maximum compression ratio recommended is 8.5.

Nitrous Injected—Good idle and daily usage with SEFI-type nitrous system. Good midrange torque and horsepower with 2,400–2,800 cruise rpm range; 1.7 ratio rocker arms and stock 9.2 compression ratio recommended.

44225 is 50-state legal covering 1985–1993 (CARB EO # D-225-46), and the effective (basic) rpm range is between 2,000 and 5,500 rpm.

Part number 444231:

Naturally Aspirated—Fair idle, good midrange and strong top-end power. Requires modified mass airflow meter, aftermarket intake, high-performance cylinder heads, and headers. Manual transmission and 3.55 or numerically higher rear gears are recommended. Requires Crane springs and retainers.

Forced Induction—Fair idle. Moderate performance usage with supercharger generating maximum 15 pounds of boost. Good mid- to upper rpm torque and horsepower. Modified mass airflow meter; intake, cylinder heads, and headers are recommended; 8.0 maximum compression ratio.

Nitrous Injected—Fair idle. Moderate performance usage with SEFI-type nitrous system. Good mid- to upper rpm torque and horsepower. Modified mass airflow meter, cylinder heads, and headers are recommended. Delivers 2,600–3,000 cruise rpm. Stock 9.2 compression ratio.

44231 is 50-state legal covering 1985–1993 (CARB EO # D-225-46), and the effective (basic) rpm range is between 2,400 and 6,000 rpm.

Part number 449601:

Naturally Aspirated—449601 is not recommended for EFI engines utilizing the stock computer. An aftermarket fully programmable processor or a sophisticated programmable piggyback processor is required.

Forced Induction—Fair idle. Moderate performance usage with a blower generating maximum 18 pounds of boost. Good mid- to upper rpm torque and horsepower. Automatic transmission with a 2,500-plus stall converter. This cam provides a 3,000–3,400 cruise rpm. An 8.0 maximum compression ratio is advised.

Nitrous Injected—Fair idle. Moderate performance usage with SEFI-type or manifold nitrous system. Good mid- to upper rpm torque and horsepower. Automatic transmission with 2,500-plus stall converter. Expect a 3,000–3,400 cruise rpm range. A 9.0 to 10.75 compression ratio is recommended.

449601 is not a street-legal cam. The effective (basic) range of operation is from 2,500 to 6,000 rpm.

Part number 449761:

Naturally Aspirated—449761 is not recommended for EFI engines utilizing the stock computer. An aftermarket fully programmable processor or a sophisticated programmable piggyback processor is required.

Forced Induction—Fair idle. Moderate performance usage with positive-displacement blower generating maximum 20 pounds of boost. Good mid- to upper rpm torque and horsepower. Automatic transmission

with a 2,500-plus stall converter. This cam provides a 3,200–3,600 cruise rpm range. A maximum 8.0 compression ratio is advised.

Nitrous Injected—Fair idle. Moderate performance usage with SEFI-type or manifold nitrous system. Good mid- to upper rpm torque and horsepower; 340-plus ci recommended. Automatic transmission with a 2,500-rpm stall converter; 3,200–3,600 curse rpm range. A 10.0 to 11.5 compression ratio is advised.

449761 is not a street-legal cam. The effective (basic) range of operation is from 3,000 to 6,500 rpm.

Part number 449581:

Naturally Aspirated—449581 is not recommended for EFI engines utilizing the stock computer. An aftermarket fully programmable processor or a sophisticated programmable piggyback processor is required.

Forced Induction—Rough idle. Performance usage with a positive-displacement blower generating a maximum 22 pounds of boost. Good upper rpm horsepower. 340-plus ci recommended. Automatic transmission with 3,000-rpm stall converter; 3,400–3,800 cruise rpm. An 8.0 maximum compression ratio is advised.

Nitrous Injected—Rough idle. Performance usage with a large nitrous system. Good upper rpm horsepower, 340-plus cubic inch displacement, automatic transmission with 3,000-rpm stall converter, 3,400–3,800 cruise rpm; 11.5 minimum compression ratio advised.

449581 is not a street-legal cam. The effective (basic) range of operation is from 3,500 to 7,000 rpm.

Computer Cams

Although computer camshafts are designed using a computer or ground

Part Number	Degrees of Duration @ .050-inch lift Int/Ext	Degrees of Advertisied Duration Int/Exh	Degrees of Lobe Separtation	Open/Close at .050-inch Cam Lift Int/Ext	Gross Lift Int/Ext
444211	208/216	262/270	112	(3), 31/45, (9)	.530/.530
444221	216/220	270/278	112	1, 35/47, (7)	.533/.544
444225	214/220	276/282	112	0, 34/47, (7)	.513/.529*
444231	220/220	282/282	110	0, 40/40, 0	.498/.498
449601	224/232	286/294	112	5, 39/53, (1)	.542/.563
449761	232/244	294/306	112	9, 43/59, 5	.563/.595
449581	244/256	306/318	110	17, 47/63, 13	.595/.595

* Gross Lift with 1.7 ratio rocker arms

on a computerized machine, the term refers to a camshaft designed for a computer-controlled engine. Factory computer controls are a limiting factor when selecting a camshaft profile.

Factory computers like consistent intake manifold vacuum, which means they don't like valve overlap. Excessive valve overlap causes an engine to run rough at slow speeds—hence the choppy, rough idle inherent in racing camshafts. Overlap causes low, inconsistent intake manifold vacuum when the engine is running at slow speed. A number of computer controls, such as the mass airflow sensor, for example, react poorly to low intake vacuum and reversion.

Also, a sophisticated electronic engine control is a feedback system that makes decisions based on a series of inputs. The computer is constantly adjusting fuel delivery and timing lead in response to the feedback it receives from such monitoring devices such as the oxygen sensor(s). Excessive valve overlap allows a small amount of unburned fuel to escape into the exhaust. The oxygen sensors interpret the reading as an extremely rich air/fuel condition. The computer reduces the amount of fuel entering the cylinders in response to the false reading. The engine runs worse, as the computer becomes more confused.

Overlap is inherent to performance cams. Opening the valves farther and holding them open longer improves VE at high rpm when veloc-ity in the intake manifold is high. Opening the valves farther requires a higher (taller) lobe, and holding the valve open longer requires a fatter (wider) lobe. Increasing girth to a lobe adds surface area (distance), which lengthens the time the valve is held off the seat. It is physically impossible to increase duration without increasing overlap. Lobe separation (the distance between the toe of the intake and exhaust lobes) also influences overlap. Although a range from 106 degrees to as much as 116 degrees is doable, a centerline should be fairly close to 110 degrees for a typical computer-controlled engine.

Roller tappet camshafts provide a measure of latitude not obtainable with a flat tappet grind. Aside from a tremendous reduction in frictional loss (parasitic drag), that's one reason original-equipment manufacturers converted to roller. As a result, factory roller cams are extremely efficient, and they make good power with very little (if any) overlap. Which brings up another point—stock cam grinds work well with forced induction.

An Ideal Compromise

There is no such thing as a perfect cam profile. All camshafts levy a degree of compromise, although stock factory cams offer the most overall performance with the least sacrifice. As you can see by the following progression from mild to wild, low-end performance suffers as the power curve migrates toward the upper end of the rpm range. Power above 3,000 rpm goes up at the sacrifice of performance below 3,000 rpm.

Compromising power for the expense of low-end performance is one issue—low-speed fuel mileage is another. EFI helps, but the cam profile remains the dominating factor. Low-speed drivability and fuel mileage become important features when a vehicle is street driven everyday. Piloting an unruly vehicle that bucks, back-fires, and stalls at slow speed gets old too. Forced induction has the ability to improve power with little or no sacrifice to low-speed performance, providing the chosen cam profile supports low-end performance. A street-legal cam profile will:

- Provide good overall drivability
- Keep emissions under legal limits
- Offer good fuel mileage under nonboost conditions
- Generate good power under boost
- Generate good power at part-throttle
- Offer a lower cruise rpm

Each of these features is compromised as the cam profile moves from mild toward wild. A driver's thrust for power and his or her tolerance for sacrifice will ultimately influence cam selection.

Blower cams are normally split-profile grinds, meaning the specifications for the intake lobe differ from the exhaust lobe. Forced induction feeds the engine a denser air/fuel charge, which creates more spent gases—more air and fuel in, more exhaust out. Favoring the exhaust, that is, opening the exhaust valve farther and/or holding it open longer, will usually net good results. Coincidentally, small-block Ford engines also respond to a larger exhaust profile because they have inherently small exhaust ports. All but one of the cams favors the exhaust valve. In the examples above, 444231 is a single profile cam. The first four cams are 50-state street-legal grinds.

Crane Camshaft Specification Card

Part Number:	**444211**	
Grind Number:	**COMPUCAM 2020 COMPUCAM HYDRAULIC ROLLER**	
Engine Ident:	**1985-UP FORD-MERCURY V-8 302 CU.IN. H.O.**	

VALVE SETTING: INTAKE **.000** EXHAUST **.000** ----> **HOT**

LIFT:					
	INTAKE @CAM	**3313**	@VALVE	**530**	ROCKER ARM RATIO
	EXHAUST @CAM	**3313**	@VALVE	**530**	**1.60**

ALL LIFTS ARE BASED ON ZERO LASH AND THEORETICAL ROCKER ARM RATIOS

CAM TIMING			OPENS	CLOSES	ADV DURATION	
@	----	INTAKE	----	----	**262**	°
----	LIFT	EXHAUST	----	----	**270**	°

SPRING REQUIREMENTS

	TRIPLE	DUAL	OUTER	INNER	RECOMMENDED RPM RANGE WITH MATCHING COMPONENTS
PART NUMBER		**99841**			MINIMUM RPM ----
LOADS:	CLOSED **120**		LBS @ **1.940** OR **1 15/16**		MAXIMUM RPM ----
	OPEN **347**		LBS @ **1.440**		VALVE FLOAT **6500**

CAM TIMING			OPENS	CLOSES	MAX LIFT		DURATION	
@	**.050**	INTAKE	**(3) ATDC**	**31 ABDC**	**107**	°ATDC	**208**	°
TAPPET	LIFT	EXHAUST	**45 BBDC**	**(9) BTDC**	**117**	°BTDC	**216**	°

REMARKS:

   FIRING ORDER: 1-3-7-2-6-5-4-8

Pertinent information is spelled out on the camshaft specification card included with the cam. Besides the lift and duration, the card lists the cam timing events—when each valve opens and closes in relationship to crank angle. Thus, 444211 opens the intake valve 3 degrees before top dead center (BTDC) and allows it to close 31 degrees after bottom dead center (ABDC), and opens the exhaust valve 45 degrees before bottom dead center (BBDC) and holds it open until 9 degrees BTDC.

The difference between the exhaust valve closing and the intake valve opening is overlap—the amount of time (in crankshaft degrees) both valves are open. In this example, because the exhaust valve closes 9 degrees BTDC and the intake valve doesn't open until 3 degrees ATDC, there is no overlap at .050-inch tappet lift. By comparison, the 449581

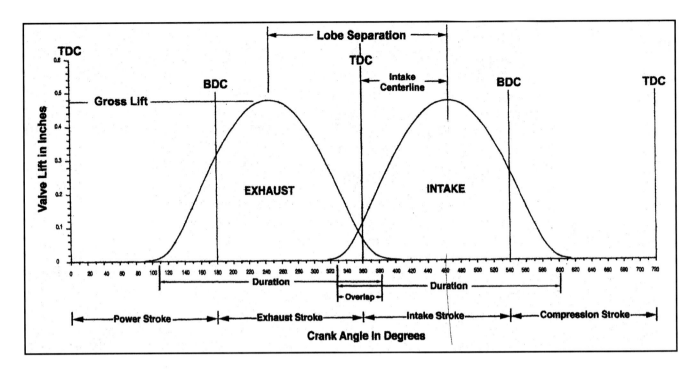

The following labels appear on the figure: TDC, BDC, Lobe Separation, TDC, Intake Centerline, BDC, TDC, Gross Lift, EXHAUST, INTAKE, Valve Lift in Inches, Duration, Overlap, Duration, Power Stroke, Exhaust Stroke, Intake Stroke, Compression Stroke, Crank Angle in Degrees

camshaft opens the intake valve 17 degrees BTDC while holding the exhaust valve open until 13 degrees ATDC, which produces 30 degrees of valve overlap.

A lobe separation of 112 camshaft degrees is equal to 224 crankshaft degrees. Lobe separation is a fixed value and cannot be changed. The intake centerline is given in crankshaft degrees and is used to "degree" the camshaft, that is, to check to ensure that the camshaft and crankshaft are synchronized so the events occur on schedule. Advancing the camshaft (reducing the intake centerline) causes all of the events to occur earlier in the cycle. Retarding the cam causes all of the events to occur later in the cycle. Advancing the camshaft shifts the power band lower in the rpm range and vise versa. For example, advancing the camshaft 4 degrees will move the beginning of the power band approximately 200 rpm lower in the range.

Lobe separation determines when peak torque will occur in the power band. A smaller (tighter) lobe separation (110 degrees compared to 112 degrees) shifts peak torque lower in the power band but also reduces its total range of effectiveness. Torque will build quickly and peak out early. A broader (longer) lobe separation spreads torque over a wider range of operation, which also enhances upper rpm power.

Appendix One
Holley/Weiand Superchargers

Holley/Weiand Superchargers

The Holley/Weiand Web site lists the following components, systems, and accompanying hardware.

Holley Supercharger Kits

In short, these charger kits provide a good match to the intended application, eliminating a lot of tuning headaches. If you want a Roots sticking through the hood, Holley/Weiand offers bolt-on-and-drive simplicity. Individual superchargers in either satin (natural aluminum) or polished (show quality) finish are listed below.

P/N 90500 - Powercharger 144 for Chevrolet S/B 302, 327, 350, 383, 400 cid, Short or Long Water Pump (satin finish)

P/N 90500-2 - Street-legal Powercharger 144 for 1988–1995 350 cid Chevrolet S/B - w/ TBI (automatic trans. only) (satin finish)

P/N 90513 - Powercharger 144 for Chevrolet S/B 302, 327, 350, 383, 400 cid, Short or Long Water Pump (polished)

P/N 90513-2 - Street-legal Powercharger 144 for 1988–1995 350 cid Chevrolet S/B - w/ TBI (automatic trans. only) (satin finish)

P/N 90550 - Powercharger 174 Chevrolet B/B- Long or Short Water Pump (satin finish)

P/N 90862 - Powercharger 174 for Ford 289, 302 cid S/B (1969 and earlier requires crank spacer) (satin finish)

P/N 90863 - Powercharger 174 for Ford 289, 302 cid S/B (1969 and earlier requires crank spacer) (polished)

P/N 91060 - Powercharger 250 for 302, 327, 350, 383, 400 cid Chevrolet S/B - Short Water Pump (satin finish)

P/N 91069 - Powercharger 250 for 302, 327, 350, 383, 400 cid Chevrolet S/B - Short Water Pump (polished)

P/N 94002 - 420 Megablower for 302, 327, 350, 383, 400 cid Chevrolet S/B - Short Water Pump (polished)

P/N 94004 - 420 Megablower for 396, 427, 454, 502 cid Chevrolet B/B - Short Water Pump (polished)

Weiand Supercharger Kits all but eliminate the task of matching components. Engineers designed, tuned, and tested these application-specific kits on the most popular small- and big-block Ford and Chevy engine profiles. Some have California Air Research Board (CARB) Exemption Order (EO) numbers, meaning they are street-legal in all 50 states. Novice tuners should research a Holley/Weiand blower kit, then build the ideal engine following their recommendations. (Note: Long and Short Nose refers to the length of the blower drive.)

P/N 6500 - Chevrolet S/B, Long Nose (satin finish)

P/N 6502 - Chevrolet S/B, Long Nose for 1969–1985 CARB EO D-256-2 (satin finish)

P/N 6503 - Chevrolet S/B, Short Nose for 1969–1985 CARB EO D-256-2 (satin finish)

P/N 6504 - Chevrolet S/B, Long Nose for 1986 only CARB EO D-256-2 (satin finish)

P/N 6505 - Chevrolet S/B, Short Nose for 1962–1968 (10-rib Drive Standard) (satin finish)

P/N 6506 - Chevrolet S/B, Short Nose for 1962–1968 (10-rib Drive Standard) (polished)

P/N 6507 - Chevrolet S/B, Long Nose for 1969–1985 CARB EO D-256-2 (polished)

P/N 6508 - Chevrolet S/B, Short Nose for 1969–1985 CARB EO D-256-2 (polished)

P/N 6509 - Chevrolet S/B, Long Nose for 1986 only CARB EO D-256-2 (polished)

P/N 6510 - Chevrolet S/B, Long Nose (polished)

P/N 6512 - Chevrolet S/B, Long Nose for 1969–1986 (10-rib Drive Standard) (satin finish)

P/N 6512 - Chevrolet S/B, Long Nose for 1969–1986 (10-rib Drive Standard) (satin finish)

P/N 6513 - Chevrolet S/B, Long Nose for 1969–1986 (10-rib Drive Standard) (polished)

P/N 6520 - Chevrolet S/B, Long Nose Oval Port (polished)

P/N 6521 - Chevrolet S/B, Long Nose Oval Port (satin finish)

P/N 6522 - Chevrolet S/B, Short Nose Oval Port (satin finish)

P/N 6523 - Chevrolet S/B, Short Nose Oval Port (polished)

P/N 6530 - Chevrolet S/B, Long Nose Rectangular Port (satin finish)

P/N 6531 - Chevrolet S/B, Long Nose Rectangular Port (polished)

P/N 6532 - Chevrolet S/B, Short Nose Rectangular Port (satin finish)

P/N 6533 - Chevrolet S/B, Short Nose Rectangular Port (polished)

P/N 6540 - Chevrolet S/B, Long Nose Rectangular Port (16-rib Drive Standard) (satin finish)

P/N 6541 - Chevrolet S/B, Long Nose Rectangular Port (16-rib Drive Standard) (polished)

P/N 7180 - Chrysler 426 Hemi (polished)

P/N 7180P - Chrysler 426 Hemi (polished)

P/N 7181 - Chrysler 392 Hemi (satin finish)

P/N 7181P - Chrysler 392 Hemi (polished)

P/N 7182 - Chrysler S/B 1955–1986 (satin finish)

P/N 7182P - Chrysler S/B 1955–1986 (polished)

P/N 7183 - Chrysler B/B 396-502 (satin finish)

P/N 7183P - Chrysler B/B 396-502 (polished)

P/N 7185 - Chevrolet S/B 1955–1986 (satin finish)

P/N 7185P - Chevrolet S/B 1955–1986 (polished)

P/N 7186 - Chevrolet 396–502 (satin finish)

P/N 7186P - Chevrolet 396–502 (polished)

P/N 7187 - Chevrolet S/B 1955–1987 (satin finish)

P/N 7187P - Chevrolet S/B 1955–1987 (polished)

P/N 7188 - Chevrolet B/B 396–502 (satin finish)

P/N 7188P - Chevrolet B/B 396–502 (polished)

P/N 7192P - Chevrolet B/B 396–502 for 1471 (polished)

P/N 7193P - Chevrolet B/B 396–502 for 1271 (polished)

P/N 7194P - Chevrolet B/B 396–502 for 1071 (polished)

Blower Manifolds (included in kits) Satin Finish

Cast-aluminum blower manifolds are engineered to adapt the supercharger to the engine as simply as possible. Essentially, they provide a ridged mount for the blower that ensures that the drive will align correctly with the crankshaft. Satin-finished components can be color coordinated with other engine components or powder coated.
P/N 6100 - Chevrolet S/B, 142 EO

P/N 6110 - Chevrolet S/B, 142

P/N 6120 - Chevrolet B/B, Oval Port 177

P/N 6130 - Chevrolet B/B, Rectangular Port 177

P/N 6140 - Chevrolet B/B, Rectangular Port 256

P/N 6150 - Chevrolet S/B, 177

P/N 7136 - Chevrolet S/B, 1955–1986

P/N 7138 - Chrysler 331–354–392 Hemi

P/N 7150 - Chrysler 426 Hemi

P/N 7151 - Chevrolet B/B, 396–502

P/N 7152 - Chevrolet B/B, 396–502 tall deck

Blower Manifolds (included in kits) Polished Finish

Polished components are a good value for those who desire a custom show look. A budget-minded builder with lots of time and patience can save some bucks by polishing a satin-finished part, but I don't recommend it.

P/N 6101 - Chevrolet S/B, 142 EO

P/N 6111 - Chevrolet S/B, 142

P/N 6121 - Chevrolet B/B, Oval Port 177

P/N 6131 - Chevrolet B/B, Rectangular Port 177

P/N 6141 - Chevrolet B/B, Rectangular Port 256

P/N 6151 - Chevrolet S/B, 177

P/N 7136P - Chevrolet S/B, 1955–1986

P/N 7138P - Chrysler 331–354–392 Hemi

P/N 7150P - Chrysler 426 Hemi

P/N 7151P - Chevrolet B/B, 396–502

P/N 7152P - Chevrolet B/B, 396–502 tall deck

Blower Carburetors

Naturally aspirated carburetors are difficult to calibrate on a good day. Adding a blower increases the level of difficulty at least two grades. Blower carburetors must provide smooth idle, quick off-idle response, acceptable fuel mileage at cruise rpm, and they must deliver enough fuel to compensate for a large increase in air density when the driver calls for full power. Forgo a polished assembly if you must, but don't skimp here. A quality blower carburetor will make more power and generally improve your driving experience. Anything else can cause a mountain of grief.

P/N 0-80572S - Chevrolet, Model 4150, 700 cfm

P/N 0-80573S - Chevrolet, Model 4150, 750 cfm

P/N 0-80574S - Chevrolet, Model 4150, 800 cfm

P/N 0-80575 - Chevrolet, Model 4150 HP, 600 cfm

P/N 0-80576 - Chevrolet/Chrysler, Model 4150, 750 cfm

P/N 0-80577 - Chevrolet, Model 4150 HP, 950 cfm

P/N 0-80578 - Chevrolet, Model 4500 Dominator HP, 1,150 cfm

Blower Camshaft Kits

Purchasing a quality forced-induction package is like hiring the best high-performance engine engineers to modify your engine for a fraction of the cost. Matching the right blower with the right carburetor with the right cam can turn into a part-time job. An inexperienced tuner can prevent a lot of headaches by purchasing matched components from one manufacturer. Holley/Weiand blower cams are engineered to complement their superchargers.

Mild
P/N 8130 - Chevrolet 262-400 P/N 8133 - Chevrolet 396–502

Aggressive
P/N 8131 - Chevrolet 262–400

Wild
P/N 8132 - Chevrolet 262–400
P/N 8134 - Chevrolet 396–502

Appendix Two
GReddy Turbo Applications

(Part Number, Application, Year, and Type)

Honda
198751   CIVIC VTEC 1992–1995 TD04H-8.5CM

Toyota
321220   MR2 Turbo 1990–1996 TD06S 20G-8CM
321303   Supra 1987–1992 TD06SH 20G-14CM
321325   Supra TT 1993-1997 T-78 33D-17CM Single

Nissan
323652   300ZX TT 1990–1996 TD05 16G Twin
323653   300ZX TT 1990–1996 TD04H 15C Twin

Mazda
323818   MIATA 1.6L 1989–1993 TD04 15C-8.5CM
323803   RX-7 TURBO 1987–1989 TD06SH 20G-16CM
323604   RX-7 TURBO 1990–1992 TD06SH 20G-16CM
323815   RX7 TT 1993–1996 TD06SH 20G-16CM
333023   3000GT VR4 1990–1996 TD04L 13G-6CM Twin

Mitsubishi
333023   3000GT VR4 1990-1996 TD046 13G-6CM Twin

Civic and Miata systems are CARB certified

Intercooler Kits
12050000 Honda Civic SOHC EX/Si FRONT MOUNT 1992-2000
         Honda Civic SOHC EX/Si LG FRONT MOUNT 1992-2000
         Honda Civic DOHC EX/Si FRONT MOUNT 1999–2000
         Honda Civie DOHC EX/Si LG FRONT MOUNT 1999–2000
         Acura Integra GSR FRONT MOUNT 1994–2000
         Acura Integra GSR FRONT MOUNT 1994–2000
12010000 Toyota MR2 Turbo Stock Location 1990–1996
12010011 Toyota Supra Turbo Front Mount 1987–1992
12010020 Supra T/T Stock Location 1993–1997
12010024 Supra T/T Front Mount Std. Turbo 1993–1997
12010022 Toyota Supra Front Mount, Single Turbo 1993–1997
12010025 Toyota Supra 4-Row Mount, Single Turbo 1993–1997
12020200 Nissan 300ZX T/T Stock Location 1990–1996
12040030 Mazda RX-7 T/T Front Mount 1987–1989
12040031 RX-7 T/T Front Mount 1990–1992
12040050 RX-7 T/T Stock Location, Std Location 1993–1996
12040051 RX-7 Single Turbo, Stock Piping T-78, Front Mount 1993–1996
12040052 RX-7 Greddy Piping T-78 Front Mount 1993–1996
12030000 Mitsubishi Eclipse Turbo Front Mount 1995–1999
         Mitsubishi Eclipse Turbo Lg. Front Mount 1995–1999

Intercooler Set-Up Kits
Honda
Civic EX/Si SOHC Front Mount 1992–2000
Civic EX/Si SOHC Large Front Mount 1992–2000

Acura
Integra GS-R Front Mount 1994–2000
Integra GS-R Large Front Mount 1994–2000
Integra/RS Front Mount 1994–2000
Integra LS/RS Large Front Mount 1994–2000

Mitsubishi
EclipseTurbo Large Front Mount 1995–1999

Intercooler Piping Kits
12050900 Honda Civic EX/Si SOHC 1992–1995 With PN 198751
12040900 Mazda RX-7 T/T 3pcs. 1993–1996 STD. I/C W/O Injector
12040901 MAZDA RX-7 T/T 2pcs. 1993–1996 GREDDY W/O Injector
13540491 MAZDA RX-7 T/T 2pcs. 1993–1996 GREDDY W/ Injector
13540492 MAZDA RX-7 T/T 3pcs. 1993–1996 STD. I/C W/Injector
12030900 Mitsu Eclipse Turbo 1995–1998
12001505 Universal 50mm Piping Kit
12001506 Universal 60mm Piping Kit

Turbo Timer
Greddy's Turbo Timer keeps the engine idling for a brief period to allow the turbocharger to cool down.

Applications
15500011 Turbo Timer (Black)

TURBO TIMER HARNESSES
15910001 Toyota MR-2 S/C 1985–1989 TT-14-11
15910003 Toyota MR-2 Turbo 1990–1992 TT-14-13
15910001 Toyota Celica All-Trac 198--1992 TT-14-11
15910001 Toyota Supra Turbo 1987–1992 TT-14-11
15910004 Toyota Supra Twin Turbo 1993–1996 TT-14-14
15920001 Nissan 280SX Turbo 1981–1983 TT-14-21
15920002 Nissan 300ZX Turbo 1984–1989 TT-14-22
15920002M Nissan300ZX Twin Turbo 1990–1996 TT-14-22M
15940002 Mazda RX-7 Turbo 1987–1991 TT-14-32
15940003 Mazda RX-7 Twin Turbo 1993–1996 TT-14-33
15930002 Mitsubishi Eclipse 1989–1994 TT-14-42
15930003 Mitsubishi Eclipse 1989–1994 TT-14-43
15930003M Mitsubishi Eclipse 1995–1997 TT-14-43M

GReddy Turbo Electronic Fuel Management Systems

Rebic IV

The Rebic IV is an auxiliary fuel-injector controller that can manage up to 8 additional injectors without assistance from the factory electronic control unit. GReddy's "black box" can be installed on any forced induction system to supply more fuel during high boost conditions.

PRofec

The PRofec is a proactive electronic boost control that employs fuzzy logic to anticipate boost spikes. In "learn mode" the hardware and software process data from the vehicle to generate interactive maps that control the high speed stepping motor.

PRofec B-Spec

The PRofec B is a boost controller that is less expensive and equally less demanding compared to the PRofec. PRofec B works well on street driven vehicles and applications with sequential turbocharger systems. It is not recommended for large-displacement engines with small or quick-response turbochargers. Features include: solenoid valve to adjust boost pressure, high-boost and low-boost selection points, no extensive programming needed, dip switches select for integral or external wastegates.

GReddy's Full Line of Pressure and Fuel Controls for Turbo Applications

15500110 Rebic IV
15500203 Profec(Fuzzy Logic Boost Controller)
15500202 Profec B-Spec (Electronic Boost Controller)
15500351 Remote Switch For Profec And Profec B-Spec.
15500361 Remote Switching Optional Harness 5-Volt
15500362 Remote Switching Optional Harness 12-Volt
11501700 T.V.V.C. (Mechanical Boost Controller)
15900512 Profec Wire Harness 4.5 Meters
15900526-4 Profec Replacement Filter 4mm
15900526-6 Profec Replacement Filter 6mm
15900012 Additional Injector Driver Harness
15900013 Additional Injector Harness
15900016 Injector Driver Harness 2.5 METERS

Turbocharger Wastegate Valves

11501500 External Wastegate Type S
11501528 External Wastegate Type R 0.8-1.2 KG/CM2
11501531 External Wastegate Type R 1.1-1.5 KG/CM2
11501534 External Wastegate Type R 1.4-ON KG/CM2
11501548 External Wastegate Type C
11501560 External Wastegate Type C HIGH FLOW
11501600 Actuator P565 11 PSI
11501610 Actuator P765 14 PSI
11900260 Spring Type-R/C 0.8-1.2 KG/CM2
11900261 Spring Type-R/C 1.1-1.5 KG/CM2
11900262 Spring Type-R/C 1.4-ON KG/CM2

Turbocharger Blow Off Valves and Accessories

11501710 Relief Valve
11501650 Blow Off Valve Type S"
11501661 Blow Off Valve Type "R"
11511000 Toyota MR-2 Turbo B.O.V. Kit 1990–1996
11511011 Toyota Supra Turbo B.O.V. Kit 1987–1992
11511050 Toyota Supra T/T B.O.V. Kit 1993–1997
11541010 Mazda RX-7 Turbo B.O.V. Kit 1987–1992
11541011 Mazda RX-7 T/T B.O.V. Kit 1993–1996
11531010 Mitsubishi Eclipse B.O.V. Kit 1995–1997
11900510 Stiff Spring
11900450 Steel Mounting Flange
11900451 Outlet Adapter 40mm For Type "R"
11900490 Outlet Adapter 40mm For Type "R"
11900491 Outlet Adapter 45mm For Type "R"
11900470 Outlet Adapter 19-21mm For Type "R"
11900471 Outlet Adapter 28-35mm For Type "R"
11900481 Outlet Adapter 16mm For Type "S"
11900482 Outlet Adapter 19mm For Type "S"
11900483 Outlet Adapter 29mm For Type "S"
99900061 Type-S Replacement Diaphragm
99900062 Type-R Replacement Diaphragm
11900520 Relief Valve Adapter

Turbocharger Boost Cut Controllers

15510006 Toyota MR-2 Turbo 1990–1996
15540001 Mazda RX-7 Turbo 1990–1991
15540006 MazdaRX-7 Twin Turbo 1993–1996

Turbocharger Speed Limiter Cut Controllers

15510201 Toyota Supra Turbo 1987–1992 T-1
15510202 Toyota MR-2 Turbo 1990–1996 T-1
15520201 Nissan 300ZX Twin Turbo 5M/T 1990-1996 N-1
15520202 Nissan 300ZX Twin Turbo 4A/T 1990-1996 N-2

NOTE: Some products are for off-road use only.

Appendix Three
Sources and Resources

Following is a list of parts suppliers and manufacturers who contributed information for this book. They are excellent resources for parts and insight for any supercharging, turbocharging, or nitrous oxide project.

Computer Programs
Allan Lockheed & Associates
Engine Expert/DynoMation
(303) 238-2414

Electronic Controls
C & M Racing Systems
(313) 480-4028

Electromotive Inc.
(703) 331-0100
www.electromotive-inc.com
techinfo@electromotive-inc.com

ETAS Inc.
(888) 382-7462
sales@etasinc.com

Hypertech
(901) 382-7752
www.hypertech.com
webmaster@hypertech.com

Jacobs Electronics
(800) 627-8800
www.jacobselectronics.com

Jet Performance Products
(714) 848-5515
(800) 535-1161
www.jetchip.com
sales@jetchip.com

Mr. Gasket Performance Group
Accel/DFI
(216) 688-8300
www.mrgasket.com

MSD Ignition
(915) 855-7123
www.msdignition.com
msdtech@msdignition.com

Racetech, Inc.
(403) 274-0154
www.sdsefi.com
racetech@cadivision.com

Split Second
(949) 863-1363
www.splitsec.com
splitsec@pacbell.net

Superchips, Inc.
(888) CAR-CHIP
www.superchips.com

Engine
Auto Specialties Performance
(281) 261-5811
www.aspracing.com
asp@aspracing.com

Competition Cams
(901) 795-2400
www.compcams.com
compcams@compcams.com

Crane Cams
(904) 252-1151
Tech: (904) 258-6174
www.cranecams.com

Crower
(619) 422-1191
www.crower.com
crowertech@crower.com

Edelbrock
(310) 781-2222
Tech: (800) 416-8628
www.edelbrock.com
efitech@edelbrock.com

Engine Systems
(404) 491-0583
www.enginesystems.com

ESI
(619) 229-7765

Federal-Mogul Engine Bearings
(248) 354-7700

Ford Motorsports Performance Equipment
Tech: (810) 468-1356

Holley Performance Products
(270) 782-2900
Tech: (270) 781-9741
www.holley.com

Hooker Headers,
A Holley Performance Brand
(270) 782-2900
www.nosnitrous.com/HiOctn/ProdLine/
Hooker.html
flowtech@support.holley.com

Lingenfelter Performance Engineering
(219) 724-2552
www.lingenfelter.com
sales@lingenfelter.com

Performance by Paul
(909) 359-3893
ppitzonka@aol.com

RPM
(877) 776-3644
www.rpmengines.com
gustavov@rpmengines.com

Nitrous Oxide Systems
Nitrous Express
(940) 767-7694
www.nitrousexpress.com

Nitrous Oxide Systems,
A Holley Performance Brand
(270) 782-2900
www.nosnitrous.com
nos@support.holley.com

Organizations
SAE International
(724) 776-4841
www.sae.org

Superchargers

Accessible Technologies, Inc.
(913) 338-2886
www.ProCharger.com

BBK Performance, Inc.
(909) 735-2400

Blower Drive Service
(310) 693-4302
www.blowerdriveservice.com
info@blowerdriveservice.com

Eaton Corporation
Supercharger Division
(616) 781-0200
www.automotive.eaton.com

Hansen Supercharger Corporation
(888) 234-1234
www.hscsupercharger.com
hscsupercharger@uswest.net

Jackson Racing Performance Products
(888) 888-4079
www.jacksonracing.com

Kenne Bell
Orders: (909) 941-6646
Fax: 909-944-4883

Magnuson Products
(805) 642-8833
www.magnuson-products.com
info@magnusonproducts.com

Neuspeed
(805) 388-7171
www.neuspeed.com

OPCON AB
(Sweden)
Tel: +46 532 611 00
www.opconab.com
info@opcon.se

Paxton Automotive Corporation
(888) 9-PAXTON
www.paxtonauto.com

Powerdyne
(661) 723-2800
www.powerdyne.com
powerdyne@powerdyne.com

Vortech Engineering, Inc.
(805) 247-0226
www.vortechsuperchargers.com

Weiand Superchargers,
A Holley Performance Brand
(270) 782-2900
www.nosnitrous.com/HiOctn/ProdLine/AV/SC/SC.html#WSCK
help@support.holley.com

Whipple Supercharger Systems
(559) 442-1261
www.whipplesuperchargers.com

Turbochargers

Advanced Vehicle Operations (Australia)
(61-39) 584-4499
www.avoturbo.com

Allied Signal Turbocharging Systems/Garrett
(800) 707-4555
www.honeywell.com

Bell Engineering Group, Inc.
CarTech: (830) 438-2890

GReddy Performance Products, Inc.
(949) 588-8300
www.greddy.com

HKS Performance Products
(310) 763-9600
www.hksusaa.com

Knight Engineering
(661) 940-1215

Ray Hall Turbocharging
(617) 4051-6672
www.turbofast.com
rayhall@internetnorth.com.au

Speed Innovations
(713) 681-7333
www.speedinnovations.com
speedinnovations@mindspring.com

Turbo City
(714) 639-4933
www.turbocity.com
turbocity@sprynet.com

Turbo Clutch
(818) 993-9174
www.turboclutch.com

Turbonetics/Spearco
(805) 581-0333
www.turbonetics.com
info@turbonetics.com

Turbo Technology
(253) 475-8319
www.turbotechnologyinc.com

Topics and Publications of Interest

Bell, Corky. *Maximum Boost: Designing, Testing and Installing Turbocharger Systems.* Cambridge: Robert Bentley, 1997.

Haile, Joe. *Motorcycle Turbocharging, Supercharging & Nitrous Oxide.* North Conway, NH: Whitehorse Press, 1997.

Heywood, John B. *Internal Combustion Engine Fundamentals.* New York: McGraw-Hill, 1988.

Macinnes, Hugh. *Turbochargers.* New York: HP Books, 1984.

Pettitt, Joe. *How to Install and Use Nitrous Oxide Injection Systems For Maximum Horsepower.* North Branch, MN: CarTech, 1998.

Pettitt, Joe. *High Performance Honda Builder's Handbook.* North Branch, MN: CarTech, 1996.

Probst, Charles O. *How to Understand, Service and Modify Ford Fuel Injection & Electronic Engine Control.* Cambridge: Robert Bentley, 1993.

Yule, John-David, ed. *Concise Encyclopedia of The Sciences.* New York: Van Nostrand Reinhold, 1978.

The World of Automobiles, An Illustrated Encyclopedia of the Motorcar. 22 vols. London, Orbis Publishing, 1974.

Index

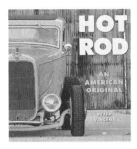

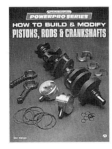
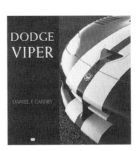
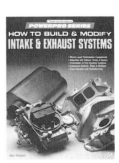